WAITROSE
FOOD
FOR ALL SEASONS

A year of delicious recipes

LONDON, NEW YORK, MELBOURNE,
MUNICH, DELHI

Editor Janice Anderson
Designer Briony Chappell
Managing Art Editor Marianne
Markham
Managing Editor Penny Warren
DTP designer Sonia Charbonnier
Production Controller Wendy Penn

First published in
Great Britain in 2005 by
Dorling Kindersley Limited
80 Strand, London WC2R 0RL

A Penguin Company

2 4 8 10 9 7 5 3 1

Copyright © John Brown Citrus
Publishing Ltd 2005

Waitrose Food Illustrated is published
by John Brown Citrus Publishing,
www.jbcp.co.uk

Recipes by Sybil Kapoor, copyright
© Sybil Kapoor 2005

A CIP catalogue record for this book
is available from the British Library

ISBN 1 4053 1164 9

Colour reproduction by GRB Italy
Printed and bound in China
by SNP Lee Fung

Discover more at
www.dk.com

CONTENTS

INTRODUCTION

At Waitrose Food Illustrated, *we're very proud of the fact that we've earned the title of world's most beautiful food magazine. It's a plaudit we intend to keep, and that means striving to bring our readers the most delicious, inspiring recipes every month.*

To do this, we make sure we work with the finest cooks and food writers in the world. Time after time, these experts tell us that the way to get the very best from your cooking is to shop and eat in tune with the seasons. Not only does that mean you can enjoy fresh fruit, vegetables, herbs and dairy produce when they are at peak quality, but it creates a fantastic rhythm to the year. Cook seasonally and you'll feel a genuine excitement when the first asparagus, strawberries, peas or Seville oranges appear. After all, there's nothing nicer than rediscovering the flavour of foods you love when you haven't eaten them for a while.

So when we decided to create a cookbook, of course we felt that it had to be themed around the seasons. The result, I hope you will agree, is a mouth-watering journey through the year, from the first green shoots of spring, through the lush fruits of summer, to the hearty baking of winter. We've selected our favourite dishes from our favourite cooks and I'd like to extend particular thanks to the highly talented Sybil Kapoor, whose exquisite recipes fill so many of these pages.

Moreover, because we wanted this to be more than just a recipe book, we've included introductions to each season's cooking from four of our best-loved writers, bringing you a taste of the food journalism for which *Waitrose Food Illustrated* has become famous. Together, I hope the words, images and irresistible recipes collected here will inspire you to cook simple, delicious food throughout the year, every year.

William Sitwell

Editor, *Waitrose Food Illustrated*

SPRING

As the earth warms up and the hours of daylight grow longer, the first fresh green vegetables are harvested, making spring the most exciting time of the year for seasonal cooking.

SERVES 8
PREPARATION TIME 10 MINUTES
COOKING TIME 20 MINUTES

INGREDIENTS

2 leeks, trimmed

3 tbsp olive oil

1.5 litres (2³/₄ pints) chicken stock

2 baking potatoes, peeled and finely chopped

1kg (2¹/₄lb) asparagus, washed

handful of chervil

400ml (14fl oz) double cream

salt and freshly ground black pepper

ASPARAGUS & CHERVIL SOUP

This delicious soup is a good way of using stems left over from dishes such as tempura that require only asparagus tips. It is equally good served hot or cold.

METHOD

Remove the outer leaves of the leeks and finely slice. Wash thoroughly and leave to drain. Heat the oil in a large pan and fry the leeks until very soft. Add the stock and potatoes, increase the heat slightly, return to the boil and cook for 10 minutes.

Meanwhile, trim the asparagus stems, discarding any tough ends. Slice off the tips from 20 pieces of asparagus and set aside for another dish. Slice the asparagus stems and remaining tips into 2.5cm (1in) pieces and add to the potatoes. Boil for a further 7 minutes or until tender.

Strip the chervil leaves from their stems. Add the stems to the soup, then liquidize it in a blender or food processor. Strain it into a bowl or saucepan, depending on whether it is to be served cold or hot. Finely chop the chervil leaves, reserving a few for garnish, and stir into the soup with the cream. Season to taste and thin with water if wished. Garnish with the reserved chervil leaves. Serve hot or cold.

If serving cold, you can garnish the soup with ice. Line a shallow baking dish with cling film, and cover with a very thin layer of water. Freeze. Lift off the film, break into large pieces and scatter in the cold soup.

IN SEASON

ASPARAGUS

When buying asparagus, whatever the variety, look for crisp, succulent stems and compact tips. Cook and eat asparagus soon after buying to enjoy its delicate flavour at its best. To prepare asparagus, trim the tough ends from the stalks and lightly peel the tougher lower sections, leaving the tops and tips alone. Thin stems are ideal for stir-fries and salads, thicker ones are better eaten on their own, dipped into melted butter or hollandaise sauce.

SERVES 4
PREPARATION TIME 10 MINUTES
COOKING TIME 40 MINUTES

INGREDIENTS

1 medium cauliflower

30g (1 oz) butter

450ml (15 fl oz) chicken stock

280ml (9 fl oz) double cream

1 bay leaf

100ml (3½ fl oz) milk

salt and freshly ground black pepper

juice of ½ lemon

small bunch of chives, finely chopped,
plus whole chives to garnish

CREAMY CAULIFLOWER & CHIVE SOUP

This delicate soup is made by gently cooking cauliflower florets in butter before simmering them in chicken stock and cream. Chives and lemon juice add an extra tang.

METHOD

Cut the cauliflower into small florets, discarding the thickest stalks, and wash the florets thoroughly.

Melt the butter in a saucepan over a medium-low heat. Add the cauliflower florets, cover and gently sweat for 10 minutes, or until they begin to soften. Do not let them colour. Add the stock, cream and bay leaf and bring to the boil. Cover the pan and simmer gently for 30 minutes. Remove the bay leaf. Pour the contents of the pan into a blender or food processor and blend to a purée. If necessary, thin the purée with the milk. Season to taste with salt and pepper.

To serve, reheat the soup, then add the lemon juice and chives. Ladle the soup into warmed bowls and garnish with a few uncut chives.

IN SEASON

CHIVES

These pretty stems have a mild oniony flavour that, although it grows in intensity as the herb matures, is still less pungent than that of other alliums, such as onions and shallots. Chives go particularly well with dairy products such as butter and soured cream and taste great with eggs and sweetish roots such as carrots and beetroot. They make a good garnish for creamy soups. Chives bruise easily, so snip them with scissors rather than cut them with a knife.

SERVES 4
PREPARATION TIME 5 MINUTES
COOKING TIME 20 MINUTES

INGREDIENTS

2 x 400g (14 oz) cans cannellini beans

120ml (4 fl oz) extra virgin olive oil

6 shallots, finely sliced

2 tsp Dijon mustard

3 tbsp red wine vinegar

salt and freshly ground black pepper

2 tsp roughly chopped lemon thyme

2 handfuls flat-leaf parsley,
roughly chopped

small bunch of chives, finely snipped

450g (1lb) baby spinach

100g (3½ oz) soft goat's cheese

WHITE BEAN SALAD

This salad can be served as a satisfying light lunch on its own or alongside grilled meat or chicken. For a really good flavour, look for an organic soft goat's cheese.

METHOD

Drain and rinse the cannellini beans and leave to drain in a colander. Meanwhile, measure 4 tablespoons of the olive oil into a wide saucepan over a medium heat. Add the shallots and gently cook them until golden. While they are cooking, whisk together the mustard and red wine vinegar.

Once the shallots are golden, add the drained cannellini beans to the pan. Stir occasionally until the beans are piping hot, then stir in the mustard and vinegar mixture and the remaining olive oil. Once everything is heated through, season to taste and mix in the herbs and spinach leaves. Keep stirring until most of the spinach has collapsed and wilted, then remove from the heat. Divide the beans among 4 plates, crumble over the goat's cheese and serve immediately.

SERVES 4
PREPARATION TIME 10 MINUTES
COOKING TIME 30 MINUTES

INGREDIENTS

4 tbsp light vegetable oil

$\frac{1}{3}$ of a day-old baguette, cut into 2cm (1in) chunks

200g (7oz) bacon lardons

1 tbsp Dijon mustard

1 tbsp white wine vinegar

2 tbsp extra virgin olive oil

2 long-leaved lettuce hearts, such as romaine, separated into leaves

4 eggs

SALAD WITH LARDONS & OEUFS MOLLET

This beautiful egg and bacon salad features oeufs mollets — the French term for soft-boiled eggs, shelled whole. Once cut, they release their gorgeous golden yolk into the salad.

METHOD

Heat 3 tablespoons of the vegetable oil in a frying pan over a medium heat. Add the bread and fry, turning, for about 10 minutes until the croutons are golden and crisp. Remove and set aside on kitchen paper.

Wipe the pan, add the remaining vegetable oil and heat it over moderate heat. Add the bacon lardons and fry for about 15 minutes until crisp and golden. Take out of the pan with a draining spoon and drain on kitchen paper. Put the Dijon mustard, white wine vinegar, extra virgin olive oil and seasoning in a small bowl and whisk together well. Drizzle this dressing over the lettuce leaves in a large bowl and toss to coat the leaves in the dressing.

Divide the lettuce among four plates. Scatter the croutons and lardons on top. Bring a pan of water to the boil, add the eggs, and simmer for exactly 4 minutes. Immediately put the eggs under cold running water to cool them. Peel the eggs very carefully, taking care not to break the whites. Place one egg on top of each salad and break it open so that the yolk runs out. Serve immediately.

IN SEASON

ROMAINE LETTUCE

Lettuce is the mainstay of many a spring salad, the green leaves providing a foil for many other ingredients, from avocados, tomatoes and onions to prawns and diced bacon. There are three main varieties of lettuce: crisphead, such as iceberg; cabbage or round; and the cos or romaine variety, which includes the little gem. This variety has elongated, firm leaves which hold up well under heavy dressings so that they make beautifully crisp salads.

SERVES 4 AS A STARTER
PREPARATION TIME 10 MINUTES,
PLUS CLEANING THE SQUID, IF
NECESSARY
COOKING TIME 10 MINUTES

INGREDIENTS

450g (1lb) fresh squid

sunflower oil for deep-frying
(see method)

55g (2oz) plain flour

salt and freshly ground black pepper

lemon halves, to serve

freshly chopped parsley to garnish
(optional)

DEEP-FRIED CALAMARI

Sliced squid is tossed in seasoned flour and deep-fried until crisp and golden. This quickly made dish is ideal as part of a leisurely lunch, served with lemon wedges, alongside a salad of spring leaves tossed in a light dressing.

METHOD

If you have to clean the squid, keep the tentacles as well as the bodies. Even if you have bought ready-cleaned squid, rinse the bodies inside and out, making sure that any sand or messy bits are washed away. Trim the tentacles of any extraneous squid matter, and rinse them too.

Preheat a deep layer of the oil in a deep pan or deep-fat fryer to 180°C (350°F), or until a cube of bread turns golden in 30 seconds. Meanwhile, slice the squid bodies into thick rounds. Thoroughly dry all the prepared squid, including the tentacles, by layering it in kitchen paper. If it is not sufficiently dry, too much flour will adhere to it and it is more liable to spit in the hot fat.

Put the flour in a large mixing bowl and season it with salt and black pepper. Mix in one-third of the squid pieces, then lift them out, shaking any excess flour back into the bowl. Carefully put the squid into the pan of hot oil. Fry them for about 3 minutes or until golden, then remove from the pan with a draining spoon and set aside. Repeat the process with the remaining squid, in two batches.

Serve the fried squid immediately with the lemon halves and, if you wish, some chopped parsley scattered over.

SERVES 4
PREPARATION TIME 10 MINUTES
COOKING TIME 12–15 MINUTES

INGREDIENTS

1 tender stem lemon grass, roughly chopped

2 garlic cloves

3 spring onions, chopped

grated zest of 1 lime

250g (8½ oz) skinless, boneless chicken breasts

1 bunch watercress

salt and freshly ground black pepper

FOR THE MISO BROTH

3 tbsp groundnut oil

3cm (1½ in) piece fresh ginger, peeled and thinly sliced

4 shallots, sliced into rings

2 garlic cloves, thinly sliced

1 bunch spring onions, cut into 3cm (1½ in) lengths

1-2 red chilies, sliced finely into rings

1 litre (1¾ pints) miso soup stock (made with 4 sachets miso paste)

1 tbsp fish sauce

2 tbsp soy sauce

2 tbsp Japanese rice vinegar

150g (5½ oz) shiitake mushrooms, stalks removed

large handful of broccoli florets

CHICKEN DUMPLINGS WITH MISO BROTH

Miso soup paste is a great storecupboard stand-by, which comes into its own as an instant, Oriental-style stock base. Chicken dumplings turn miso broth into a main dish.

METHOD

For the dumplings, put the lemon grass, garlic and spring onions into a food processor and process until finely chopped. Transfer to a bowl and stir in the lime zest. Put the chicken breasts in the food processor and pulse briefly until coarsely chopped. Add to the bowl. Finely chop a small handful of the watercress and stir it into the chicken mixture. Season and form into small dumplings, about the size of a walnut. Cook in a steamer for 5–6 minutes, until cooked through.

Meanwhile, make the broth. Heat the oil in a large saucepan over a gentle heat, add the ginger, shallots and garlic and fry until soft but not coloured. Add the remaining broth ingredients and bring to the boil. Reduce the heat and simmer for 2–3 minutes until the mushrooms and broccoli are just cooked. Stir in the remaining watercress and serve with the dumplings.

SERVES 4
PREPARATION TIME 25 MINUTES
COOKING TIME 25 MINUTES

INGREDIENTS

250g (8½ oz) baby beetroot, washed and leaves trimmed off

4 little gem lettuces

1 bunch chives, snipped

handful of mint leaves, roughly ripped

55g (2 oz) walnut halves, roughly chopped

200g (7 oz) feta cheese, diced

1 tsp clear honey

2 tbsp lemon juice

5 tbsp walnut oil

salt and freshly ground black pepper

1 tbsp roughly chopped dill

IN SEASON

BABY BEETROOT

The tiny, purple globes of early beetroot that appear in spring are sweet, juicy, and very beautiful. Scrub them well, but do not peel – the skins are still thin and edible, and this also helps preserve their colour. Boil or roast them whole, smother with butter or olive oil, sprinkle with parsley (which balances their intense sweetness) and serve alongside cold meats. Or let them cool and toss into salads where they will enhance salty ingredients such as feta or bacon.

FETA, BEETROOT & WALNUT SALAD

Combine fresh-tasting, salty feta cheese with sweet beetroot and bitter walnuts for a delicious salad. A simple honey, lemon and walnut oil dressing adds an exciting final zing.

METHOD

Put the beetroot in a saucepan. Cover with water and bring to the boil. Cover the pan and boil for 20 minutes, or until tender when pierced with a knife. Drain and, when cool enough to handle, peel off the skin. Cut the beetroot into quarters.

Meanwhile, separate, wash and dry the lettuce leaves. Put in a large mixing bowl with the chives, mint, walnuts and feta.

Whisk together the honey, lemon juice and walnut oil and season to taste. Toss the warm beetroot in half this vinaigrette mixture. Add the chopped dill.

Divide the lettuce mixture among 4 plates, add the dressed beetroot and serve immediately with the remaining vinaigrette served separately.

SERVES 4
PREPARATION TIME 10 MINUTES,
PLUS MARINATING
COOKING TIME 5 MINUTES

INGREDIENTS

24 freshwater prawns

FOR THE MARINADE

2 tsp peeled and finely diced
fresh ginger

finely grated zest of 2 limes

1 tbsp lime juice

1 tbsp runny honey

1 tbsp soy sauce

1 tbsp roasted sesame oil

FOR THE SALSA

1 papaya, peeled, seeded and
finely diced

juice of 1 lime

2 tbsp finely chopped coriander

1/4 small red chili, finely diced

salt and freshly ground black pepper

GRILLED GINGER PRAWNS WITH PAPAYA

This is a lovely starter for a springtime meal, making use of ingredients such as papaya that are particularly good at this time of year. Serve it with young lettuce leaves, if you wish.

METHOD

Peel the prawns. Cut a shallow slit down the length of their backs and pull away the black digestive cord (if it is there). Rinse the prawns and pat dry. Mix all the ingredients for the marinade in a bowl, add the prawns and stir well to coat them in the marinade. Chill in the refrigerator for 20 minutes.

Mix the diced papaya with the lime juice and the coriander. Add the chili and season with salt and pepper.

Preheat a ribbed, cast-iron grill pan over a high heat. Thread the prawns, still coated in the marinade, onto skewers and put them on the grill pan. (You could put them straight on the pan, if you prefer.) As soon as they turn pink, flip them and cook for a further 2–3 minutes. They take about 5 minutes in all to cook.

Serve the prawns hot, warm or cold with the papaya salsa.

SERVES 4
PREPARATION TIME 10 MINUTES,
PLUS MARINATING
COOKING TIME 20–25 MINUTES

INGREDIENTS

3 chicken breasts, about
140g (5oz) each, skinned

1 egg white

6 tsp cornflour

1½ dried hot red chilies, seeded

450ml (15 fl oz) water

4 tbsp sunflower oil

2 tbsp soy sauce

85g (3oz) cashew nuts

1 tsp sugar

2 tsp white wine vinegar

6 spring onions, finely sliced

IN SEASON

SPRING ONIONS

The spring onion, or salad onion as it
is also called, is an allium – in fact, an
immature form of the ordinary onion.
Spring onions give crisply sharp top
notes to mixed salads, sandwiches and
many cooked dishes, including those
based on the cooking of south-east
Asia. Choose spring onions with taut,
succulent green top leaves and fresh-
looking roots. Droopy, softish leaves and
dry, brown roots indicate spring onions
that are past their best.

STIR-FRIED SZECHUAN CHICKEN & CASHEWS

*Diced chicken breast takes on a velvety, yet succulent texture
when marinated in egg white and cornflour, before being
stir-fried in a spicy chili and soy sauce. This dish is good
served with stir-fried broccoli and steamed rice.*

METHOD

Cut the chicken breasts into 1cm (½in) dice. Place in a bowl and mix in the egg
white. Sprinkle in 4 teaspoons of the cornflour, and stir everything together well
to ensure the chicken pieces are well coated in the marinade. Cover and chill for
at least an hour, or up to 3 hours.

Meanwhile, put the chilies in a saucepan with 300ml (10fl oz) of the water and
1 tablespoon of the sunflower oil. Bring to the boil and simmer for 10–15 minutes.
Drain the chilies, and when they are cool, finely dice them.

To make the sauce, mix the remaining cornflour with the soy sauce and the
remaining water in a bowl and set aside.

Heat 1 tablespoon of the sunflower oil in a non-stick frying pan or wok. Add the
cashew nuts and a pinch of salt and stir-fry for a few seconds until the nuts are
golden brown. Set aside.

Return the pan to the heat, and add the remaining oil. Once it is hot, add the
diced chilies, the chicken and sugar. Stir-fry briskly for a few minutes until the
chicken is golden and cooked, then stir in the vinegar and allow it to evaporate.
Immediately add the sauce, the cashew nuts and spring onions. Add more salt
and pepper to taste, or an extra sprinkle of sugar, if you like. Serve the dish as soon
as the sauce has thickened.

SERVES 8
PREPARATION TIME 1 HOUR
15 MINUTES

INGREDIENTS

2 bread (tortilla) wraps

oil for brushing

10 long-leaved lettuce leaves, coarsely shredded

55g (2oz) rocket

4 tomatoes, diced

6 small radishes, thinly sliced

4 spring onions, finely sliced

$^1/_2$ small red pepper, cored, seeded and diced

$^1/_4$ cucumber, diced

1 tbsp chopped mint

1 tbsp chopped coriander

1 tbsp chopped flat-leaf parsley

2 tbsp sumac (optional)

salt and freshly ground black pepper

FOR THE DRESSING

5 tbsp lemon juice

5 tbsp extra virgin olive oil

FOR THE BABA GANOUSH

2 large aubergines, about 675g (1$^1/_2$ lb) total weight

2 garlic cloves

2 tbsp lemon juice

2 tbsp tahine

large pinch of ground cumin

pinch of ground white pepper

2 tbsp plain yogurt (optional)

extra virgin olive oil

chopped flat-leaf parsley, to garnish

FATTOUSH WITH BABA GANOUSH

Fattoush is a traditional Lebanese salad that usually includes sumac, a tangy spice made from dried berries. If it is not available, the salad is still delicious without it, especially when served with baba ganoush, a Lebanese aubergine dip.

METHOD

To make the baba ganoush, preheat the grill to high. Prick the aubergines with a fork and grill them, turning occasionally, until the skin blisters and blackens all over. When cool, peel off the skin. Cut the aubergine flesh into chunks and put in a colander for 15 minutes to drain off excess liquid. Pound the garlic and a pinch of salt together until smooth, then transfer to a food processor. Add the aubergine flesh, lemon juice, tahine, cumin, pepper and yogurt, if using. (The yogurt mellows the flavour of the dip.) Process to a thick purée. Transfer to a bowl, taste and adjust the seasoning. Set the baba ganoush aside while you make the fattoush.

Preheat the grill to medium. Lightly brush one of the bread wraps with olive oil and put it on a baking sheet. Toast under the grill until lightly browned and crisp on both sides. Repeat with the second wrap. When the wraps are cool, break them into jagged pieces.

Put all the remaining salad ingredients into a large bowl and season well with salt and pepper. Mix the lemon juice and oil for the dressing, season, and add it to the salad, tossing well to distribute the dressing. Cover the salad with the broken bread pieces, and serve at once. Drizzle olive oil over the baba ganoush, garnish it with parsley and serve separately.

SERVES 6
PREPARATION TIME 1 1/2 HOURS
COOKING TIME 40–60 MINUTES

INGREDIENTS

200ml (7fl oz) olive oil

1 onion, finely diced

1 garlic clove, finely diced

1/4 tsp ground cinnamon

pinch of ground allspice

450g (1lb) minced lamb

200ml (7fl oz) white wine

400g (14oz) can chopped tomatoes

finely grated zest of 1 lemon

2 tbsp finely chopped parsley

1 tbsp roughly chopped fresh oregano

salt and freshly ground black pepper

30g (1oz) finely grated Parmesan

1kg (2 1/4 lb) aubergines, trimmed

FOR THE WHITE SAUCE TOPPING

570ml (18fl oz) milk

1 bay leaf

3 black peppercorns

75g (2 1/2 oz) butter

75g (2 1/2 oz) plain flour

2 egg yolks

30g (1oz) finely grated Parmesan

IN SEASON

LAMB

Tender spring lamb is delicious cooked simply, with olive oil, lemon thyme or a squeeze of lemon and a sprinkling of sea salt. But it is also excellent used in more complicated dishes with other flavourful ingredients, such as this Moussaka. Either way, serve it with simple condiments and vegetables, or just a leafy green salad.

MOUSSAKA

This traditional Greek dish perfectly combines sweetly-flavoured lamb and aubergines, topped with a creamy white sauce. It takes a while to make, but can be prepared in advance.

METHOD

Heat 2 tablespoons of the olive oil in a saucepan over a low heat. Add the onion and garlic and gently fry until soft. Add the cinnamon and allspice and continue to fry for 2 minutes. Mix in the minced lamb, increase the heat slightly and stir-fry the meat briskly until it separates into small granules and turns brown. Add the wine, tomatoes, lemon zest, parsley and oregano and bring to the boil. Adjust the seasoning and reduce the heat. Simmer gently for 30 minutes, or until rich and thick, then beat in the Parmesan and season with salt and pepper.

For the white sauce, put the milk, bay leaf and peppercorns into a saucepan. Set over a low heat, and 'scald' the milk by bringing it up to boiling point then removing from the heat. Cover the pan and set aside to infuse for 20 minutes.

Cut the aubergines lengthways into slices about 7.5mm (1/3 in) thick. Pour a little of the remaining olive oil into a non-stick frying pan and set over a medium-high heat. When the oil is hot, add a single layer of aubergine slices and fry briskly until pale gold on both sides. Remove from the pan and drain on kitchen paper. Repeat the process with the remaining aubergine slices and oil. Lightly season the aubergine. Preheat the oven to 190°C (375°F, gas 5).

Finish the white sauce by melting the butter in a saucepan over a low heat. Stir in the flour, to make a roux, and cook for about 3 minutes. Strain the flavoured milk and, using a wooden spoon, slowly stir it into the roux, only adding more milk as the first addition is smoothly absorbed into the roux. Simmer this thick sauce over a very low heat for 5 minutes, stirring regularly. Remove from the heat and beat in the two egg yolks. Add salt to taste.

Line the bottom of a 25cm (10in) square, 10cm (4in) deep baking dish (or a 30 x 25cm/12 x 10in lasagne pan) with half the aubergine slices. Cover with the meat, followed by the remaining aubergine. Then evenly spread the warm white sauce over the top and scatter over the remaining Parmesan. Bake in the oven for 40 minutes, or until the topping has formed a thick, golden crust. Leave to stand for 5 minutes before serving in slices.

If the dish is being made in advance, leave the uncooked Moussaka to cool, then cover and chill until needed. Bake the chilled Moussaka for 40 minutes covered with foil, then for a further 20 minutes uncovered.

SERVES 4
PREPARATION TIME 35 MINUTES
COOKING TIME 25 MINUTES

INGREDIENTS

450g (1 lb) asparagus

1 litre (1³/₄ pints) chicken stock

3 tbsp olive oil

1 onion, finely diced

30g (1 oz) butter

300g (10¹/₂ oz) risotto rice, such as carnaroli

30g (1 oz) freshly grated Parmesan

salt and freshly ground black pepper

ASPARAGUS RISOTTO

The season for asparagus is relatively brief, so enjoy it while you can. Here, the thicker parts of the stems are simmered in stock and puréed before being added to the rice, giving an extra layer of asparagus flavour to this creamy risotto.

METHOD

Thoroughly wash the asparagus to remove any grit. Cut off the hard stalk-ends and, using a potato peeler, pare off the tough skin on the lower part of the stems. Discard the trimmings, and cut each stem in half across the middle. Roughly slice the lower halves of the stems.

Divide the stock between 2 saucepans and bring both to the boil. Add the sliced asparagus stalks to one, return to the boil, then cover and simmer for 10 minutes or until tender. Keep the other pan of stock simmering gently.

Meanwhile, pour the oil into a wide sauté or frying pan and set over a low heat. Add the diced onion and gently fry until soft. Cut off the tips of the remaining raw asparagus and slice the stems into pea-sized rounds. Add both rounds and tips to the sautéed onion with the butter and cook for 2 minutes before stirring in the rice, making sure it is well coated in the oil. Fry for 2 more minutes, then stir in 2–3 ladles of the plain simmering stock. Keep stirring regularly, adding more stock as the rice absorbs the liquid.

Meanwhile, pour the chopped asparagus stems with the stock they have been simmering in into a blender or food processor and blend to a purée. Strain back into the pan. When you have finished adding the plain stock to the rice, slowly add the asparagus purée stock to the rice. After about 20 minutes, all the stock will be absorbed and the rice will be cooked, though retaining a slight bite. Stir in the Parmesan, season and serve. Add some extra lightly cooked whole asparagus to each serving, if you like.

SERVES 6
PREPARATION TIME 15 MINUTES
COOKING TIME UP TO 2 HOURS

INGREDIENTS

4 sprigs rosemary

1 lemon

100g (3$^{1}/_{2}$oz) butter, softened

salt and freshly ground black pepper

1 leg of lamb, about 1.8–2kg (4–4$^{1}/_{2}$lb)

8 garlic cloves (unpeeled)

1.25kg (2$^{3}/_{4}$lb) new potatoes, scrubbed

FOR THE GRAVY

150ml (5fl oz) red wine

2 tbsp redcurrant jelly

300ml (10fl oz) beef or lamb stock

BUTTERY ROAST LAMB WITH NEW POTATOES

Here is a dish perfectly planned to welcome the first rays of spring sunshine. New potatoes, sprinkled with rosemary, are roasted round the lamb to make a superb spring meal.

METHOD

Preheat the oven to 230°C (450°F, gas 8).

Strip the leaves from half the rosemary and chop them. Grate the zest from the lemon. Mix both into the butter. Season the lamb, smear with the butter and put it in a roasting tin large enough to take the lamb and the potatoes.

Put in the oven and roast for 20 minutes. Reduce the oven temperature to 200°C (400°F, gas 6), baste the lamb and continue roasting for 15 minutes per 450g (1lb) for medium-rare, 20 minutes for medium and 25 minutes for well-done meat. Forty-five minutes before the end of cooking, sprinkle the potatoes with salt and put them and the remaining rosemary and garlic around the lamb, basting them with the juices. Cut the zested lemon in quarters and add them, too.

When the lamb is cooked, transfer it to a warm serving dish with the potatoes and leave to rest for 10 minutes in a warm place while you make the gravy.

Remove the rosemary and lemon pieces from the roasting tin. Skim all but 3 tablespoons of the fat from the tin. Squeeze the garlic cloves out of their skins into the tin. Put the tin over a low heat, add the wine and deglaze the tin, stirring to make sure all the crisp, caramelized bits are mixed into the wine. Once the wine is bubbling, stir in the redcurrant jelly. Stir until it has melted, then add the stock. Cook over a medium heat for 10–15 minutes until bubbling and slightly thickened. Strain into a warmed jug and serve with the lamb and potatoes.

SERVES 4
PREPARATION TIME 20 MINUTES,
PLUS MARINATING
COOKING TIME 16 MINUTES

INGREDIENTS

4 chicken breasts, skinned

2 tablespoons olive oil

2 sprigs tarragon

finely sliced zest of 1 lemon, plus
2 tbsp lemon juice

salt and freshly ground black pepper

FOR THE GREEN
OLIVE BUTTER

55g (2oz) unsalted butter, softened

2 tsp lemon juice

$\frac{1}{2}$ tsp finely chopped tarragon leaves

3 fat green olives, finely diced

IN SEASON

CHICKEN

Few meats are as versatile as chicken. Although it is available all year round, it's ideally suited to spring cooking with all its delicate flavours. It is worth spending more on an organic bird, and it will give you several meals: roast it with lemon and serve with purple sprouting broccoli, then use the cold leftovers in a salad with new potatoes, mayonnaise and herbs. Finally, boil up the carcass for a tasty stock – the ideal base for a vernal risotto of asparagus and petits pois.

GRILLED CHICKEN WITH GREEN OLIVE BUTTER

This is a quick and easy way to enliven chicken breast. The meat is beaten into an escalope before being soaked in olive oil, tarragon, and lemon zest and juice. Add a dollop of green olive butter and you have a wonderful dinner party dish.

METHOD

Remove the fillets and any sinews or discoloured pieces from the chicken breasts, keeping the fillets for another dish. Place each breast between 2 sheets of cling film. Gently beat the meat into thin escalopes with a rolling pin.

Mix together the olive oil, tarragon, lemon zest and juice, and a twist of black pepper in a bowl. Add the chicken breasts, turning them to ensure that they are well coated in the mixture. Set aside and chill, covered, for 30 minutes.

To make the green olive butter, beat together the butter, lemon juice and tarragon leaves, then mix in the diced olives and season to taste. Spoon the mixture on to wet greaseproof paper, and shape into a rough sausage. Roll up into a cylinder and chill until needed.

Preheat a ridged grill pan over a medium-high heat. Add 2 of the escalopes, and grill on each side for 4 minutes. Set aside and keep warm while you cook the other two. Serve with a slice of olive butter melting on top. This is delicious with salad and chips or new potatoes.

SERVES 4
PREPARATION TIME 10 MINUTES
COOKING TIME 10 MINUTES

INGREDIENTS

4 oatcakes, crushed to fine crumbs

1 tsp mustard powder

4 trout fillets

4 tsp coarse sea salt

FOR THE SAUCE

150ml (5 fl oz) soured cream
or crème fraîche

2 tbsp honey mustard (or 1 tbsp English
mustard mixed with 1 tbsp honey)

1 tbsp snipped chives

TROUT IN MUSTARD OVERCOATS

This is perfect as a light lunch or supper dish, or for Sunday-morning brunch. Trout are oily fish whose natural butteriness crisps up the oatmeal jacket, even on a dry pan. Herring also works really well in this recipe. Replace the oatcake crumbs with fine-milled oatmeal or pinhead oatmeal, if you like.

METHOD

Make the sauce by lightly beating the cream or crème fraîche with the mustard and chives. Do not overbeat or the sauce will be too liquid. Chill until needed.

Spread the oatmeal crumbs on a plate and mix in the mustard powder. Flip the trout fillets through the crumbs, pressing them down to ensure that their skin is thoroughly coated.

Put a heavy-based frying pan over a high heat, and sprinkle in 2 teaspoons of the salt. Put 2 of the coated fish fillets on the salt – if it is hot, you won't need any extra fat to fry the fish. Keep shaking the pan to stop the fillets sticking. Turn the fillets once, cooking them for 2–3 minutes on each side. Remove to a warm plate and keep warm. Wipe the pan clean and repeat with the remaining salt and fish.

If you prefer to grill the fish, dot the fillets with a few pieces of butter to prevent the oat crumbs burning. Cooking time is much the same.

Slip each fish fillet on to a warm plate and serve with the chilled mustard sauce.

SERVES 6
PREPARATION TIME 15 MINUTES
COOKING TIME 40 MINUTES

INGREDIENTS

5 tbsp vegetable oil

3 onions, finely sliced

3 tsp finely chopped fresh ginger

3 garlic cloves, chopped

2–3 green chilies (or to taste),
finely sliced

1 tbsp ground coriander

1$\frac{1}{2}$ tsp ground turmeric

pinch of chili powder

salt and freshly ground black pepper

juice of 1$\frac{1}{2}$ lemons

300ml (10fl oz) water

1.35kg (3lb) peeled, raw tiger prawns

600ml (1 pint) coconut milk

2 handfuls coriander leaves, roughly
chopped

CURRIED COCONUT KING PRAWNS

For this quickly made curry, succulent tiger prawns are cooked in a caramelized onion sauce flavoured with fragrant oriental spices, including chili, plus lemon and coconut milk.

METHOD

Heat the oil in a wide-based saucepan over a high heat and add the onions. When the onions are sizzling, reduce the heat and fry, stirring regularly, until they are soft and golden. Add the ginger, garlic and chilies and cook for 2 minutes. Add the coriander, turmeric, chili powder and a generous pinch of black pepper. Fry for 3 minutes. Mix in the lemon juice and water. Bring to the boil and simmer briskly for 5–10 minutes, or until the water has evaporated and you can see the oil being released from the onion.

The dish can be prepared in advance up to this point and set aside, covered, in the fridge until needed.

To finish cooking, turn the heat to high under the onion mixture and add half the prawns. Stir-fry until the prawns are pink and cooked, then remove them from the pan with a draining spoon (you'll take a few onions with them). Repeat the process with the remaining prawns.

Add the coconut milk to the pan, bring to the boil and cook until the sauce has thickened slightly. Return the prawns to the pan and continue cooking gently for a minute or two until they are heated through. Taste and adjust the seasoning, if necessary. Scatter the coriander over the dish. Serve with rice.

SERVES 4
PREPARATION TIME 10 MINUTES
COOKING TIME 5 MINUTES

INGREDIENTS

55g (2oz) unsalted butter, softened

1 red chili, seeded and finely chopped

2 tbsp finely chopped parsley

grated zest and juice of 1 lime

salt and freshly ground black pepper

2–4 sea bream, scaled and filleted

3 tbsp olive oil

PAN-FRIED SEA BREAM & CHILI LIME BUTTER

The delicate, sweet flesh of sea bream is wonderful pan-fried in olive oil so that it retains its succulence. Add a curl of chili lime butter and its subtle flavours are even more delicious. This recipe can be adapted to other similar white-fleshed fish.

METHOD

First, make the chili lime butter. Beat together the butter, chopped chili and parsley. Add the lime zest, then beat in 2 tablespoons of the lime juice, discarding any that is left. Season to taste with salt and pepper.

Put the butter on a piece of greaseproof paper and shape into a sausage. Roll up the paper and gently roll the butter in it to form a smooth cylinder with no pockets of air. Chill until needed.

Cut three diagonal slashes into the skin of each fish fillet. This stops them curling up as they cook. Put a non-stick frying pan over a medium-high heat and add the oil. Lightly season the fillets and place flesh-side down in the oil. Fry until golden and no longer sticking, then turn over and cook, skin-side down. They should take 5–6 minutes in all, but you may need to cook them in batches.

Slice the butter into 5mm (1/4in) discs. As soon as the fish has been put on warmed plates, put a couple of discs of chili butter on each fillet. This dish is delicious served with wilted spinach.

SERVES 6
PREPARATION TIME 25 MINUTES
COOKING TIME 10–20 MINUTES

INGREDIENTS

400g (14 oz) can black beans
or kidney beans

juice of 1 lime

6 tbsp extra virgin olive oil

1 small chili, or to taste, finely diced

1 bunch coriander, roughly chopped

1 small red onion, diced

salt and freshly ground pepper

225g (8 oz) tomatoes

1 small ripe avocado

FOR THE SPICED SWORDFISH

6 swordfish steaks, about
200g (7oz) each

6 tbsp olive oil

3 tbsp paprika

1 tbsp ground cumin

1 tbsp garlic granules

1 tbsp dried thyme

3 limes, halved

SPICED SWORDFISH WITH A BEAN RELISH

The meaty texture of swordfish lends itself to strong flavourings and searing heat. Here, the fish is coated in a spicy paprika-based mixture before it is seared and served with a tart, spicy avocado and bean relish.

METHOD

To make the relish, drain the beans into a sieve and rinse thoroughly under cold running water. Shake dry and set aside to drain. Put the lime juice and olive oil into a medium-sized bowl. Whisk well then add the chili, coriander and red onion. Season with salt and pepper and mix in the beans.

Cut a small cross in the base of each tomato, put in a bowl and cover with boiling water. Leave for a minute, then drain. Peel off the tomatoes' skin. Halve the tomatoes, cut into small dice and mix with the beans. Finally, halve, stone and peel the avocado. Cut into dice, slightly larger than the beans, and gently mix into the relish. Adjust the seasoning and set aside.

Preheat a ridged grill pan over a medium-high heat. To prepare the swordfish steaks, cut off any skin and remove any particularly dark-coloured areas of flesh, as they can taste bitter. Toss the steaks in the olive oil. In a separate bowl, mix the paprika, cumin, garlic granules and thyme with a generous seasoning of salt and pepper. Sprinkle the spice mixture over the oiled fish, making sure the steaks are evenly coated. Put on the hot grill pan and cook for about 4 minutes on each side. If this has to be done in two batches, slightly undercook the first batch of fish and keep it warm in a low oven while the second batch is cooked.

Put the cooked swordfish steaks on warmed plates and top with the avocado and bean relish. Garnish with the lime halves and serve.

SERVES 6
PREPARATION TIME 30 MINUTES
COOKING TIME 30 MINUTES

INGREDIENTS

900g (2lb) rhubarb (trimmed weight), cut into chunks

170g (6oz) caster sugar, or to taste

1 vanilla pod, broken into 2 or 3 pieces

370g (13oz) fresh raspberries

FOR THE SCONE TOPPING

340g (12oz) self-raising flour

pinch of salt

125g (4^1/$_2$oz) cold butter, diced

85g (3oz) caster sugar

2 small eggs, beaten

100ml (3^1/$_2$fl oz) full fat milk, plus extra for brushing

2 tbsp granulated sugar

RHUBARB & RASPBERRY COBBLER

Cobblers are a homely sort of fruit pie, topped with a scone mixture cut out to resemble cobblestones. Serve the cobbler hot, warm or cold, with cream or crème fraîche.

METHOD

Preheat the oven to 180°C (350°F, gas 4). Mix the rhubarb, sugar and vanilla pod in a 1.5 litre (2^3/$_4$ pints) pie dish. Bake in the oven for 10–15 minutes, depending on the thickness of the rhubarb. Remove from the oven and discard the vanilla pod.

Sift the flour and salt into a mixing bowl and rub in the butter, or pulse in a food processor, until the mixture forms fine crumbs. Stir in the caster sugar. Put the eggs in a measuring jug and make up to 200ml (7fl oz) with the milk. Pour into the flour and mix into a lumpy dough.

Transfer the dough to a floured surface and lightly knead until smooth. Roll out to a 1cm (^{1}/$_2$in) thickness, and cut scones with a 5cm (2in) floured cutter. Mix the raspberries into the rhubarb and arrange the scones in just-overlapping circles on top. Brush with milk and scatter over the sugar. Bake in the oven for 30 minutes, until the cobbler is golden and oozing with juice.

MAKES 6 LARGE TARTLETS OR 10–12
SMALL ONES
PREPARATION TIME 20 MINUTES,
PLUS CHILLING
COOKING TIME 20 MINUTES,
PLUS COOLING

INGREDIENTS

150g (5¹/₂oz) '00' pasta flour,
or plain flour

pinch of salt

75g (2¹/₂oz) cold butter, diced

1 large egg yolk

2–3 tbsp ice-cold water

FOR THE RHUBARB TOPPING

6 sticks rhubarb, cut into pieces

2–3 tbsp water

2 tbsp sugar

maple syrup, to taste

FOR THE FILLING

250g (8¹/₂oz) cream cheese

55g (2oz) icing sugar, sifted

115g (4oz) crème fraîche

120ml (4fl oz) double cream

IN SEASON

RHUBARB

Technically, rhubarb, which is thought
to be a native of Tibet, is a vegetable,
which is how one or two Middle Eastern
cuisines use it. In the West it is used
mainly as a fruit in tarts, pies, preserves
and even wines. By the middle of spring,
outdoor rhubarb, which is thicker and a
darker pink than early rhubarb, is widely
available. When using rhubarb always
cut off the leaves, which are poisonous.
Cut the stalks into same-sized lengths or
chunks so that they cook evenly.

FRUIT TARTLETS

These simply made tartlets, using a rich shortcrust pastry, are delicious with rhubarb, but could be topped with other fruits. Use berry fruits, which need no cooking, and the tartlets will not take as long to make.

METHOD

Put the flour and salt into a bowl or food processor. Add the butter and rub in with the fingertips, or pulse in the food processor, until the mixture resembles fine crumbs. Add the egg yolk and mix in lightly. Add just enough ice-cold water to bring the mix together into a dough. Knead very lightly on a floured surface, then form into a flat disc, wrap and chill for 30 minutes.

Preheat the oven to 200°C (400°F, gas 6). Roll out the pastry thinly and cut out to line either six 10cm (4in) tartlet tins or ten to twelve 5cm (2in) tartlet tins. Prick the base of each pastry case with a fork. Bake for 15 minutes, or until golden. Remove the pastry cases from the oven and leave to cool in the tins.

To make the rhubarb topping, put the rhubarb in a saucepan with the water and sugar. Cook over a very low heat for about 10–15 minutes, until soft. Leave to cool.

For the filling, beat the cream cheese, sugar and crème fraîche together. Whip the cream until it holds soft peaks and fold into the cream cheese mixture. Spoon the mixture into the tart cases, top with the rhubarb (or fruit of your choice), and drizzle over the maple syrup. Serve at once.

MAKES 16 PIECES
PREPARATION TIME 40 MINUTES,
PLUS COOLING
COOKING TIME 35 MINUTES,
PLUS COOLING

INGREDIENTS

400g (14oz) whole shelled almonds, roughly chopped in batches in a food processor

3 tbsp caster sugar

400g (14oz) pack filo pastry

200g (7oz) unsalted butter, melted, plus extra for greasing

FOR THE SYRUP

340g (12oz) caster sugar

finely pared zest of 1 lemon

1½ tbsp lemon juice

2½ cinnamon sticks, roughly broken

450ml (15fl oz) water

BAKLAVA

This famous Greek sweet pastry is time-consuming but easy to make. If any filo pastry is left over after it is completed, roll it up and chill or freeze for later use.

METHOD

The syrup is best made the day before and kept in the fridge. Put all the ingredients for the syrup in a small saucepan. Set over a medium heat and stir occasionally until the sugar has dissolved. Lower the heat and simmer gently for about 20 minutes, or until the mixture forms a thin syrup. Remove from the heat, tip into a bowl, cover and cool, but do not strain. Chill when cold.

Preheat the oven to 160°C (325°F, gas 3). Liberally butter a 30 x 20cm (12 x 8in), 5cm (2in) deep baking dish.

Mix the chopped almonds with the caster sugar and set aside.

Unwrap the filo pastry and, if necessary, roughly measure and trim the sheets to ensure that they fit the prepared baking dish. They will shrink slightly, so allow an extra 1cm (½in). Brush the first sheet with plenty of melted butter and spread over the base of the baking dish. Continue to butter and layer the sheets until you have about 5 layers, completely covering the base, then scatter them with one-third of the almonds. Cover with 3 more layers of pastry, then sprinkle with half the remaining almonds before covering with another 3 layers of pastry. Scatter with the remaining almonds then top with another 7 or 8 layers of pastry. Liberally brush the top with melted butter.

With a sharp knife, gently cut through the top layers of pastry to mark out about 16 squares, diamonds or rectangles. Do not cut all the way through. This will help when you come to serve the baklava.

Put the baklava in the oven and bake for 30 minutes, then increase the oven temperature to 200°C (400°F, gas 6) and bake for another 10 minutes. The baklava is ready when it looks golden and cooked through.

Meanwhile, remove the lemon zest and cinnamon from the syrup. As soon as the baklava is taken out of the oven, quickly but evenly pour over the cold syrup. Leave to cool. When cold, cut the pieces along the original lines, but right through the pastry layers this time. Serve with strong coffee. The baklava improves and becomes more sticky if it is served the day after it is made.

SERVES 6
PREPARATION TIME 30 MINUTES
COOKING TIME 30 MINUTES, PLUS
COOLING

INGREDIENTS

8 egg yolks

55g (2oz) caster sugar

575ml (18fl oz) double cream

1 vanilla pod, split

icing sugar, to finish

CREME BRULEE

This much-loved dessert, whose name literally means 'burnt cream', has long been popular in Britain and France. Use the best eggs, sugar and cream, and you'll be stunned by the result.

METHOD

Preheat the oven to 180°C (350°F, gas 4).

Put the egg yolks and caster sugar in a large bowl and whisk together until the two are well combined.

Put the cream and vanilla pod in a heavy-based saucepan and bring just to boiling point, being careful not to let the cream boil. Remove the pan from the heat and take out the vanilla pod. Split the pod and scrape its seeds back into the cream. Discard the pod. Whisk the cream slowly into the egg yolk mixture.

Bring a pan of water to simmering point and reduce the heat to low. Sit the bowl with the egg and cream mixture over the simmering water and heat, stirring constantly with a wooden spoon, for about 15 minutes, until the mixture thickens into a custard with the consistency of single cream.

Strain the custard through a sieve into six 7.5cm (3in) ramekins or moulds. Sit these in a roasting tin. Pour warm water into the tin to come three-quarters of the way up the sides of the ramekins. Bake in the oven for 20–30 minutes, until just set. To test, remove one of the custards from the tin after 20 minutes and shake gently. There should be slight movement in the centre of the custard. If it is still runny, put the custards back in the oven for 5 minutes. When ready, remove from the oven, remove the ramekins from the roasting tin and allow to cool, but do not put them in the fridge.

Sift a thin layer of icing sugar over the cooled custards. Heat the sugar with a cook's blow torch until just dissolved but not coloured. Add another thin layer of sugar and heat with the torch again. It will bubble and start to colour. Stop when it is just turning golden. Add a third layer and heat again until it is deep golden brown. You may feel you need one more layer but keep it thin – a millimetre, less than a sixteenth of an inch, is too thick. The sugar topping can be caramelized under a very hot grill, keeping the ramekins as close to the heat as possible, but a blow torch gives much more control. Leave the topping to set, then serve at room temperature.

SUMMER

This is the most bountiful season. Many fresh foods are at their absolute, flavour-packed peak, which means they need minimal preparation, leaving cooks with plenty of time to relax and enjoy the fruits of their labours.

COURGETTES Mix green and yellow to make beautiful summer dishes.

MELONS The most fragrant and refreshing of summer fruits.

PEAS When very young and fresh, these are delicious raw.

SUMMER
FOODS IN SEASON

Warm and slow-paced, scented and ripe, summer is the sexiest season, when Nature is at her most provocative. The season is our reward for having battled through the cold and dark of winter, and is the fulfilment of spring's fertile promise.

Instead of being cocooned in a fug of boiling, braising and casseroling, the summer kitchen subtly changes character, and may even move outside. Whereas earlier in the year, slow-cooking was the order of the day, now most summer foods need only threatening with heat, or can even be served in a trice in all their raw glory.

'Ah, barbecue!' is the stock approach to treating meat when temperatures rise, but there is more to summer suppers than char-grilled protein (although massaging sweet-sour, chili-mustard stickiness over a poussin or a chicken joint is as much of a pleasure as eating the result). Instead of simply slapping it on the grill, allow good lean beef the time and luxury to wallow in a spicy aromatic marinade, then administer the *coup-de-grâce* by searing it for seconds and finishing the dish with the crispest, pertest green beans.

From the comfort of our sun loungers, we can believe that farmers' fingers, once chillblained and rough from winning tubers and roots from cold, rutted earth, are now soft and

NECTARINES Along with peaches, these are incredibly elegant, raw or cooked.

BASIL A great summer herb, with an aniseed-tinged flavour. Try it with fruit.

STRAWBERRIES Delicious and packed with antioxidants and vitamin C.

green, having gently plucked for us innocent baby broad beans to be whizzed into soup, and fresh peas to be podded and popped into tarts.

The bright colours of summer produce speak for themselves. Where once tomatoes murmured, now they cry redly of their soft, rich flavour, pleading sweetly to be sliced or stuffed or concassed into an elegant gazpacho. Red onions striated in shades ranging from Schiaparelli pink to darkest aubergine compete for our affections with green courgettes and super-sweet, sun-yellow corn cobs. Fragrant canteloupe melons, the essence of orange evening sunshine, and cooling, moist watermelons marry superbly with many summer foods, such as bright white feta cheese, or prawns and dill.

Now, instead of braving mountainous seas in search of dark, deep catches, fishermen put out into off-shore waters in bright day boats, lifting for us cloches filled with juicy crabs. Or they put out lines to lure small sardines and bright-eyed sole. These are to be kissed with bright spices or fresh herbs and (yet another) glass of pale wheat beer or fragrant Riesling – it is summer, after all.

Tree and berry fruits no longer need to be bullied to give up their best, but bring their true bright flavours to fools and soups, soufflés and tarts. Mealtimes need not start at eight sharp, for summer softens time and this season's foods are patient and fresh. Nature now clasps us to her ample bosom and whispers: 'Enjoy!'

KEVIN GOULD

Contributing editor, *Waitrose Food Illustrated*

SERVES 4
PREPARATION TIME 15 MINUTES
COOKING TIME 30 MINUTES

INGREDIENTS

3 tbsp olive oil

2 small onions, roughly chopped

2 garlic cloves, roughly chopped

1 litre (1³/₄ pints) chicken stock

675g (1¹/₂lb) shelled broad beans
(about 2kg /4¹/₂lb in pods)

2 large sage leaves, roughly chopped

200ml (7fl oz) crème fraîche

salt and freshly ground black pepper

pinch of caster sugar (optional)

TO SERVE

4 tbsp crème fraîche

4 sage leaves or 2 tbsp finely
snipped chives

BROAD BEAN SOUP WITH CREME FRAICHE & SAGE

This simple, fragrant soup of puréed fresh broad beans, chicken stock and crème fraîche is surely the taste of summer. It is equally good eaten hot, warm or cold, which makes it an ideal soup for a busy cook organizing a lunch party.

METHOD

Heat the olive oil in a large saucepan over a low heat, add the onions and garlic and gently fry them for about 10 minutes, or until soft. Add the stock, increase the heat and bring to the boil. Add the beans and return to the boil. Cook briskly for 12 minutes, or until the beans are meltingly soft.

Remove the pan from the heat and add the chopped sage. Liquidize the mixture in a food processor or blender while still piping hot. Strain the soup through a sieve and stir in the crème fraîche. Season to taste with salt, pepper and, if liked, a pinch of sugar.

If you are eating the soup straight away, reheat it now. Alternatively, cover and keep it in the fridge until it is needed. Whether the soup is served hot or cold, ladle it into soup bowls, add a spoonful of crème fraîche and garnish with a sage leaf or a sprinkling of snipped chives.

SERVES 6
PREPARATION TIME 25 MINUTES

INGREDIENTS

¹/₂ tbsp lime juice

1 tbsp lemon juice

3 tbsp orange juice

2 tbsp extra virgin olive oil

salt and freshly ground black pepper

4 plump cos lettuce hearts

generous handful mint leaves

generous handful coriander leaves

1 red onion, finely sliced into rings

1 ridge cucumber, peeled, halved
and sliced

200g (7oz) feta cheese, crumbled
into chunks

6 ripe peaches

PEACH, RED ONION & FETA SALAD

*Peaches make a wonderful addition to this simple salad.
A scattering of mint and coriander leaves, and a fruity citrus
dressing adds up to a fragrant, luscious dish.*

METHOD

To make the dressing, whisk together the lime, lemon and orange juices in a small
bowl with the olive oil and seasoning. Set aside.

Separate the lettuce leaves, discarding the tough outer ones. Wash and gently dry
the remaining leaves. Rip the larger ones in half and place all the leaves in a large
bowl with the mint, coriander, onion rings and sliced cucumber. Crumble the feta
into chunks and add to the leaves. Cover and set aside.

Just before serving the salad, quarter and stone the peaches. Cut each quarter
into fine slices and add to the salad. Re-whisk the dressing, pour over the salad
and mix thoroughly. Serve immediately.

SARDINE PATE

SERVES 4
PREPARATION TIME 30 MINUTES,
PLUS COOLING

INGREDIENTS

450g (1lb) sardines, cleaned and filleted

1 tbsp olive oil

100g (3½oz) unsalted butter, softened

generous pinch of cayenne pepper

salt and freshly ground black pepper

juice of 1 lemon

3 tbsp double cream

Cayenne pepper and lemon juice enhance the rich taste of grilled fresh sardines in this pâté. Served with crusty bread or toast, it is great eaten on a picnic or at an outdoor meal.

METHOD

Preheat a ridged grill pan over a medium-high heat.

Lightly oil the filleted sardines and, when the grill pan is smoking slightly, put on them on it, flesh side down. Grill for 1–2 minutes. Turn them over and grill for another minute. Transfer to a plate to cool. Once the fish is tepid, remove and discard the skin and flake the flesh, keeping a look out for stray bones. Set aside.

Meanwhile, beat the softened butter with the cayenne pepper and salt and black pepper to taste until it is light and fluffy. Mix in the lemon juice, followed by the cream. Then add the cooled, flaked fish and beat in. Alternatively, you can mix the pâté in a food processor but do not over-process it. Serve with lemon wedges and crusty bread – Irish soda bread is particularly good.

SERVES 4 AS A STARTER
PREPARATION TIME 20 MINUTES

INGREDIENTS

1 galia melon

1 cucumber

small handful of dill

12 large, cooked, peeled prawns

salt and freshly ground black pepper

juice of 1 lime

PRAWN & MELON SALAD WITH DILL

All the flavours in this light salad are very gentle and understated except for the lime, which adds a final kick that brings everything together. This is a starter salad. Just double up on the ingredients for a fine summer main course dish.

METHOD

Quarter the melon, scoop out the seeds and cut off the peel. Slice the melon into thin wedges and cut each wedge in half.

Peel the cucumber and then cut it in half lengthways. Scrape out the cucumber's seeds with a teaspoon, then cut the flesh into slices. Put the melon and cucumber in a bowl. Pluck the dill fronds from the stalks. Add the fronds to the melon and cucumber and toss gently to mix everything together.

If the prawns are very large, cut them in half lengthways. If necessary, remove the black vein running down the back. Add the prawns to the bowl with the melon. Season, add the lime juice and toss well. Serve chilled as a starter.

IN SEASON

MELONS

Fragrant, sweet, juicy and refreshing, melons are high in vitamin C, fibre and potassium. Whatever the colour and size of a melon, from the small cantaloupe and charentais to the huge watermelon, choosing a good one is simple. A ripe melon feels heavy in the hand and exudes a sweet scent, more distinctive in some melons than in others. The stalk end of a ripe melon gives a little, when pressed. Store melons at room temperature.

MAKES 10
PREPARATION TIME 30 MINUTES
COOKING TIME 1 HOUR, PLUS
COOLING

INGREDIENTS

100g (3½oz) American long-grain rice

10 large slicing tomatoes, plus
200g (7oz) extra tomatoes (any size)

6 tbsp Greek olive oil

1 onion, finely chopped

2 small courgettes, finely diced

4 spring onions, finely chopped

bunch parsley, finely chopped

small bunch dill, finely chopped

salt and freshly ground black pepper

100ml (3½fl oz) cold water

STUFFED TOMATOES

The heady taste of a Greek summer holiday can be recaptured by baking tomatoes stuffed with dill, parsley, spring onions, courgettes and rice. The same basic recipe can be adapted to produce stuffed aubergines, peppers and courgettes.

METHOD

Put the rice in a large sieve and rinse under cold running water. Shake it well and set aside to drain.

Slice off the stalk end of each slicing tomato and set aside. Cut away the central ribs and seeds and scoop them out with a teaspoon. Set aside the scooped-out flesh of 4 of the tomatoes. Finely chop the remainder of the scooped out flesh and put in a bowl with the washed rice. Put the hollow tomatoes, upside down, on a cooling rack over their baking dish to catch any excess juice.

Heat 2 tablespoons of the olive oil in a frying pan over a medium-low heat. Add the onion and fry gently until soft. Increase the heat, add the courgettes and fry briskly for 2 minutes. Tip the mixture into the rice. Add the spring onions, parsley, dill and 1 tablespoon of the olive oil. Season to taste and mix well.

Season the inside of the tomatoes with salt and pepper, then gently pack in the rice stuffing so the tomatoes are three-quarters full. Cover with their 'lids' (which may be removed before serving, if you like), and put in the baking dish. Preheat the oven to 190°C (375°F, gas 5).

Put the extra tomatoes in a bowl, pour over boiling water, and leave for 2 minutes. Remove from the water and slip off the skins. Cut the tomatoes into quarters and put in a food processor with the pulp set aside from the 4 slicing tomatoes. Process to a purée, then add the cold water and salt and pepper to taste. Pour the purée into the bottom of the tomato dish. Drizzle the remaining olive oil over the tomatoes. Put the dish in the centre of the oven and bake, uncovered, for 1 hour, basting regularly. Serve the stuffed tomatoes tepid or cold.

SERVES 4–6
PREPARATION TIME 1 ½ HOURS
COOKING TIME 25 MINUTES

INGREDIENTS

3 green courgettes, trimmed
and sliced diagonally

3 yellow courgettes, trimmed
and sliced diagonally

salt and freshly ground pepper

2 large eggs

few drops balsamic vinegar (optional)

2–3 tbsp plain flour

olive oil for shallow frying

3 buffalo mozzarella cheeses, about
225g (8oz) each, sliced

1 tbsp chopped marjoram

1 tbsp shredded basil leaves

FOR THE TOMATO SAUCE

3 tbsp olive oil

1 onion, chopped

2 garlic cloves, chopped

3 cans chopped plum tomatoes, about
400g (14oz) each, or 1.5kg (3lb 3oz)
fresh plum tomatoes, skinned and
chopped

1 tbsp tomato purée

1–2 bay leaves

pinch of sugar

IN SEASON

COURGETTES
Baby marrows they may be, but tender,
green or yellow-skinned, ivory-fleshed
courgettes have little in common with
the monster marrows of gardening
legend. The courgette's peel is edible,
they are very quick to cook, and are
perfect for slicing, grating, frittering,
adding to pasta sauces, baking, or
tossing, raw and sliced, into salads.

PARMIGIANA DI ZUCCHINE

In this delicious dish from Parma in northern Italy, both green and yellow courgettes are baked with mozzarella cheese in a herby tomato sauce. The result is a dish that is satisfying in both colour and flavour.

METHOD

Keeping the green and yellow courgette slices separate, sprinkle them lightly with salt and put in separate colanders. Leave to drain for 30 minutes. Rinse and drain.

Meanwhile, make the tomato sauce. Heat the oil in a roomy saucepan over a medium heat. Add the onion and garlic and fry gently until softened but not coloured. Add the tomatoes, tomato purée and bay leaves, bring to a simmer then reduce the heat. Cover the pan and leave to simmer for 30–40 minutes. Remove the lid for for the last 10 minutes so that the mixture can reduce to a rich, thick sauce. Season with salt, pepper and sugar to taste.

Beat the eggs with a tablespoon of water and a few drops of balsamic vinegar (if using). Pour into a shallow dish. Spread the flour on another plate and season it with salt and pepper. Pour about 1cm (½in) depth of olive oil into a frying pan and heat over a medium-high heat.

Preheat the oven to 180°C (350°F, gas 4).

Still keeping the two colours separate, dip the courgette slices in the flour and then the egg, then drop into the hot oil, a few at a time. Cook, turning once, for about 5 minutes, until golden. Remove from the pan and drain on kitchen paper. Repeat until all the courgette slices are cooked.

Layer the green courgette fritters on the base of a large gratin dish. Cover with half the tomato sauce, then half the mozzarella slices, then sprinkle over half the marjoram and basil. Add the yellow courgette fritters in a layer, and cover with the remaining tomato sauce, mozzarella, and herbs. Drizzle with a little oil and bake for 20–25 minutes, until beautifully brown and bubbling. Serve straight away with a green leaf salad, if liked.

SERVES 4
PREPARATION TIME 50 MINUTES

INGREDIENTS

450g (1lb) baby new potatoes

450g (1lb) green beans, trimmed

4 eggs

1½ tsp smooth Dijon mustard

1 garlic clove, finely chopped

3 tbsp white wine vinegar

150ml (5fl oz) extra virgin olive oil

salt and freshly ground pepper

4 tuna steaks, about 150g (5½oz) each

8 anchovy fillets, cut into strips

handful basil leaves, ripped

1 red onion, finely sliced

225g (8oz) baby plum tomatoes, halved

12 black olives

4 cos lettuce hearts, trimmed

NICOISE SALAD

The key to a good Niçoise salad is to use what looks best and freshest on the day. There are no firm rules, although traditionalists maintain that it should contain no cooked vegetables. Thus, potatoes might be replaced by sliced cucumber, and green beans by raw baby artichoke hearts.

METHOD

Put the potatoes in a saucepan and cover with cold water. Cover the pan, bring to the boil, and boil for 15 minutes, or until tender. Drain. Drop the beans into a saucepan of boiling water and cook for about 8 minutes, until very tender. Drain and spread on a plate to cool. Put the eggs in a pan, cover with cold water and bring to a simmer. Simmer for 8 minutes, drain away the water and leave under a running cold tap for 5 minutes.

For the vinaigrette dressing, whisk together the mustard, garlic, vinegar and all but 1 tablespoon of the olive oil. Season with salt and pepper. When the beans are tepid, dress them in a third of the vinaigrette. Peel the potatoes. Cut into thick slices and mix in a third of the vinaigrette.

Meanwhile, preheat a ridged grill pan on a medium-high heat. Brush the tuna steaks with the remaining olive oil and season with salt and pepper. Place on the hot grill pan and sear for about 3 minutes on each side. The time will vary according to how thick the tuna steaks are, but remove them from the pan while still slightly pink inside as they will continue to cook. Leave to cool, then break into chunks. Put in a large bowl with any juices from the grill pan.

Add the anchovies, basil, onion, tomatoes and olives to the tuna. Add the lettuce (ripping the large leaves into pieces). Peel the eggs, cut into quarters and add to the salad with the beans, potatoes and remaining dressing. Gently toss all the ingredients together to mix well, and serve.

SERVES 6
PREPARATION TIME 30 MINUTES,
PLUS CHILLING

INGREDIENTS

1.5kg (3lb 3oz) ripe strawberries

115g (4oz) caster sugar, plus 2 tbsp

200ml (7fl oz) dry champagne (brut)

pinch of salt

170g (6oz) plain fromage frais

TO SERVE

tiny mint leaves

freshly ground black pepper

STRAWBERRY SOUP WITH FROMAGE FRAIS

Blend puréed strawberries with sugar and champagne to create a refreshing summer dish. Adding a swirl of sweetened fromage frais and a sprinkling of black pepper transforms it into a suave dessert.

METHOD

Wash and hull the strawberries. Put them in a blender with the 115g (4oz) caster sugar and blend to a purée. Push the purée through a sieve into a mixing bowl. Discard the pips left in the sieve. Stir in the champagne and a pinch of salt. Cover and chill in the fridge for at least 2 hours.

Beat the fromage frais with the remaining 2 tablespoons of sugar, cover and chill.

To serve the soup, skim off the pale strawberry froth from the top before pouring it into 6 soup bowls or large cups. Place small blobs or teaspoons of sweetened fromage frais on top of each. Garnish with tiny mint leaves and finish with a small grinding of black pepper. Serve immediately.

IN SEASON

STRAWBERRIES

Although they are easy to buy all year round, it's far better to wait until early summer when these luscious berries are naturally in season and their sweet flavour is at its peak. Never serve them cold, always at room temperature, and treat them simply. Try them sliced and folded into whipped cream with crushed meringue to make Eton Mess, or macerate them in a fruity liqueur and spoon over vanilla ice cream.

SERVES 4–6
PREPARATION TIME 30 MINUTES
COOKING TIME 40 MINUTES

INGREDIENTS

large pinch of saffron (about 20 threads)

2 tbsp olive oil

1 medium onion, finely sliced

1 large garlic clove, sliced

400g (14 oz) can chopped tomatoes

150ml (5fl oz) white wine

450g (1lb) waxy potatoes, peeled and cut into chunks

450g (1lb) carrots, peeled and cut into chunks

450g (1lb) parsnips, peeled and cut into chunks

450g (1lb) turnips, cut into chunks

short stick of cinnamon

1 bay leaf

salt and freshly ground black pepper

400g (14oz) can chickpeas, drained

couscous, to serve

FOR THE FLAVOURING MIX

1 tbsp olive oil

55g (2oz) blanched almonds, roughly chopped

1 garlic clove, finely chopped

1 tbsp chopped parsley

1 tbsp fresh breadcrumbs

IN SEASON

ROOT VEGETABLES

Although they are available all year round, many root vegetables are at their best in winter, cold frosts adding to the intensity of their flavour. Smaller root vegetables, such as carrots and turnips, can be cooked whole when young. Older ones are excellent in soups and stews, or combined in purées or mashes.

VALENCIAN VEGETABLES WITH SAFFRON

This is the traditional midday dish in the farmhouses of Valencia. In summer, it is made with beans, peas and artichokes, but it is also delicious with earthy root vegetables, which are lifted by the musky flavour of the saffron.

METHOD

Soak the saffron in a splash of boiling water for 10 minutes, then crush it firmly in the water with a spoon.

Heat the oil in a large saucepan over a medium heat and add the onions and garlic. Fry gently for 10–15 minutes until they are soft and golden, but not brown. Add the tomatoes and bring to a simmer. Add the wine and simmer briskly for a couple of minutes to evaporate the alcohol. Add the vegetables and the saffron with its soaking water.

Pour enough water into the pan to barely cover the vegetables. Bring to the boil, add the cinnamon stick and bay leaf and seasoning. Cover the pan and cook for 25–30 minutes, until the vegetables are tender.

Meanwhile, prepare the flavouring mix. Heat the olive oil in a frying pan over a medium heat. Add the almonds and fry gently until they turn golden, but not brown. Stir in the garlic and parsley. Fry for another minute then stir in the breadcrumbs and fry for a further minute so that the breadcrumbs take up the oil and brown a little.

As soon as the vegetables are tender, add the chickpeas and stir in the flavouring mix. Bring to the boil and cook, uncovered, for about 10 minutes, until the liquid is reduced to a small amount of sauce. Serve the vegetables warm – the best temperature to appreciate the delicate flavour of the saffron. Serve them with couscous, as the Spanish do.

SERVES 4
PREPARATION TIME 50 MINUTES,
PLUS RESTING THE PASTA DOUGH
COOKING TIME 15–20 MINUTES

INGREDIENTS

300g (10½oz) bread flour

½ tsp salt

3 eggs

1 tsp olive oil

fine-ground semolina for dusting

FOR THE STUFFING

450g (1lb) pumpkin or squash, skinned, seeded and cubed

2 tbsp mostarda di Cremona, the fruit chopped small *or* a mixture of 1 tbsp crystallized peel, 1 tbsp honey and 1 tsp grain mustard

2–3 amaretti biscuits, crushed

4 tbsp breadcrumbs

1 small egg, lightly beaten

½ tsp nutmeg, freshly grated

2 tbsp freshly grated Parmesan

TO SERVE

75g (2½oz) unsalted butter

3-4 sage leaves

grated Parmesan

TORTELLI DI ZUCCA AL BURRO

These light and delicate pumpkin-filled ravioli are sauced with sage-infused butter, just as they are in Emilia Romagna, their Italian home. Crushed amaretti give the filling texture.

METHOD

For the pasta, mix the flour and salt together in a roomy bowl. Crack the eggs into a well in the middle, and add the oil. Work the ingredients together in a circular movement with your hand, adding enough water to create a softish dough. If you need to dry it out a little, dust your hands with a little more flour. Knead the dough thoroughly for at least 10 minutes, until it is perfectly smooth and elastic. Lightly oil the dough ball (use the palm of your hand, moistened with a little oil), put it in a plastic bag and leave to rest for 30 minutes.

Preheat the oven to 190°C (375°F, gas 5). Roast the pumpkin or squash on a baking sheet for about 30 minutes, until the flesh is tender. Skin the pumpkin and process or mash the flesh to a purée. Set aside to cool.

Divide the pasta dough in half, form each piece into a ball and dust with semolina. Roll out into two very thin strips equal in length and width. Alternatively, feed the dough through a pasta-roller, gradually decreasing the settings until the pasta is thin enough to read a newspaper through.

Mix the puréed pumpkin with the mostarda, including a little of the syrup, and work in the remaining stuffing ingredients. Drop teaspoonfuls of the mixture about 8cm (3½ in) apart on one of the pasta sheets. Brush between the piles with a little water, cover with the remaining sheet of pasta, and press between the mounds to seal. Cut with a pastry wheel or a sharp knife to give about 24 plump little pillows.

Bring a large pan of well-salted water to the boil. Slip in the tortelli in small batches, as many as will cover the surface. Cook for just 2–3 minutes – they will bob to the surface as soon as they are done. Remove from the pan with a draining spoon and place in a warm dish trickled with a little oil.

Meanwhile, melt the butter in a frying pan and then add the sage. Continue to heat until the butter sizzles and turns golden, but do not let it brown. Drizzle the tortelli with the hot butter and serve. If liked, have a bowl of grated Parmesan on the table to sprinkle over the ravioli.

SERVES 6
PREPARATION TIME 45 MINUTES
COOKING TIME 20–40 MINUTES

INGREDIENTS

4 medium potatoes, peeled and cut into 2.5cm (1 in) chunks

3 tbsp extra virgin olive oil

185g (6½ oz) back bacon, diced

1 large onion, finely sliced

2 garlic cloves, finely diced

1 tsp fresh thyme leaves

¼ tsp chili flakes (or to taste)

675g (1½ lb) Savoy cabbage, trimmed, quartered and cut into chunky dice

55g (2oz) freshly grated Parmesan

salt and freshly ground black pepper

butter for greasing

225g (8oz) taleggio cheese, diced

IN SEASON

SAVOY CABBAGE

Distinguished by its dark green, wrinkly and dimpled leaves, Savoy cabbage is one of the mildest varieties in the large brassica family, which includes curly kale, cauliflower and pak choi as well as the many different cabbages. Once blanched, Savoy cabbage leaves are ideal for stuffing. To stuff a whole Savoy cabbage, trim it and wash in salted water before removing the hard core. Savoy cabbage is traditionally stewed with partridge in France.

CHEESY BACON, POTATO & CABBAGE GRATIN

This is a robust supper dish that oozes with melted taleggio and Parmesan cheeses. It is delicious, especially when accompanied by a rich-flavoured tomato and pepper salad.

METHOD

Bring a large pan of water to the boil. Drop in the chunks of potato and return to the boil. Cover and cook for 5 minutes, or until just tender. Drain the potato chunks and put in a large bowl.

Meanwhile, heat the oil in a large saucepan. Add the bacon and fry until it is well coloured. Lower the heat and stir in the onions, garlic, thyme and chili flakes. Fry gently, stirring occasionally, until the onion is soft.

Wash the prepared cabbage, then tip a third of it, still wet, into the onion mix. Keep adding more cabbage as it wilts in the pan until all is incorporated. You may need to add a little water, to prevent the cabbage sticking. Once the cabbage has wilted, remove the pan from the heat and mix the cabbage and onion into the potatoes. Mix in about half the Parmesan and the seasoning.

Preheat the oven to 200°C (400°F, gas 6). Butter a 23cm (9 in) square baking dish, about 5cm (2 in) deep.

Spoon half the cabbage and potato mixture into the baking dish. Dot with half the taleggio. Cover with the remaining cabbage mixture and strew the top with the remaining taleggio and Parmesan. If the mixture is still warm, bake in the centre of the oven for 20 minutes – otherwise bake for 30–40 minutes – or until the vegetables are piping hot and the cheese is bubbling and flecked golden.

SERVES 4
PREPARATION TIME 30 MINUTES
COOKING TIME 45 MINUTES

INGREDIENTS

1 red onion, thickly sliced

3 tbsp quince cheese (membrillo)

2 oven-ready pheasants

salt and freshly round black pepper

30g (1oz) butter, softened

2 bay leaves

1 tbsp Marsala

150ml (5 fl oz) chicken stock

FOR THE SAVOURY BREADCRUMBS

1 tbsp olive oil

20g (³/₄ oz) butter

2 shallots, finely chopped

8 tbsp coarse, sourdough breadcrumbs

1 tbsp chopped walnuts or pine nuts

1 tbsp raisins, soaked in boiling water

IN SEASON

PHEASANT

Native to China, pheasant is a fine-tasting game bird that is easy to cook, taking half the time of a chicken. It can be roasted, stewed, braised and even cooked *en papillote*. It is available either fresh – when it is often also 'oven-ready' – or frozen. Pheasant is often sold as a brace of birds: 1 hen and 1 cock. A hen pheasant is thought to be more tender than a cock, but feeds only 2–3, whereas a cock will feed 3-4.

ROAST PHEASANT WITH QUINCE CHEESE

Pheasant is traditionally served with bread sauce and game chips but it is good to ring the changes, as here. Breadcrumbs are another traditional accompaniment and the updated version here can be made in advance and stored in a sealed container. Chicken and partridge also work well in this recipe.

METHOD

Preheat the oven to 200°C (400°F, gas 6).

Lay the sliced red onion on the bottom of a roasting tin. Put half the quince cheese inside each pheasant's cavity and season inside. Smear the butter over both birds and season again. Lay the pheasant on the onions and tuck the bay leaves under them. Roast for 45 minutes, or until the juices run clear when the thigh is pierced with a skewer.

Meanwhile, prepare the breadcrumbs. Heat the oil and butter in a frying pan over a medium heat. Add the shallots, breadcrumbs and nuts. Toss together for about 5 minutes, until the breadcrumbs have absorbed all the fat and the mix is crisp and golden. Drain on kitchen paper. When ready to use, drain the raisins, squeezing out excess moisture, and toss into the breadcrumbs.

When the pheasants are cooked, remove from the oven. Carefully tip each bird so any quince cheese left in the cavities runs out into the pan juices. Transfer the birds to a warmed plate, cover with foil and rest them in a warm place while you make the gravy.

Skim off any excess fat from the roasting tin. Remove the bay leaves and onions. Put the tin over a medium heat, pour in the Marsala and stir vigorously to lift all the caramelized bits from the tin. Add the stock and bring to the boil, then simmer for 2–3 minutes. Pour into a warmed jug. Carve the pheasants and serve with the breadcrumbs and gravy.

SERVES 4
PREPARATION TIME 20 MINUTES
PLUS DRYING OVERNIGHT
COOKING TIME 2 HOURS, 45
MINUTES

INGREDIENTS

1 oven-ready duck, about 2.25kg (5lb)

scant tbsp Cointreau

juice of 1 orange

2 oranges, segmented, all membrane
and peel removed

salt and freshly ground black pepper

3 spring onions, finely sliced

FOR THE ROASTED PUMPKIN

1 pumpkin, about1.5kg (3lb 3oz)

1½ tbsp olive oil

2 sprigs thyme, leaves only, plus extra
to garnish

finely grated zest of 1 orange

DUCK WITH THYME, ORANGE & PUMPKIN

Fruit goes well with duck because it is such a rich meat. This dish makes the most of the classic combination of duck and orange, with the fruit's colour echoed in the pumpkin.

METHOD

Put the duck in a colander and pour a kettle of boiling water over it, to help loosen the fat. Drain the duck and pat dry thoroughly, inside and out, with kitchen paper. Brush the duck with the Cointreau (this helps to dry out the skin, giving a crisper finish). To dry the duck further, put it, uncovered, in the fridge and leave for 24 hours.

When ready to roast the duck, preheat the oven to 200°C (400°F, gas 6). Put the duck on a rack in a roasting tin. Put in the oven and roast for 45 minutes, then turn the oven temperature down to 150°C (300°F, gas 2). Continue cooking for 2 hours, or until the meat is almost falling off the bone and the skin in really crisp. Remove from the oven and transfer to a warm plate. Rest for 5–10 minutes.

While the duck is roasting, prepare the pumpkin. Cut it in half, scoop out the seeds and slice the pumpkin into thin wedges. Put on a shallow roasting tray and sprinkle over the olive oil, thyme leaves, orange zest and salt and pepper. Put in the oven with the duck for the last 20 minutes of cooking time. While the duck is resting, increase the oven temperature to 200°C (400°F, gas 6) and continue roasting the pumpkin for 10 minutes, or until the flesh beings to caramelize.

Shred the duck meat and skin away from the carcass. Toss the meat in the orange juice, mixed with any duck juices left on the plates. Season. Arrange the pumpkin on a serving platter. Add the shredded duck and scatter over the orange segments and spring onions. Garnish with thyme and serve. Sautéed potatoes are a good additional accompaniment.

SERVES 6
PREPARATION TIME 40 MINUTES,
PLUS MARINATING
COOKING TIME 1 HOUR, 10 MINUTES

INGREDIENTS

1kg (2¼ lb) venison leg meat, trimmed and diced

3 strips finely pared orange zest

6 tbsp sunflower oil

225g (8 oz) dry-cure smoked back bacon, cut into lardons

1 onion, quartered and sliced

2 large carrots, cut into batons

1 small garlic clove, finely chopped

2 tbsp Grand Marnier

2 tbsp plain flour

150ml (5fl oz) chicken stock

3 stems parsley

2 sprigs thyme

salt and freshly ground black pepper

200g (7 oz) plain flour

100ml (3½ fl oz) water

2 tbsp chopped parsley

FOR THE MARINADE

1 bottle fruity red wine

1 bay leaf

3 sprigs thyme

1 large sprig parsley

1 onion, roughly sliced

2 outer sticks of celery, roughly sliced

2 large carrots, roughly sliced

1 clove

5 black peppercorns

IN SEASON

VENISON

Although farmed venison is available throughout the year, its rich flavour suits the cooking of colder months best. The simple way to cook farmed venison is to roast or grill it, then serve it with a clear gravy and a fruit jelly. It is also very good stewed and turned into a pie or pasty.

VENISON DAUBE

Traditionally, wild venison is marinated in wine to tenderize it. Today, farmed venison does not need tenderizing, but a wine and vegetable marinade can add another layer of flavour to a casserole. Here, the marinated meat is gently simmered with bacon, orange zest, carrots, onions and garlic.

METHOD

Mix all the marinade ingredients together and put with the venison in a non-metallic container. Turn the meat in the marinade to coat it well, cover the dish and chill for a minimum of 8 hours and a maximum of 24 hours.

Turn the oven on to 140°C (275°F, gas 1). Put the strips of orange zest in an ovenproof dish and place in the oven for about 10 minutes, or until the zest is curled and dry. Take out of the oven and set aside. Leave the oven on.

Drain the marinated meat and vegetables, reserving the marinade liquid. Separate the meat from the marinated vegetables, herbs and spices. Set the meat aside and discard the vegetables, herbs and spices.

Heat 3 tablespoons of the oil in a frying pan over a moderate heat. Fry the bacon for 3 minutes, then add the sliced onion, carrots and garlic. When the onions are soft and golden, transfer the vegetables from the pan to a casserole dish.

Add another 2 tablespoons of the oil to the pan and increase the heat to high. Put enough of the marinated venison into the pan to form a single layer and fry it briskly until it is well coloured. Transfer it to the casserole dish. Repeat the process, with extra oil if needed, until all the meat is browned. Pour the Grand Marnier over the venison in the casserole, set alight and stir until the flames die out.

Now stir the 2 tablespoons of plain flour into the fat in the frying pan. Cook for 1 minute then stir in about a quarter of the reserved marinade liquid. Boil until it has reduced by half. Add the remaining marinade liquid and continue to boil until it is thick, then mix into the casserole with the stock, dried orange peel, parsley stems and thyme. Season to taste.

Mix the flour and water to make a stiff dough. Roll out on a lightly floured surface into a long sausage, press around the rim of the casserole and squash the lid down on top of it. Put the casserole in the oven and bake for 1 hour, 10 minutes. Break the pastry seal, add the chopped parsley and serve the casserole.

SERVES 6
PREPARATION TIME 30 MINUTES,
PLUS 1 ½ HOURS COOKING
FINAL COOKING TIME 35 MINUTES

INGREDIENTS

3 tbsp olive oil

1kg (2¼lb) braising steak, cut into
2.5 cm (1in) cubes

1 large onion, chopped

225g (8oz) chestnut mushrooms, halved

1 heaped tbsp plain flour

1 bay leaf

2 tbsp Worcestershire sauce

1 tbsp english mustard

300ml (10fl oz) beef stock

salt and freshly ground black pepper

1 tbsp chopped parsley

300g (10½oz) shortcrust pastry

lightly beaten egg mixed with a little
water, to glaze

STEAK & MUSHROOM PIE

Beef and mushrooms are perfect together, as this traditional favourite demonstrates. You can also serve the filling by itself as a tasty stew, with mashed potatoes to mop up the sauce.

METHOD

To make the filling, heat 1 tablespoon of the oil in a large heatproof casserole. Add one-third of the steak and brown over a medium heat. Remove with a draining spoon and set aside. Repeat with the remaining oil and beef in two batches, leaving some oil in the casserole when you remove the last batch of beef.

Add the onion to the casserole and cook for about 15 minutes, until soft and caramelized. Add the mushrooms and continue to cook, stirring, for 5 minutes, or until the mushrooms begin to soften. Add the flour, stirring it into the onions and mushrooms, and cook for 2–3 minutes. Add the Worcestershire sauce, mustard and beef stock and stir until the mixture is smooth. Return the beef to the casserole, along with the bay leaf. Bring to the boil, reduce the heat, cover the casserole and simmer for about 1½ hours, or until the beef is very tender. Season to taste with salt and pepper, and add the parsley. Remove the bay leaf.

Preheat the oven to 190°C (375°F, gas 5).

Roll out the pastry to fit the top of a 1.7 litres (3 pints) pie dish. Cut a thin ribbon of pastry, brush the rim of the dish with the beaten egg and water mixture and stick the pastry strip to it.

Put the beef and mushroom filling into the pie dish. Put a pie funnel in the middle of the filling. Lay the pastry over the top, pressing the edges to seal and trimming off the excess. Make a hole for the top of the pie funnel to poke through. Cut a few decorative leaves from the pastry trimmings and stick them to the pie with the egg. Glaze the top of the pie with the remaining beaten egg. Put in the oven and bake for 35 minutes until golden brown.

SERVES 4
PREPARATION TIME 20 MINUTES
COOKING TIME 10 MINUTES

INGREDIENTS

sunflower oil for deep frying

450g (1lb) pork fillet, cut into
2.5cm (1in) cubes

1 tbsp sake

1 tbsp soy sauce

3 tbsp plain flour, sifted

1 egg, lightly beaten

2 red peppers, quartered and seeded

1 bunch spring onions, trimmed

225g (8oz) can bamboo shoots, drained
and rinsed

2 x 225g (8oz) cans unsweetened
pineapple chunks in juice, drained

1 tbsp cornflour

FOR THE SWEET AND SOUR SAUCE

2 tsp cornflour

100ml (3½fl oz) water

4 tbsp soft brown sugar

2 tbsp soy sauce

6 tbsp rice or white wine vinegar

2 tbsp tomato ketchup

SWEET & SOUR PORK

*This dish has long been a favourite in Chinese restaurants.
This recipe shows how easy it is to prepare at home. It is
delicious served with steamed or egg-fried rice.*

METHOD

If you are using a deep-fat fryer, fill it with oil and preheat to 180°C (350°F).

Put the pork cubes in a large bowl. Mix in the sake and soy sauce and set aside.

To make the batter for the pork, sift the flour into a medium-sized bowl, drop the egg into the centre and beat until the mixture is smooth. Set aside.

Cut the peppers and spring onions into 2.5cm (1in) pieces. Set aside with the bamboo shoots and pineapple chunks.

To make the sweet and sour sauce, put the cornflour in a small saucepan. Mix in the water, sugar, soy sauce, vinegar and ketchup and set the pan over a low heat. Simmer gently for about 3 minutes, or until the sauce has thickened.

Meanwhile, remove the pork from its marinade. Put it on a plate, dust with the tablespoon of cornflour, then mix it into the batter. If you are not using a deep-fat fryer, heat enough oil in a wok or sauté pan to shallow-fry the pork until it is smoking hot. Deep-fry or shallow-fry the batter-coated pork in two batches. Each batch should take 2–3 minutes. Once each batch is a deep-gold colour, remove and drain on kitchen paper.

Return all the cooked pork to the oil for another 2 minutes, while you heat 2 tablespoons of sunflower oil in a non-stick frying pan or a wok. Once sizzling hot, add the red pepper and spring onions, stir-fry briskly for a minute, then add the bamboo shoots and pineapple chunks, followed by the sauce. Bring the sauce up to a boil and as soon as it is bubbling, mix in the piping hot pork. As soon as it is coated in the sauce, pour into a serving dish and serve, with rice.

SERVES 6
PREPARATION TIME 1 HOUR,
PLUS CHILLING
COOKING TIME 30 MINUTES

INGREDIENTS

250g (8½ oz) plain flour

pinch of salt

125g (4½ oz) cold butter, diced

1 egg yolk

2 tbsp water

FOR THE FILLING

400g (14oz) pumpkin, peeled
and seeded weight

200ml (7 fl oz) water

85g (3oz) caster sugar

finely grated zest of 1 lemon

3 tbsp brandy

pinch of ground cinnamon

pinch of ground ginger

150ml (5 fl oz) double cream

5 egg yolks

icing sugar, to dust

EDWARDIAN SPICED PUMPKIN PIE

This deliciously spiced pumpkin pie could not be more authentically Edwardian. It is adapted from the 1909 edition of Mrs Beeton's Everyday Cookery.

METHOD

Put the flour, salt and butter in a mixing bowl or food processor and rub the butter into the flour with the fingertips, or pulse in the processor, to fine crumbs. Tip into a bowl and add the egg yolk and enough cold water to bind the dough. Knead lightly on a floured surface, then roll out and use to line a deep 20cm (8 in) tart tin with a removable base. Prick the base with a fork, line with greaseproof paper and baking beans. Chill for 30 minutes.

Preheat the oven to 200°C (400°F, gas 6).

Put the pumpkin flesh in a saucepan with the water. Bring to the boil, cover and simmer until the pumpkin is very soft and the water has evaporated. If necessary, add a little more water as the pumpkin cooks, but you need the final mixture to be quite dry. Purée the pumpkin, either in a food processor or through a sieve, and set aside to cool.

Put the pastry-lined tart tin in the oven and bake for 10 minutes. Remove the paper and baking beans and bake for a further 8–10 minutes, until the pastry no longer looks raw. Take the tin from the oven and reduce the oven temperature to 180°C (350°F, gas 4).

Mix the pumpkin with the sugar, lemon zest, brandy and spices. Beat together the egg yolks and cream and add to the mix. Pour into the pastry case. Return the tin to the oven and bake for 30–40 minutes or until the filling is just set, but still with a slight wobble. Serve the pie warm or cold, dusted with icing sugar.

SERVES 6
PREPARATION TIME 25 MINUTES
COOKING TIME 15 MINUTES

INGREDIENTS

1 lemon

3 sprigs rosemary

5 black peppercorns

200g (7oz) granulated sugar

200ml (7fl oz) water

100ml (3½fl oz) dessert wine, such as Beaumes de Venise

6 ripe English pears, such as Comice

5 ratafia biscuits

225g (8oz) clotted cream

PEAR COMPOTE WITH ALMOND CREAM

This is an update of the old British custom of flavouring sugar with rosemary. A light sugar syrup is infused with the herb and other ingredients and poured over sliced pears.

METHOD

Finely pare a few strips of zest from the lemon. Put in a small saucepan with the rosemary, peppercorns, sugar and water. Set over a medium heat and stir occasionally until the sugar has dissolved. Simmer for 15 minutes, or until a sticky syrup has formed.

Meanwhile, squeeze the lemon and pour the juice and the dessert wine into a bowl. Peel, quarter and core the pears. Cut each quarter into 3 or 4 lengthways slices and mix into the dessert wine. Once the syrup is ready, strain into the pears and gently mix. Set aside to cool.

To make the cream, finely crush the ratafias in a freezer bag with a rolling pin. Tip into a small bowl and mix in the clotted cream. The almond flavour will develop in intensity the longer the mixture is left. Chill until needed.

Serve the pears, which should be chilled or at room temperature, with the cream.

IN SEASON

PEARS

Perfectly ripe pears are best simply sliced and served with cheese, or drizzled with honey and partnered with almonds. Different varieties mature at different times, so shop around throughout the autumn. Slightly under-ripe pears, however, are actually better for cooking, whether poached, roasted or puréed. They have a particular affinity with chocolate – try baking them into a chocolate sponge pudding. Always peel pears before cooking.

SERVES 8
PREPARATION TIME 1 HOUR
COOKING TIME 10 MINUTES

INGREDIENTS

4 large, ripe pears, about 800g (1³/₄lb) in total

juice of 1 lemon

115g (4oz) caster sugar, plus extra for dusting

2 tbsp arrowroot

4 tbsp calvados

15g (¹/₂oz) butter, melted

4 egg whites

FOR THE CHOCOLATE SAUCE

200g (7oz) dark chocolate, broken

200ml (7fl oz) milk

2 tbsp double cream

30g (1oz) caster sugar

30g (1oz) butter, diced

HOT PEAR SOUFFLES WITH CHOCOLATE SAUCE

Serve the chocolate sauce separately, so that each guest can break into their soufflé and pour in their sauce. You only need a little because the soufflés have quite a delicate flavour.

METHOD

To make the sauce, put the chocolate in a small bowl set over a pan of simmering water and leave to melt. Put the milk, cream and sugar in a saucepan and stir over a low heat until the sugar has dissolved. Once the chocolate has melted, bring the milk mix to the boil and whisk the melted chocolate into it. Remove from the heat and gradually beat in the butter until the sauce is smooth and glossy. Keep the sauce warm if you are making the soufflés straightaway, or cool and chill it.

Peel, core and roughly dice 3 of the pears. Put the diced pears in a non-corrodible saucepan with half the lemon juice and 85g (3oz) of the sugar. Cook gently for about 15 minutes, or until the pear is soft and surrounded by juice. Pour into a blender and blend to a purée, then return to the pan. Mix the arrowroot with 3 tablespoons of the calvados and stir into the puréed fruit. Reheat and boil for 2 minutes, until the mixture thickens. Remove from the heat and cool.

Preheat the oven to 220°C (425°F, gas 7). Brush eight 150ml (5fl oz) soufflé dishes or ramekins with the melted butter and liberally coat with caster sugar. This helps the soufflés rise in the dishes. Set aside.

For the soufflé filling, peel, core and finely dice the remaining pear. Mix with the remaining calvados and the remaining lemon juice and leave to macerate while the calvados and pear purée is cooling.

Once the purée is tepid, strain the macerated diced pear and mix the juices into the purée. Whisk the egg whites until fluffy, add the remaining 30g (1oz) of caster sugar and continue to whisk until stiff. Loosen the puréed pears with one-third of the whipped whites and then gently fold in the remainder.

Spoon the mixture half way up the soufflé dishes, sprinkle with the diced pear, and top with the remaining soufflé mixture. Flatten the top of the soufflés with a palette knife, then run your thumb around the top inside edge of each soufflé dish to prevent the soufflé sticking as it cooks, which can stop it rising. Place on a hot baking sheet in the centre of the oven and immediately lower the temperature to 190°C (375°F, gas 5). Bake for 10 minutes until the soufflés are well-risen but slightly wobbly. Serve immediately with the hot sauce served separately.

SERVES 8
PREPARATION TIME 35 MINUTES,
PLUS COOLING THE SPONGE BASE
COOKING TIME 15 MINUTES

INGREDIENTS

170g (6oz) dark chocolate, broken into pieces

170g (6oz) caster sugar

5 eggs, separated

1 tsp vanilla extract

3 tbsp hot water

icing sugar to dust

FOR THE FILLING

3 tbsp icing sugar

115g (4oz) unsweetened chestnut purée

4 tbsp soured cream

100g (3½oz) cooked chestnuts, peeled and roughly chopped

2 tbsp rum

300ml (10fl oz) double cream

IN SEASON

CHESTNUTS

Inside its leathery covering, the flesh of a fresh chestnut is white and crisp, and its mildly nutty sweetness is intensified when it is cooked. To peel chestnuts, simmer in boiling water for 1 minute or roast in a hot oven for 5 minutes; peel off the skin while still hot. Cooked chestnuts, diced or puréed, work well with cream, and their delicacy is enhanced by vanilla. They are great with chocolate and make a delicious filling for sponge cakes.

CHOCOLATE CHESTNUT RUM ROULADE

A gooey chocolate sponge and an unctuously smooth chestnut purée come together to make this roulade a truly tempting pudding or tea-time treat. To save time, use pre-cooked, peeled, vacuum-packed chestnuts, if they are available.

METHOD

Preheat the oven to 180°C (350°F, gas 4) and lightly oil a shallow baking tin, measuring about 35cm x 25cm (14 x 10in). Line the baking tin with greaseproof paper, and oil the paper very lightly.

Melt the chocolate in a small bowl set over a pan of simmering water. In a separate large bowl, beat the caster sugar into the egg yolks until thick, pale and fluffy. Add the vanilla extract. Once the chocolate has melted, stir in the hot water and beat until smooth, then gradually stir into the egg mix.

Whisk the egg whites until they hold soft peaks. Quickly and gently fold them into the chocolate mixture. Pour into the prepared tin, spread evenly, and immediately put it into the oven. Bake for 15 minutes, then remove, and immediately cover with a sheet of greaseproof paper and a clean tea towel. Leave until cold.

Meanwhile, mix the icing sugar into the chestnut purée, followed by the soured cream and chopped chestnuts. Pour the rum and double cream into a large mixing bowl. Whisk until the mixture forms stiff peaks then roughly fold it into the chestnut cream so that you have a marbled effect.

Spread a large sheet of greaseproof paper on a clean working surface. Liberally dust with sifted icing sugar. Gently turn the sponge out onto the paper and peel away its layer of baking paper. Trim the edges and spread the chunky chestnut cream over the base. Using the sugared paper, carefully roll up the sponge lengthways, like a swiss roll. Trim off the ends, if you like, and lift the roulade onto a clean plate. Carefully ease away the sugared sheet. Chill the roulade in the fridge for a few hours before serving it.

SERVES 4
PREPARATION TIME 20 MINUTES
COOKING TIME 55 MINUTES

INGREDIENTS

2 large cooking apples, such as Bramley

caster sugar to taste

340g (12oz) blackberries

150g (5½oz) softened butter

6-8 medium-thick slices day-old white bread, crusts removed

BLACKBERRY & APPLE CHARLOTTE

The best blackberries for puddings and desserts are those picked early in the season, when they are at their juiciest and not too full of seeds. Other berry fruits, such as blackcurrants, are also good in this traditional pudding.

METHOD

Peel, core and roughly chop the apples. Put in a large pan with 1 tablespoon of water and put on a low heat. Cook gently for 10 minutes, until the apples are soft but not collapsed. Add sugar to taste, then add the blackberries, stir gently so as not to break up the fruit, and remove from the heat.

Preheat the oven to 180°C (350°F, gas mark 4).

Butter the slices of bread well on one side. Use two-thirds of the bread to line a 1 litre (2 pints) pie dish, placing them butter-side down and cutting to fit. Fill the dish with the apple and blackberry mix. Cut the remaining bread into rectangles and use to cover the filling, butter-side up. Sprinkle over more sugar. Put the pie dish in the oven and bake for 45 minutes, or until the bread topping is golden and crisp. Serve immediately with cream or custard.

WINTER

*This is a time, when it is cold
and grey outside, for food that
is comforting and wonderfully
warming, for dishes slow-cooked
with spices and aromatics to
a mellow richness.*

SERVES 6
PREPARATION TIME 10 MINUTES
COOKING TIME 45 MINUTES

INGREDIENTS

1.5kg (3lb 3oz) leeks, trimmed, outer leaves and dark green tops discarded

5 tbsp olive oil

3 garlic cloves, roughly chopped

8 stems lemon grass, finely sliced

2 large potatoes, peeled and diced

1.5 litres (2³/₄ pints) chicken stock or water

salt and freshly ground black pepper

300ml (10fl oz) single cream

TO GARNISH

Choose from:

finely sliced spring onions

finely snipped chives

garlic croutons

IN SEASON

LEMON GRASS

This tapering aromatic stalk of an Asian grass, available whole or in a powdered form called sereh, is a key flavouring of South-east Asian cookery that is increasingly popular in the West. It gets its name from its marked citrus scent, but there are also hints of ginger and grass. To use it in salads, soups or fish dishes, peel off the tough outer layer, bruise the stem and then use it whole, diced or sliced in cooking. Remove whole pieces before serving.

LEEK & LEMON GRASS SOUP

This delicate-tasting soup is equally good served hot or chilled. Ring the changes with the garnish, depending on your mood. Try garnishing with spring onions, as here, or with snipped chives or a few croutons.

METHOD

Cut the leeks in half lengthways and wash thoroughly under cold running water. Finely slice and put in a colander. Rinse again and set aside to drain.

Heat the olive oil in a large saucepan. Add the garlic and lemon grass and gently fry for 4 minutes. Mix in the potatoes and continue to fry over a low heat, stirring regularly, for about 8 minutes, until they begin to soften. Stir in the leeks and continue to fry for about 7 minutes, until soft.

Add the chicken stock or water and season to taste with salt and pepper. Bring to the boil, then reduce the heat to moderate and simmer for 25 minutes, or until the vegetables are very soft. Pour the contents of the saucepan into a blender or food processor and blend until very smooth. Pass the mixture through a sieve back into the saucepan. Taste and adjust the seasoning and stir in the cream.

Reheat the soup just before serving and garnish each bowl with finely sliced spring onions, snipped chives or garlic croutons.

SERVES 6
PREPARATION TIME 10 MINUTES,
PLUS SOAKING
COOKING TIME 40–45 MINUTES

INGREDIENTS HEAD

340g (12oz) red split lentils

3 tbsp vegetable oil

4 slices back bacon, finely diced,
or a ham bone

2 onions, finely diced

3 carrots, finely diced

3 sticks celery, finely diced

2 garlic cloves, roughly chopped

1 bay leaf

3 sprigs parsley

1.5 litres (2³/₄ pints) water

salt and freshly ground black pepper

chives to garnish

SCOTTISH LENTIL SOUP

A warming bowl of lentil soup is delicious eaten with crusty bread, fruit and cheese. Alternatively, eat the soup with a ham sandwich, the ham cut from the bone used to make the soup.

METHOD

Wash the lentils in a sieve under cold running water. Tip into a bowl and cover with warm water. Soak for 30 minutes.

Heat the oil in a large pan and, if using bacon, add it to the pan and fry until lightly coloured. Mix in the vegetables and garlic and stir-fry for about 10 minutes, until soft. Drain the lentils and mix into the vegetables with the herbs and water. Add the ham bone, if using. Bring to the boil then simmer gently for about 30 minutes, or until the lentils and vegetables are very soft. Remove any scum.

Remove the herbs and the ham bone, if using, pour the soup into a blender and blend to a purée. Strain through a sieve back into the saucepan and adjust the seasoning, if necessary. Reheat before serving, garnished with chives.

SERVES 4
PREPARATION TIME 10 MINUTES
COOKING TIME 25 MINUTES

INGREDIENTS

1 tbsp olive oil

1 onion, chopped

2 x 400g (14 oz) cans butter beans, drained and rinsed

200g (7oz) potato, peeled and cut into 2cm (³/₄in) cubes

750ml (1¹/₄ pints) vegetable stock

salt and freshly ground black pepper

1 tbsp pesto, plus extra to garnish

BUTTER BEAN & PESTO SOUP

This deliciously unfussy, creamy butterbean soup gets a dash of the Mediterranean, in the form of basil-rich pesto, to turn it into an immensely satisfying meal.

METHOD

Heat the oil in a large saucepan over a medium heat. Add the onion and fry gently until soft. Add the beans, potato cubes and stock. Bring to the boil, reduce the heat and simmer gently, uncovered, for 20 minutes, or until the potato is tender. Add the pesto, stirring it in well.

Pour the soup into a blender and liquidize it to a creamy purée. Return to the pan, season to taste with salt and pepper and reheat gently. To garnish, thin a little pesto down with some olive oil and drizzle on to the soup in warmed bowls.

SERVES 4–6
PREPARATION TIME 35 MINUTES,
PLUS CHILLING

INGREDIENTS

8 navel oranges

1 pomegranate

150g (5¹/₂ oz) caster sugar

150ml (5 fl oz) water

handful of small mint leaves

ORANGE, POMEGRANATE & MINT SALAD

This finely flavoured mix of orange and pomegranate seeds dressed with orange zest syrup and mint makes a refreshing breakfast dish, but can also be served as a beautiful dessert.

METHOD

Finely pare the zest from 2 of the oranges, taking care to leave behind the bitter white pith of the orange. Cut the pared strips of zest into matchsticks. Put in a small saucepan and cover with cold water. Bring to the boil, drain immediately and cover with fresh cold water again. Return to the boil and simmer for 25 minutes, or until tender. Drain and set aside.

Meanwhile, take a sharp, serrated knife and cut off the top and bottom of each orange. Then cut away the pith and peel. Slice the oranges horizontally into thin discs and lay in a shallow dish, with any excess juice. Remove any pips.

Cut open the pomegranate and carefully extract its juicy pink seeds with a teaspoon, saving their juice as you do so. Discard any of the cream-coloured membrane as this tastes very bitter. Scatter the pomegranate seeds over the oranges, along with any juice.

Put the sugar and water in a small, heavy-based saucepan. Set over a low heat and stir until the sugar has dissolved, then bring to the boil and add the blanched orange zest. Simmer briskly for 5 minutes or until the orange strips look translucent. Remove from the heat and pour over the oranges. Once cool, scatter over the mint leaves and chill the salad until needed.

INGREDIENTS

4 large oranges, peeled and segmented

400g (14 oz) feta cheese, cubed or crumbled (and preferably marinated, see right)

2 large bunches watercress, torn into sprigs

FOR THE HONEY-ROAST ALMONDS

3 tbsp butter

150g (5½ oz) flaked almonds

3 tbsp set honey

pinch of salt

FOR THE DRESSING

5 tbsp extra virgin olive oil

1 tbsp sherry vinegar

pinch of sugar

salt and freshly ground black pepper

FETA, ORANGE & WATERCRESS SALAD

To give feta an extra layer of flavour, marinate cubed or crumbled feta for a few days in olive oil to which 2 sprigs of fresh thyme and a few black peppercorns have been added.

METHOD

Lightly oil a baking tray. Melt the butter for the almonds in a saucepan over a medium heat. Toss in the almonds. Cook for a minute or so, until the almonds are beginning to colour. Stir in the honey and salt and cook for a further 2–3 minutes, or until the almonds are golden and the honey has caramelized. Spread the nuts out in a thin, even layer on the baking tray. Leave until set, then break into clusters.

Whisk the dressing ingredients together and season with salt and pepper.

Put the orange segments into a large bowl with the crumbled feta and watercress then toss with the dressing. Divide the salad among 4 plates, scatter over the roast almond clusters, and serve immediately.

SERVES 6
PREPARATION TIME 45 MINUTES
COOKING TIME 2¹/₄ HOURS,
PLUS COOLING

INGREDIENTS

100g (3¹/₂ oz) butter, softened

6 sprigs thyme

1 lemon, halved

2 oven-ready pheasants, wiped
inside and out

freshly grated nutmeg

cayenne pepper

salt and freshly ground black pepper

100g (3¹/₂oz) smoked ham,
fat trimmed off

FOR THE TOPPING

500g (1lb 2oz) butter

TO GARNISH

sprigs of fresh thyme

finely pared lemon zest

POTTED PHEASANT

A great way of using an older, perhaps slightly tough, bird.

METHOD

Preheat the oven to 140°C (275°F, gas 1). Put a knob of butter, 3 thyme sprigs and a lemon half inside each pheasant. Mix a pinch of the nutmeg, cayenne, salt and pepper and rub over each bird. Put in a casserole dish and press the remaining butter over them. Cover, put in the oven and roast for 2 hours, 10 minutes, turning the birds and basting with the butter several times. Set aside to cool. Melt the butter for the topping. Line a sieve with wet muslin and put over a bowl. When the butter has produced a pale scum, pour the clear liquid through the cloth, leaving the dregs in the pan. Set aside the strained butter and discard the rest. If it solidifies, remelt it. Pull the meat off the cooled pheasants, discarding skin, fat or sinew. Put the ham and pheasant in a processor and pulse briefly to chop. Season with more nutmeg, cayenne, salt and pepper and add two-thirds of the melted butter. Process again to form a rough paste. Pack into six 150ml (5fl oz) ramekins. Press the paste down, then pour over the remaining butter in a thin layer. When firm, cover and chill. Keep for up to 4 days in the fridge. Serve garnished with thyme and lemon zest.

SERVES 4, AS A STARTER
PREPARATION TIME 20 MINUTES,
PLUS MARINATING
COOKING TIME 10 MINUTES

INGREDIENTS

1 medium cauliflower, trimmed
and broken into small florets

FOR THE DRESSING

3 tbsp sherry vinegar

4 tbsp olive oil

1 garlic clove, finely chopped

2 tbsp finely-chopped marjoram
or parsley

2 tbsp stuffed olives, sliced

salt

freshly ground pepper, or dried
chili flakes

TO FINISH

2 tbsp olive oil

2 tbsp fresh breadcrumbs

55g (2oz) serrano ham, diced small,
optional

1 tsp sherry vinegar

1 tbsp paprika (preferably smoked)

SHERRY-BODEGA CAULIFLOWER

The sherry makers of Jerez like to use their vinegar in a dressing for this winter tapa. The crisply aromatic topping counterpoints the texture and flavour of the cauliflower.

METHOD

Cook the cauliflower florets in a large saucepan of boiling, lightly salted water for 5–6 minutes, until tender but not mushy. Drain well. Mix all the ingredients for the dressing together in a large bowl. Add the warm cauliflower and mix gently to coat with the dressing. Set aside for an hour or two for the cauliflower to take up the flavours of the dressing.

To finish, heat the olive oil in a small pan over a medium-high heat. Add the breadcrumbs and fry for a minute or two, stirring to make sure they brown evenly. Toss in the diced ham (if using), remove the pan from the heat, sprinkle with the vinegar and paprika and tip the contents of the pan over the cauliflower. Serve at once, perhaps with a glass of amontillado sherry.

IN SEASON

CAULIFLOWER

Cauliflower is a brassica, which means it is descended from the wild cabbage, the ancestor of all cabbages. Unlike its relatives, the cauliflower is prized for its flowers, or 'curds', rather than its leaves. Cauliflower can be eaten raw, in a salad or with a tangy dip. Cooked, it marries beautifully with hard cheeses like Cheddar or Parmesan, either in a sauce or grated and mixed with breadcrumbs as a crispy topping. Choose cauliflowers with tightly packed, creamy white curds.

SERVES 6
PREPARATION TIME 40 MINUTES
COOKING TIME 20 MINUTES

INGREDIENTS

750g (1lb 10oz) ready-rolled
puff pastry

300g (10½oz) leeks, trimmed
and washed

45g (1½oz) butter

2 tsp clear honey

1 tsp chopped rosemary

salt and freshly ground black pepper

200g (7oz) Wensleydale cheese

1 egg, beaten

LEEK & WENSLEYDALE PITHIVIERS

Wensleydale is a hard cheese with a creamy flavour and a crumbly, almost feta-like texture. Here, it is partnered with buttery leeks and parcelled in puff pastry. Serve the pithiviers with a spicy, fruit chutney alongside them for a great lunch.

METHOD

Spread out the puff pastry on a floured surface and, using a small coffee saucer as a guide, cut out 12 discs, each about about 12cm (5in) in diameter. Chill the discs while making the filling.

Slice the leeks thinly. Melt the butter in a saucepan over a medium heat, add the leeks and fry for about 10 minutes, until soft but not coloured. Stir in the honey and rosemary. Season to taste with salt and pepper and leave to cool. Crumble the cheese and stir into the leek mixture.

Preheat the oven to 200˚C (400°F, gas 6).

Lay 6 of the pastry discs on a baking sheet and divide the leek mixture evenly among them, spooning it into a neat mound in the centre, leaving a rim of about 1cm (½in) around the edges. Brush the borders with the beaten egg and cover with the remaining discs. Crimp the edges to seal. Score a pattern of radiating lines from the centre of the parcels outwards, taking care not to cut through the pastry. Brush with more beaten egg.

Put into the oven and bake for about 20 minutes, until puffed up and golden. Serve hot or warm with a spicy fruit chutney on the side. If necessary, the pithiviers can be made a few hours ahead of time and reheated.

SERVES 6 AS PART OF A MEAL
PREPARATION TIME 10 MINUTES
COOKING TIME 12 MINUTES

INGREDIENTS

500g (1lb 2oz) tofu

sunflower oil for deep-frying

1 tbsp finely chopped fresh ginger

3 garlic cloves, finely sliced

1 tsp red chili flakes, or to taste

5 spring onions, finely sliced

2 tbsp soy sauce

1½ tbsp white wine vinegar

SPICY-SOUR BEAN CURD

Serve this deliciously piquant dish of crisp-coated, soft-centred bean curd as part of a Chinese-based meal. It is good with steamed fish and stir-fried greens.

METHOD

Drain the tofu and pat dry with kitchen paper before cutting it into 2cm (³/₄in) cubes. Pat the cubes dry on kitchen paper.

Heat the oil in a deep fat fryer to 200°C (400°F). Alternatively, pour a deep layer of the oil into a large, heavy-based saucepan until it is hot enough for a cube of bread, dropped in, to turn golden brown in a few seconds. Slowly lower half the tofu cubes into the oil. They will foam violently as you do so. Deep fry for 4–5 minutes, gently loosening the tofu from the basket. The tofu cubes will gradually float up to the surface and the foaming will subside. Scoop the crisp, golden tofu from the hot oil with a draining spoon and leave to drain in a sieve over a bowl. Repeat the process with the second batch of tofu cubes.

Heat a wok over a medium-high heat and add 1 tablespoon of sunflower oil. Stir in the ginger, garlic and chili flakes and after a couple of seconds, stir in the fried tofu, followed by the spring onions, soy sauce and vinegar. As soon as the sauce has been absorbed and the tofu is hot, serve it.

IN SEASON

TOFU

An essential ingredient of Chinese and Japanese cooking, tofu, or bean curd, as it is often called in the West, is made from puréed soy beans. Soft and white, with a cheese-like texture, tofu comes in several forms, ranging from firm to 'silken'. Normally sold packed in brine, fresh tofu will keep for 1–2 weeks in the fridge, if unopened. As soy beans are high in protein and very low in fat, tofu is highly nutritious and is an excellent standby ingredient for warming, spicy dishes.

SERVES 4
PREPARATION TIME 30 MINUTES
COOKING TIME 10 MINUTES

INGREDIENTS

8–12 large, moderately hot chili peppers, such as anaheim

300g (10^1/$_2$oz) crumbly white cheese, such as Cheshire, Caerphilly or feta, cut into small 'fingers'

400ml (14 fl oz) whipping cream

salt and freshly ground black pepper

RAJAS POBLANAS

A Mexican dish for which it is always hard to find a recipe – because all Mexican cooks know how to make it. If you can't get anaheim chilies, use six glossy red romano chilies.

METHOD

Preheat the grill to hot. Wipe the chilies and hold them in a gas flame with tongs (or grill under a fierce heat or roast in the highest possible oven) until the skin blisters and blackens a little. Put them in a plastic or paper bag for 10 minutes or so to loosen the skins, then peel. Pick the 4 best chilies, make a slit in the side of each and slip in a finger of the cheese. Seed the remaining chilies and slice into ribbons – these are the rajas.

Arrange the whole chilies in a shallow flameproof dish and fill in the gaps with the ribbons. Crumble in the remaining cheese and pour in the cream. Season with a little salt and pepper. Slip under a very hot grill until deliciously brown and bubbling. Serve piping hot, with soft tortillas for mopping up the cream and maybe a shot of frozen tequila to aid the digestion. Very Mexicano.

IN SEASON

CHILIES

The chili gets its fiery nature from an alkaloid called capsaicin, present in varying amounts depending on the variety of chili – and there are hundreds. When choosing fresh chilies, red or green, look for shiny, firm skin without black patches. Dried chilies, whether whole, ground or flaked, should retain a bright, intense colour.

HONEY-ROAST HAM

SERVES 8–10
PREPARATION TIME 15 MINUTES
COOKING TIME 1¹/₂–2 HOURS,
PLUS COOLING

INGREDIENTS

1.5–2kg (3lb 3oz–4¹/₂lb) joint
unsmoked gammon

2 tbsp clear honey

2 tbsp sherry

1 tbsp demerara sugar

If you choose a gammon joint on the bone, you will have the bone left for soup when you have eaten the ham. But a boned gammon will taste just as good when it is roasted.

METHOD

Preheat the oven to 180°C (350°F, gas 4). Spread a large piece of foil in a roasting tin. Put the gammon joint on top, rind side uppermost. Bring the foil up around it and crimp the edges together to enclose the meat, being careful not to wrap it too tightly. Put in the oven and roast for 25 minutes per 450g (1lb).

Take the ham out of the oven and increase the heat to 200°C (400°F, gas 6). Carefully fold back the foil and cut the rind and string from the gammon, leaving the layer of fat. Score the fat in a diamond pattern with a sharp knife. Mix the honey, sherry and sugar together and spoon over the fat. Leaving the sides of the meat protected by the foil, but the top open, return the ham to the oven and bake for 20 minutes, or until golden brown. Leave to cool and set before carving.

SERVES 4–6
PREPARATION TIME 15 MINUTES
PREPARATION TIME 1 HOUR,
15 MINUTES

INGREDIENTS

2 large onions, finely sliced

1 salt-pickled lemon, cut in chunks
(or 1 fresh lemon, chopped small)

1 chicken, about 1.5kg (3lb 3oz)

20g (³/₄oz) butter

¹/₂ tsp saffron threads, lightly toasted
in a dry pan

¹/₂ cinnamon stick

12 green olives (preferably unpitted
and in brine)

salt and freshly ground black pepper

30g (1oz) raisins or pitted and
chopped prunes

1–2 large potatoes, peeled and cut
in chunks

400g (14oz) can chickpeas, drained

TO SERVE

couscous

1–2 tbsp harissa paste

LEMON CHICKEN TAGINE WITH HARISSA

A chicken, cooked whole in an aromatic broth coloured with saffron and flavoured with lemon, cinnamon and olives, is served with a sauce made of harissa, a hot chili paste.

METHOD

Put the onion and chopped lemon in a heavy-based flameproof casserole. Set the chicken on top, dot with butter, and add enough water to come half-way up the sides of the chicken. Add the saffron, cinnamon, olives and salt and pepper to taste. Put the casserole on the hob, bring to the boil, turn down the heat, cover and simmer gently for 30 minutes. Add the raisins or prunes, potatoes and chickpeas. Continue to simmer for another 30 minutes, checking the casserole and adding a little more boiling water if it looks like drying out, until the chicken is golden and perfectly tender. Taste and adjust the seasoning.

To make a harissa sauce to serve with the chicken, strain a ladleful of hot broth from the casserole and stir in the harissa. Set aside in a small jug or bowl.

Carve the chicken and serve it on a bed of steamed couscous in individual bowls, with the other ingredients from the casserole and a spoonful or two of the broth. Serve the harissa sauce separately.

SERVES 8
PREPARATION TIME 1 HOUR,
PLUS 4 HOURS FOR THE STOCK
FINAL COOKING TIME 15 MINUTES

INGREDIENTS

2 oven-ready ducks

2 tsp sea salt

SAUCE

2 onions, chopped

4 garlic cloves, chopped

4 carrots, chopped

4 sticks celery, chopped

1 bottle red wine

5 black peppercorns

juice and finely pared zest
of 1 Seville orange

HONEY GLAZE

1/2 tsp ground cinnamon

4 tbsp clear honey

juice and finely grated zest
of 1 Seville orange

IN SEASON

SEVILLE ORANGES

The short-seasoned Seville orange is too bitter-tasting to eat raw. Softened by long cooking and then sweetened with sugar, its peel and juice make superb marmalade, but it also adds a fragrant piquancy to meat and fish dishes. Seville orange peel has a number of uses. Candied or dried in the oven, it can be used to flavour stews and stir-fries. Its oil is used in liqueurs.

HONEY, ORANGE & CINNAMON ROAST DUCK

Do not be discouraged by the length of this recipe. Time must be allowed for chilling the duck and simmering the stock but each stage is very easy and the results are impressive.

METHOD

Preheat the oven to its highest setting. Remove any pin feathers from the ducks and lightly prick the birds all over with a fork. Rub the salt into the ducks' skin and place the birds upside down in a roasting tin. Put in the oven and roast for 10 minutes, then turn breast-side up and roast for another 10 minutes. Remove from the oven and set aside to cool.

Carve each cooled bird into 4 pieces. Begin by cutting away the breast meat from one side of the breast bone and rib cage then continue to work the knife around the carcass so that the breast and leg come away in one piece. Repeat the process on the other side. Now cut the leg away from the breast and trim each portion, cutting way the wings beyond the first joint. Lightly score the skin in a diamond pattern. Cover and chill until needed.

Roughly chop the duck carcasses and place in a large saucepan over a low heat to release their fat and to colour. Once all the bones are coloured, stir in the vegetables for the sauce and cook until softened. Add the wine, peppercorns, orange zest (reserving 4 pieces of zest for finishing the sauce) and enough water to cover. Bring to the boil, skim off any froth and simmer gently for 4 hours, until the liquid has reduced by two-thirds. Strain into a clean container, cool and chill.

On the day of serving, remove and discard any fat from the top of the stock and transfer the stock to a small pan. Add the reserved orange zest and boil vigorously until reduced by half. Mix in the orange juice and continue to boil until about 200ml (7fl oz) of well-flavoured, dark-brown sauce is left. Set aside until needed.

While the stock is reducing, mix the glaze ingredients together. Coat the duck joints in this and chill, covered, until needed.

Preheat the grill to medium-high. Put the duck leg pieces, skin-side up, under the grill for 5 minutes. Then add the duck breasts, skin-side up, and turn over the legs. Spoon over some more glaze. Cook for 5 minutes, then turn all the pieces over, spoon over more glaze and cook for another 5 minutes. This cooking time renders the legs well done and the breasts slightly pink. If you like all the meat well done, cook all the pieces for the same length of time. Serve with the piping hot sauce.

SERVES 4
PREPARATION TIME 10 HOUR
COOKING TIME 15–20 MINUTES

INGREDIENTS

2 tbsp olive oil

2 shallots, finely sliced

salt and freshly ground black pepper

675g (1½lb) haddock fillet, skinned
and cut into 4 portions

1 tsp finely chopped tarragon

200g (7oz) cherry tomatoes, thickly
sliced

2 tbsp capers, drained, rinsed
and patted dry

200ml (7fl oz) crème fraîche

30g (1oz) freshly grated Parmesan

CHEESY BAKED HADDOCK

This scrumptious supper dish is best served golden brown and sizzling and eaten with creamy mashed potatoes and steamed spinach. The combination of tarragon, cherry tomatoes and capers perfectly balances the richness of the crème fraîche and Parmesan topping.

METHOD

Preheat the oven to 220°C (425°F, gas 7). Heat 1 tablespoon of the oil in a small frying pan, add the shallots and fry gently until soft.

Brush a baking dish with the remaining olive oil. Scatter the shallots over its base, then lightly season the fish pieces with salt and pepper and arrange them in a single layer in the dish.

Scatter over the tarragon, sliced cherry tomatoes and capers. Beat the crème fraîche to make it more liquid and spoon it evenly all over the top. Sprinkle over the cheese.

Put the dish in the oven and bake for 15–20 minutes, or until the fish is cooked and the dish is sizzling golden-brown. Serve at once.

SERVES 6
PREPARATION TIME 12 MINUTES
COOKING TIME 20-25 MINUTES

INGREDIENTS

6 salmon fillet portions, each about 140g (5oz)

2 tbsp extra virgin olive oil

juice of 1/2 lemon

salt and freshly ground black pepper

6 small sprigs rosemary

18 baby leeks, about 600g (1lb 6oz), trimmed

olive oil

FOR THE PARSLEY AND ANCHOVY VINAIGRETTE

4 anchovy fillets, finely diced

1 tbsp finely chopped parsley

1 tbsp white wine vinegar

5 tbsp extra virgin olive oil

BAKED SALMON WITH ANCHOVY VINAIGRETTE

Fresh salmon, baked with rosemary and lemon, has a delicate flavour that is complemented by fresh-tasting leeks and a tart anchovy and parsley dressing. Serve the salmon hot or cold, with warm new potatoes.

METHOD

Preheat the oven to 180°C (350°F, gas 4). Whisk together in a small bowl all the ingredients for the vinaigrette. Season with a little black pepper and set aside. The flavour will intensify if the vinaigrette sits for about 15 minutes.

Lightly oil the fish, then season each fillet with the lemon juice and pepper. Lightly oil a large sheet of foil. Lay the fish in a row and tuck a sprig of rosemary under each fillet. Add a little more lemon juice and wrap into a large baggy parcel. Put the parcel on a baking tray and bake in the oven for 20–25 minutes.

Remove any tough outer layers from the leeks. To clean them, slice in half vertically from the green end downwards, stopping one-third of the way down, so that the green part of the leek splays out. Rinse thoroughly under cold running water. Drop into a pan of boiling water and cook for 3 minutes, or until tender. Cool the leeks under cold running water and pat dry with kitchen paper.

Preheat a ridged grill pan over a medium-low heat, or preheat the grill. Rub the leeks with a little olive oil and season lightly. Put them on the grill pan, or under the grill, and grill, turning regularly, until they are flecked golden.

Remove the salmon from its foil wrapping and arrange on 6 plates with the leeks. Spoon over the parsley-anchovy vinaigrette and serve.

SERVES 6
PREPARATION TIME 15 MINUTES
COOKING TIME 10 MINUTES

INGREDIENTS

1kg (2¼lb) sea bass fillets, skinned

salt

2 tbsp sultanas

good pinch of saffron strands

4 tbsp amontillado sherry

3 tbsp pine nuts

120ml (4fl oz) water

SEA BASS WITH SAFFRON, SHERRY & PINE NUTS

Easy and quick to make, this dish is a wonderfully balanced mixture of flavours, the delicate taste of the sea bass enhanced by amontillado sherry and saffron, and given extra texture by pine nuts and sultanas.

METHOD

Cut the fish fillets into smaller pieces, and sprinkle lightly with salt.

Put the sultanas in a bowl and strew with the saffron. Warm the sherry and pour it over the sultanas and saffron.

Heat a heavy-based frying pan on a medium-low heat, add the pine nuts and toss them in the pan until they take on a deep-gold colour and give off their waxy, aromatic scent. Pour on to a plate and set aside.

Take the pan off the heat and pour in the sultanas in their saffroned sherry. Add the water, return the pan to the heat, and bring to a simmer. Add the fish fillet pieces in a single layer. (The fish may have to be cooked in batches.) If the fish pieces are not almost submerged, add more water. After simmering for about 1 minute, turn the pieces over with spatulas. They cook very quickly and if over-cooked, they may break into flakes as they are turned. Cook for another minute or so on the second side and remove to a plate.

Continue until all the fish has been cooked, adding more water as necessary. When all the fish has been cooked and removed from the pan, use a spatula to remove as many sultanas as you can and add them to the cooked fish on the plate. Turn the heat under the frying pan to high and let the sherry-saffron juices reduce to a just-liquid yellow syrup. Pour this over the fish, then scatter over the toasted pine nuts. Serve with simply cooked puy lentils and rice.

SERVES 8
PREPARATION TIME 30 MINUTES,
PLUS CHILLING

INGREDIENTS

3 tbsp vodka or water

11g (¼oz) sachet powdered gelatine

finely grated zest and juice
of 1 grapefruit

3 large eggs, separated

150g (5½oz) caster sugar

3 tbsp lemon juice

300ml (10fl oz) double cream

FOR THE DECORATION (OPTIONAL)

1 grapefruit

55g (2oz) caster sugar

4 tbsp water

IN SEASON

GRAPEFRUIT

Like other citrus fruits, grapefruit, a native of the West Indies, contains potassium and many valuable vitamins, including C, B and E. Its acidic juice is wonderfully refreshing, especially at breakfast time, when the whole fruit is also a splendid addition to the meal. The juice and the whole fruit are also invaluable in marinades and dressings and help bring out the fresh sweetness in shellfish, salad leaves and creamy desserts. Choose grapefruit that feel heavy in their skins.

GRAPEFRUIT MOUSSE

Add vodka to grapefruit zest and juice and you get a mousse sophisticated enough for a dinner party. Because it contains raw eggs, it should not be served to small children, the elderly or infirm, or pregnant women.

METHOD

Pour the vodka or water into a small bowl and sprinkle over the gelatine. Put the bowl in a larger bowl, then pour boiling water into the larger bowl so the bowl of vodka gelatine is gently heated. Set aside.

Put the grapefruit zest in a large mixing bowl with the egg yolks and 100g (3½oz) of the caster sugar. Whisk with an electric whisk until the mixture is pale and thick.

Stir the gelatine to ensure that it is fully dissolved. Mix the grapefruit juice into the gelatine then stir the mixture into the beaten egg yolks with the lemon juice. Put the mixture in the fridge, stirring regularly, for 10–15 minutes, until it begins to thicken and set. Stirring helps make sure that the mixture sets evenly.

Whip the cream until it holds very soft, floppy peaks. Using a metal spoon, gently fold the cream into the grapefruit gelatine mixture. If it seems a little floppy, chill until it thickens a little. As soon as the mixture is just holding its shape, whisk the egg whites until they form soft peaks then whisk in the remaining sugar. Immediately fold the sweetened egg whites into the mousse and spoon the frothy mixture into 8 individual soufflé dishes or ramekins. Chill until needed.

To make a grapefruit zest decoration, if you wish, finely pare the zest from the second grapefruit with a lemon peeler. Cut away any bitter white pith and cut the strips into fine matchsticks. Drop into a pan of boiling water, leave for 30 seconds, then drain. Repeat this process twice, using fresh water each time. Dissolve the sugar in the water in a small pan and add the blanched grapefruit zest. Simmer for 5 minutes until the zest is sticky. Remove the zest from the syrup with a fork, put it on a plate and leave to cool.

Before serving the mousses, sprinkle a little of the grapefruit zest over each.

MAKES 12
PREPARATION TIME 15 MINUTES
COOKING TIME 25–30 MINUTES,
PLUS COOLING

INGREDIENTS

100g (3½oz) macadamia nuts

170g (6oz) softened unsalted butter,
plus extra for greasing

150g (5½oz) caster sugar

175ml (6fl oz) maple syrup

2 eggs

1 tsp vanilla extract

175g (6oz) plain flour

pinch of salt

MAPLE & ROAST MACADAMIA BLONDIES

These delicious blondies should be dense and sticky, so be careful not to overcook them. Be careful with the macadamia nuts, too. Being high in oil, they burn easily.

METHOD

Preheat the oven to 190°C (375°F, gas 5). Line the base of a 20cm (8in) square cake tin with non-stick baking parchment, and butter the sides.

Spread the macadamia nuts on a baking tray, put in the oven and roast for 5–10 minutes, shaking once or twice, until they are nicely browned, but not burnt. Set aside to cool, then roughly chop them. Leave the oven turned on.

Put the butter in a heavy-based saucepan large enough to hold all the ingredients, and melt it over a low heat. Remove from the heat. Stir in the sugar and maple syrup, then whisk in the eggs, one at a time, followed by the vanilla extract. Sift the flour and salt into the pan and beat in – not too vigorously, as a slightly lumpy batter makes a finer blondie than a perfectly smooth one. Finally, mix in the chopped nuts.

Pour into the prepared tin and bake in the oven for 25–30 minutes, until just about firm. Test by inserting a skewer into the centre. If it comes out almost clean, but with the odd moist crumb adhering to it, then the blondies are cooked.

Cool for 10 minutes in the tin, then cut into 12 squares. Eat the blondies warm or cool them on a wire rack and store in an airtight container.

SERVES 6
PREPARATION TIME 20 MINUTES,
PLUS CHILLING

INGREDIENTS

pinch of saffron (about 12 threads)

juice and finely grated zest of 1 orange

8 ginger biscuits or 12 amaretti biscuits

3 dried apricots, cut into small dice

600ml (1 pint) whipping cream

3 tbsp caster sugar

150ml (5fl oz) dry sherry

SAFFRON, ORANGE & APRICOT SYLLABUB

Early recipes for syllabub called for the cow to be milked directly into a pitcher of sweetened wine, producing a frothy head, the syllabub, which could be scooped off and eaten with a spoon. Here is a simpler way to make this delicious dessert.

METHOD

Toast the saffron threads in a dry pan over a medium heat for a few seconds to release their flavour. Add the saffron to the juice and zest of the orange and leave to infuse in a warm place for 30 minutes.

Roughly crush the biscuits, leaving them a little crunchy, and mix with the chopped apricots. Divide the mixture among 6 tall glasses.

Whisk the cream until it holds stiff peaks. Whisk in the sugar and sherry and the saffron and orange mixture. Spoon the syllabub over the biscuit base in the glasses and put in the fridge to chill for an hour or two before serving.

IN SEASON

SAFFRON

Saffron is the dried stigma of an autumn-flowering crocus, *crocus sativus*. The spice is expensive because it takes 85,000 flowers to make just 450g (1lb) of saffron. Its unique, musty flavour, perfumed scent and intense yellow colour are essential in many of the great dishes of the Mediterranean, from paella to bouillabaise. Saffron is available as a powder and as the dried stigmas (threads). A 'good pinch' of saffron is 12–14 threads.

SERVES 4
PREPARATION TIME 30 MINUTES,
PLUS RESTING
COOKING TIME 10 MINUTES

INGREDIENTS

125g (4½oz) plain flour

pinch of salt

1 egg, beaten

200ml (7fl oz) milk

60ml (2fl oz)

1 tbsp sunflower oil

2 tbsp brandy (optional)

FOR THE ORANGE BUTTER

125g (4½oz) butter

55g (2oz) caster sugar

juice and zest of 2 oranges

3 tbsp Grand Marnier

TO FLAMBE THE CREPES

1 tbsp caster sugar

2 tbsp Grand Marnier

2 tbsp brandy

CREPES SUZETTE

The pancakes for this classic recipe can be made in advance and frozen or chilled, before being reheated in an irresistible mixture of orange juice, butter, sugar and Grand Marnier. The final flambé adds an amazing bitter-sour note.

METHOD

Sift the flour and salt into a bowl. Make a well in the centre and add the egg. Mix the milk with the water and slowly add to the egg, beating to incorporate all the flour. Beat until smooth. Stir in the oil and brandy and strain the mixture through a sieve into a clean bowl. Leave to rest for 30 minutes.

Heat a frying pan over a medium-high heat. Rub the pan with a wad of oil-soaked kitchen paper. Remove from the heat and pour in about one-eighth of the batter. Quickly rotate the pan so it is evenly coated with a thin layer and return to the heat. As soon as the pancake begins to set, loosen the edges and flip it over. Cook for 1 minute, then transfer to a warm plate. Cover with greaseproof paper. Grease the pan and repeat, until all the batter is used up. The recipe makes 8 pancakes.

Set a large, heavy-based frying pan over a gentle heat and put in the ingredients for the orange butter. When melted, simmer briefly. Add one pancake at a time to the pan. Carefully fold in half and then in half again, using a spoon and fork. Push to the side of the pan and repeat with the remaining pancakes.

To flambé, sprinkle the pancakes with the sugar, pour on the alcohol, and light with a match. Give the pan a couple of good shakes. When the flames have died down, divide the folded pancakes among 4 plates, putting 2 on each plate, pour some of the pan juices over each plate and serve at once.

SERVES 6
PREPARATION TIME 10 MINUTES

INGREDIENTS

450g (1lb) ricotta

2 tbsp icing sugar, sifted

1 tsp ground cinnamon

coriander honey

2 tbsp pine nuts, lightly toasted

12 amaretti biscuits, to serve

CINNAMON RICOTTA & CORIANDER HONEY

Woody, aromatic cinnamon enhances the creamy texture of Italy's ricotta cheese in this elegant, easily prepared dessert. If you can't find coriander honey, any clear, floral honey will do.

METHOD

Put the ricotta in a mixing bowl, add the icing sugar and ground cinnamon and beat well together.

Spoon a small mound of the ricotta mixture on 6 shallow dessert dishes, drizzle over the coriander honey, and sprinkle over the toasted pine nuts. Put 2 amaretti biscuits on each dish and serve.

Accompany the Cinnamon Ricotta with coffee or a small glass of dessert wine, such as an Italian vino santo.

IN SEASON

CINNAMON

It takes just a whiff of this aromatic spice to conjure up thoughts of log fires and indoors warmth, so often is it used in winter-time foods and drinks. Cinnamon is the dried inner bark of a laurel-like tree native to Sri Lanka. As the bark dries it is rolled into tight quills, or sticks, that are sold whole or ground. Cinnamon can be used in sweet or savoury recipes, from sticky buns to mulled wine. Always store it in air-tight jars in a dark place, and discard it when its aroma fades.

MAKES 18
PREPARATION TIME 30 MINUTES
COOKING TIME 30 MINUTES,
PLUS COOLING

INGREDIENTS

8 large egg whites

pinch of salt

500g (1lb 2 oz) caster sugar

1 tbsp cornflour

2 tsp white wine vinegar

1 tsp rosewater (optional)

4 pomegranates

juice of 1 lemon

750ml (1¼ pints) double cream

IN SEASON

POMEGRANATE

The intensely flavoured pomegranate is one of the world's oldest fruits and is greatly valued for its juice and deep-red seeds. Split open the pomegranate and use a teaspoon to scoop its seeds into a bowl, saving any juice. Alternatively, whack the fruit with a spoon to dislodge the seeds. Discard the creamy membrane, which is very bitter. The seeds can then be mixed into a winter salad or scattered over orange segments in a dessert.

POMEGRANATE MINI-PAVLOVAS

Chewy meringue, downy cream, fragrant seeds — how much more blissfully delicious could a cold-weather dessert get? The meringues keep well in an airtight tin for a week or so, but if fewer are wanted, halve the recipe quantities.

METHOD

Preheat the oven to 180°C (350°F, gas 4). Line 3 baking trays with baking paper. Draw six 10cm (4 in) circles on each.

Beat the egg whites and salt until satiny peaks form. Beat in the sugar, a spoonful at a time, until the meringue is stiff and shiny. Sprinkle over the cornflour, vinegar and rosewater, if using. Fold in. Mound onto the baking trays within the circles, smoothing the tops and sides. Put in the oven and immediately reduce the temperature to 150°C (300°F, gas 2). Cook for 30 minutes. Turn off the oven. Leave the pavlovas inside to cool completely. If the oven is electric, open the door.

Halve 2 of the pomegranates and juice them. This is easy with an electric juicer, but manageable with a normal citrus juicer. Put the juice into a small pan with the lemon juice. Bring to the boil and simmer for a few minutes or until the mixture has become syrupy. Set aside to cool.

Whip the cream until thick but not stiff. Remove the cooled meringues from the baking sheets and place on serving plates. Pile on the cream.

Halve the remaining pomegranates. Hold one pomegranate half at a time over a bowl and bash with a wooden spoon so the seeds fall out. Scatter the seeds generously over the meringues. Drizzle about half a teaspoonful of the pomegranate syrup over each, and serve at once.

INDEX

Contents

Fresh vistas
The Industrial Revolution drew heavily on the progress of technology, and the status of scientists rose accordingly. Figures like Britain's Michael Faraday, Sweden's Alfred Nobel and France's Francois Arago became international celebrities. Arago was for ten years the director of the Paris Observatory, whose refractor, dating from 1845, is shown here.

Introduction

The end of the Napoleonic Wars left Europe at peace, reborn after a long period of turmoil. Yet a different kind of upheaval was in the offing. Political and economic stability laid the groundwork for a time of extraordinary growth that would draw on all the scientific and technological advances of the age. The industrial era was gathering pace.

Progress in medicine and hygiene, together with the mechanisation of agriculture, helped to rein back the epidemics and famines that had earlier ravaged Europe. Across the Continent nations experienced a social revolution that gradually emptied the countryside, driving villagers to the cities in search of work and a new way of life. Coal mining and iron and steel manufacture came to the fore, first in Britain, then elsewhere in Europe and in America. This was the golden age of steam, used to power turbines, locomotives and ships, making everything faster. Telegraph lines began to link up a world that was already growing smaller.

Buoyed by success, the European great powers threw themselves into the adventure of colonialism, which served as an outlet for the growing nationalism of the day. A new kind of society came into being, urban and middle-class. The way in which people saw themselves also changed. The new photography recorded their faces permanently, while writers turned their gaze on society, detailing changing characters and customs. It was an age of realism and pragmatism in the arts.

Yet alongside the material progress there was another, less positive side to the age. In the slums of the great cities lived a whole class of people who had suffered from the mechanisation of labour and the rationalisation of work. Faced with the growth of a proletarian underclass, thinking people realised that liberal economic ideas required a framework, urbanism had to be thought through and education spread more widely. The Age of Reason and the industrial era had to make common cause.

The editors

▲ The German scientist Joseph von Fraunhofer drew on Newton's work on colour and light to establish the discipline of spectroscopy, an important tool in physics

▲ Samuel Colt invented the revolver in 1835; the cartridge followed in 1850 and a rebounding hammer was added to the gun 16 years later

The 19th century opened onto a remarkable vista of emerging knowledge. In the realm of the very small, the newly invented spectroscope could break light into its constituent parts, a discovery that ranked alongside those of John Dalton, the first

▶ Auguste Siebe's 1837 diving helmet helped to facilitate underwater exploration

▼ An early example of an ammeter, designed to measure the strength of an electric current; the implement was named after André Marie Ampère, who established electrodynamics, a new branch of the science of electricity

▲ A notebook that once belonged to John Dalton, the scientist who first propounded the atomic theory of matter and who is also remembered for discovering colour blindness, a condition still sometimes referred to as 'daltonism'

scientist to weigh atoms, and André Marie Ampère, who measured electric current. The era saw many developments of huge practical significance, such as the first suspension bridges, steamships that ploughed the world's oceans at unprecedented speeds and the

▲ The railway age began on 17 September, 1825, when George Stephenson pioneered the world's first passenger service on a stretch of the line linking Darlington to Stockton-on-Tees

◄ Department stores made their first appearance in Paris in the 1820s; this magnificent glass dome is in Printemps, which was founded there in 1865

▲ A steam-powered vehicle of 1834 demonstrates a practical application of the Carnot cycle, which explained the theory of how steam engines work and founded the science of thermodynamics

laying down of railway lines that stretched for hundreds of miles. Fast and powerful steam trains transported whole new categories of goods and also began to serve the needs of growing numbers of passengers. Above all, this was the age of industrialisation

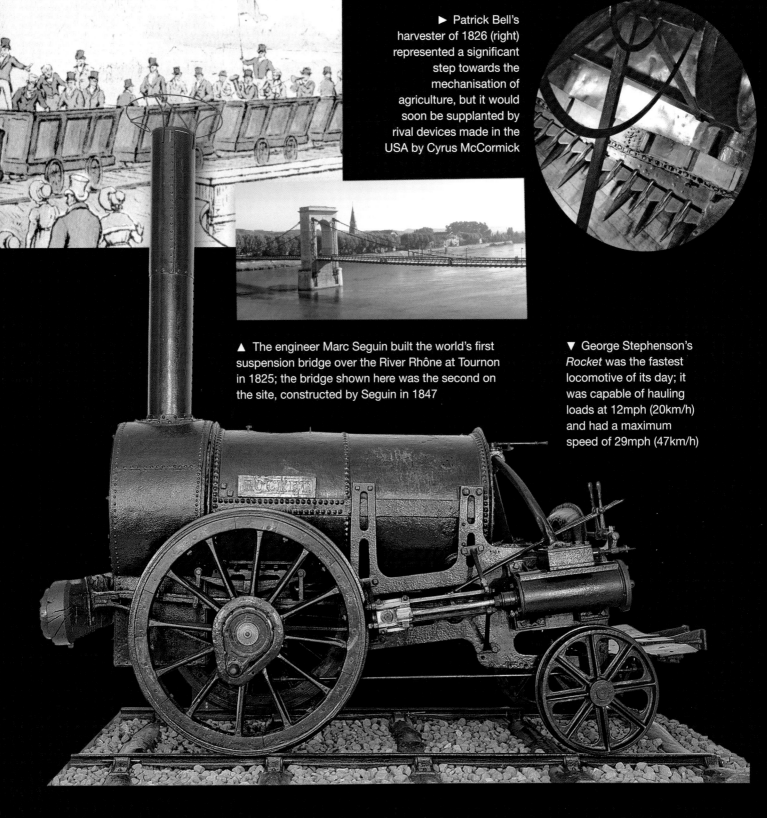

▶ Patrick Bell's harvester of 1826 (right) represented a significant step towards the mechanisation of agriculture, but it would soon be supplanted by rival devices made in the USA by Cyrus McCormick

▲ The engineer Marc Seguin built the world's first suspension bridge over the River Rhône at Tournon in 1825; the bridge shown here was the second on the site, constructed by Seguin in 1847

▼ George Stephenson's *Rocket* was the fastest locomotive of its day; it was capable of hauling loads at 12mph (20km/h) and had a maximum speed of 29mph (47km/h)

when the exodus from the countryside that swelled the population of cities brought in its wake new forms of urban transport and new ways of buying and selling. The first public bus and tram services were seen at this time, and department stores appeared, bringing

▶ The turbine (right), invented by French engineer Benoît Fourneyron in 1827, proved far more efficient than old-fashioned water wheels (above)

◀ Barthélemy Thimonnier's 1830 sewing machine was the first of a series of sewing devices, steadily improved over the years, that made the mass-production of clothes possible, bringing fashion within the range of people on modest incomes

the latest consumer goods together under one roof. Meanwhile, mechanisation and the use of fertilisers dramatically increased agricultural yields. Medicine combated diseases with new tools and procedures, among them the stethoscope, endoscope,

◀ Photographic equipment of the kind used from the 1830s by Jacques Daguerre and his successors to capture images on silver-coated copper plates

▼ William Fox Talbot (below, on the right) was a pioneer of photography who developed the calotype process, a rival to the daguerrotype

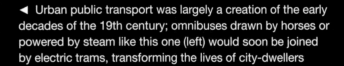

◀ Urban public transport was largely a creation of the early decades of the 19th century; omnibuses drawn by horses or powered by steam like this one (left) would soon be joined by electric trams, transforming the lives of city-dwellers

hypodermic syringe and blood transfusion, now successful for the first time. The spirit of the age was optimistic and pragmatic, as inventors sought to make life easier with useful devices such as sewing machines, matches and the safety pin. At the same time,

▼ Following Anselme Payen's isolation of cellulose in 1837 the discovery was exploited to make a number of fibre-based products, as in this early paper mill

▼ This prototype electric motor was made by Michael Faraday in 1821 to demonstrate the link between electricity and magnetism

▼ The SS *Great Britain*, designed by Isambard Kingdom Brunel and launched in 1845, was powered by steam-driven propeller, a device inspired by the Archimedes' screw

scientists were listened to with respect – François Arago, for example, has gone down in history as much for his Republican politics as for his work on electromagnetism. Philosophically as well as scientifically, the age bore within it the seeds of much that

▶ Charles Goodyear on his quest to make a usable form of rubber; the process of vulcanisation, which he discovered in 1837, made rubber hard but pliable and resistant to changes in temperature

▲ An electromagnetic telegraph machine developed in the late 1830s by Samuel Morse, using the code that still bears his name; simple and cheap to operate, the system first connected cities, then crossed national boundaries and eventually oceans to connect far-flung nations

would be new about the modern world. Alongside the industrial revolution went a breakthrough in communications, marked first by the invention of photography and then the telegraph. Michael Faraday demonstrated the link between electricity and magnetism

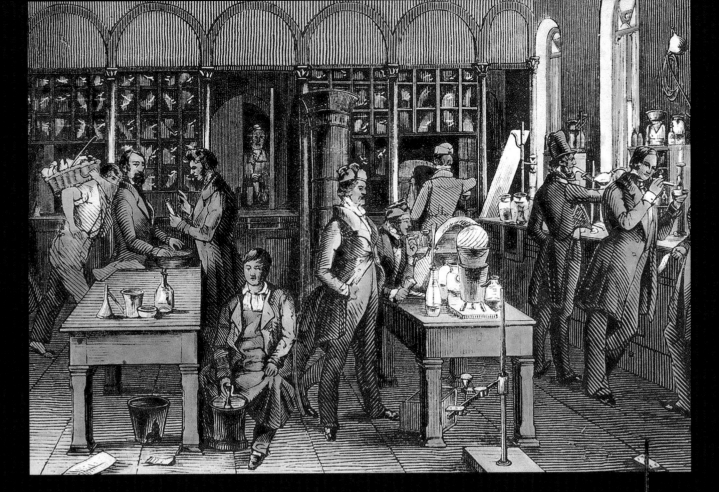

▲ The world's first chemistry laboratory was founded in the 1820s at Giessen University in Germany by Justus von Liebig, the chief early promoter of the use of fertilisers in agriculture

▼ Equipment developed in 1836 by James Marsh to test for the presence of arsenic; the Marsh Test is still used by forensic scientists today

◀ Having already developed a reliable detonator, Swedish chemist Alfred Nobel found a way of stabilising nitroglycerine in 1866, then put the two together to make dynamite, which he patented in 1887

that by the century's end would give people control over electric currents. Charles Goodyear's vulcanisation process for rubber would be seized upon in the coming motor age, but the photovoltaic effect – the principle behind capturing energy from the

▶ The eight planets of the Solar System that were known in 1846, with Mercury at the top and newly discovered Neptune at the bottom; the Earth's moon is at top right

◀ Early equipment for the inhalation of anaesthetic, first demonstrated by William Morton in the 1840s

▶ Hexham station on the Newcastle to Carlisle railway line, built between 1830 and 1838 at a time when the development of railways was helping to transform the nation's economy through the spread of industrialisation

Sun, discovered in 1839 – would not be exploited for another century or more. The world was becoming more efficient in many ways, including the power to kill and destroy, as the success of revolvers and nitroglycerine would show. Yet the scientists of this

▲ A hypodermic syringe used on a patient by Charles Gabriel Pravaz in 1853; the device made it possible to inject a drug into a patient without cutting flesh

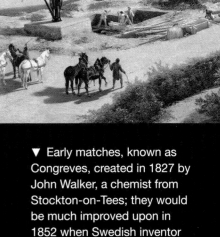

▼ Early matches, known as Congreves, created in 1827 by John Walker, a chemist from Stockton-on-Tees; they would be much improved upon in 1852 when Swedish inventor Johan Edvard Lundström came up with the safety match

▲ Equipment used by Léon Foucault in his celebrated pendulum experiment to demonstrate the rotation of the Earth

period were not just visionary in practical matters, they also proved prophetic on a wider scale. Léon Foucault demonstrated irrefutably that the Earth rotates; the speed of light was measured; William Thomson developed the Kelvin scale for assessing absolute

▼ In 1849 French physicist Hippolyte Fizeau used the equipment below to estimate the speed of light, which he calculated to be 315,350km/s; modern laser interferometry has now refined the figure to 299,792km/s, or 186,287.48 miles a second

▲ The Borsig factory in Berlin; in the first half of the 19th century a rapid burst of industrialisation led to new factories springing up all over the Prussian capital

▶ Brandenburg Gate, Berlin's best-known monument located at the western end of the Unter den Linden ('Under the Lime Trees'), the city's famous boulevard

temperatures; and the discovery of an eighth planet, Neptune, expanded the Solar System. As industrialisation left its mark on the landscape, the bond between humankind and nature became stretched – a trend that would continue in the years ahead

THE STORY OF INVENTIONS

It all began with water. Heated by coal, transformed into steam, driven by turbines, it powered factories, trains and ships. Steam power replaced horse power as railways spread across the countryside in place of farmtracks and engine drivers took the jobs of coachmen. Used at first to shift goods, railways were soon also transporting passengers, who quickly overcame their initial terror of the puffing monsters to be won over by the speed, comfort and affordability of trains.

THE SPECTROSCOPE – 1814
Lessons from light

Born out of the researches of the German optician Joseph von Fraunhofer, spectroscopy followed on from Newton's analysis of light and colour of 150 years before. By breaking down different spectra to determine the properties of their light sources, it would have an immense impact on physics, illuminating scientific mysteries from the structure of the atom to the composition of the universe.

The instrument resembled a small astronomical telescope, pivoting up and around a fixed tripod. But there was one big difference: a prism set a few centimetres behind the objective lens captured light from the stars.

The year was 1814 and this first spectroscope – designed and made by Joseph von Fraunhofer, a talented optician in charge of glass and lens-making at the Optical Institute at Benediktbeuern – was destined to transform astronomy, physics and all other fields in which light could be used as a method of analysis. The age of spectroscopy was getting under way and it would do for light what the microscope had done for matter.

Earlier breakthroughs

In 1672 Isaac Newton had shown that prisms could refract white light into a spectrum of seven separate colours – the colours of the rainbow. He had also noted, without understanding why, that each colour exhibited a different degree of refrangibility – that is, each colour was deflected by refraction to a different extent.

In 1801 William Herschel discovered infrared radiation while attempting to measure the temperature of the solar spectrum. That same year the German physicist Johann Wilhelm Ritter happened upon the ultraviolet

Analysing light
Joseph von Fraunhofer (above centre) demonstrates his spectroscope to colleagues.

part of the spectrum in the course of studying the effects of its colours on the darkening of paper soaked in a silver chloride solution. Meanwhile, an English scientist named William Hyde Wollaston reported the unexpected presence of a number of dark lines in the solar spectrum when looked at through a prism, but he did not pursued the subject further.

A PLETHORA OF APPLICATIONS

Today, interest in spectroscopy stretches well beyond the realm of pure physics and the spectra investigated are no longer limited to what can be seen with the naked eye. Spectroscopy is used to study an increasingly vast range of phenomena, from radio waves and microwaves to infrared, X and gamma rays. Laboratories and factories use a variety of instruments, each associated with a particular wavelength band and a specific technology, such as emission or nuclear magnetic resonance spectroscopy or mass spectrometry. One such application, for example, enables criminologists to tease out hard evidence from tiny traces of dust gathered at a crime scene.

WAVES OF COLOUR

Colour is determined by a light ray's wavelength – that is, by the distance between two successive crests of the wave.

'Fraunhofer lines' in his honour. Meanwhile, he continued to perfect the spectroscope, which was unveiled in 1814. Seven years later he replaced the prism inside the instrument with a grill – the diffraction grating – which enabled him to analyse the spectrum of other heavenly bodies, notably the double star Sirius, the brightest object in the night sky.

The universe in a spectroscope

Fraunhofer died of tuberculosis in 1826, aged just 39, leaving the mystery contained within the black lines unsolved. His spectroscope would go on to play as significant a role in the future of astronomy as the telescopes devised by Galileo and Newton, opening the way first for the science of astrophysics and then to physical cosmology and quantum physics.

Spectroscopy has enabled scientists to study the chemical composition of the visible bodies of the universe, just as clearly as if they could be brought down to Earth for laboratory analysis. It has revealed, for example, that there is methane on Venus and carbon dioxide on Mars. Even more extraordinary, it has enabled astronomers to identify the gases that make up objects as distant as Betelgeuse, a red supergiant in the constellation of Orion, and the Crab Nebula thousands of light years away with the same degree of certainty as if they had visited such distant destinations in person.

Rainbow hues
Human eyes can only distinguish the seven main colours of the rainbow. In reality, a rainbow is formed of a continuous succession of hues, ranging from red to violet.

Multiple vision
A spectroscope with seven separate prisms (above). It was made in the late 19th century for the English astronomer Norman Lockyer.

Cosmic chemistry

In around 1813, while researching different kinds of glass for lenses, Fraunhofer discovered the same dark lines seen by Wollaston. He was used to working by candlelight, which provided a continuous spectrum, and was quick to grasp that the lines were significant as interstices in the solar spectrum, carrying information about the nature of the Sun itself. Fraunhofer prepared a detailed list of 576 lines in the solar spectrum, noting their exact spacing; they would eventually be named

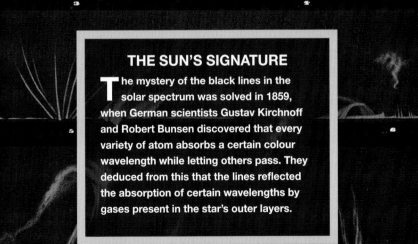

THE SUN'S SIGNATURE

The mystery of the black lines in the solar spectrum was solved in 1859, when German scientists Gustav Kirchnoff and Robert Bunsen discovered that every variety of atom absorbs a certain colour wavelength while letting others pass. They deduced from this that the lines reflected the absorption of certain wavelengths by gases present in the star's outer layers.

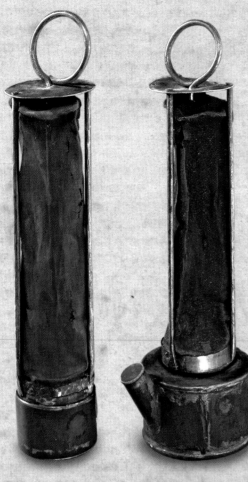

The miner's lamp 1816

Lifesaver
Sir Humphry Davy invented the lamp that came to bear his name in the wake of an explosion that killed 92 men in a pit at Felling, County Durham, in 1812.

Working underground in mines was not only physically challenging but also highly dangerous because of firedamp – the mixture of methane and other explosive gases produced as a by-product of coal extraction. The oil lamps originally used to light the tunnels and galleries had naked flames, which were always likely to ignite a blast. At the instigation of the mine owners, inventors took up the challenge of devising a safer means of illumination. In 1815 Sir Humphry Davy came up with the idea of enclosing the flame within a double mesh of wire gauze, which effectively prevented chance ignition. Patented the next year, his invention was an immediate success. The Davy lamp and its derivatives remained in use for more than a century, during which time many improvements were made to the basic design, notably the addition in about 1840 of an inner chimney to increase the draft. The lamps only became redundant when electric lighting was installed in pits in around 1900.

The metronome 1816

A CUMBERSOME PRECURSOR

The earliest known device for regulating musical time-keeping was a chronometer devised in the late 17th century by a French musician named Étienne Loulié. Employing a standard pendulum, it stood more than 2m high.

Seated at his desk, Ludwig van Beethoven was intent on the task of noting down a musical score. Keeping time at his side was a singular device recently sent to him by his fellow-German, Johann Maelzel. It was a metronome – a slender pyramid-shaped wooden box, weighted at the base and containing a clock mechanism that worked a graduated upward-pointing pendulum. The composer had only to slide the counterweight on the pendulum to set the tempo at whatever he required – 72 beats a minute, for example, for the *allegro con brio* of the final movement of his Seventh Symphony. Maelzel patented his invention in 1816, then sought to popularise it by sending examples to 200 composers. It was the support of Beethoven, then at the height of his powers, that won Maelzel the best publicity. From 1817 on the master used it to establish the tempo for performances of all his earlier symphonies, and henceforth the metronome was an indispensable tool for musicians. It was not dethroned until electronic devices performing the same function became available in the late 20th century.

Elegant timekeeper
Decorated with painted iron and gilded bronze, this metronome was built to Johann Maelzel's design in 1815.

The stethoscope 1816

In 1816, shortly after he had taken up a new position at the Hospital Necker in Paris, a 35-year-old doctor named René Laennec was at the bedside of a young woman suffering from a cardiac condition. He needed to check the beating of her heart, but found himself too embarrassed to do so. In his quandary he had the idea of rolling up a sheaf of paper and putting one end on the woman's chest and the other to his ear. On doing so, he was surprised to hear her heartbeats more clearly than if he had put his ear directly to her breast.

Laennec determined to improve on his chance discovery, replacing the tube of paper first with a solid rod and then with a hollow cylinder of beechwood. Initially, he called his invention a *pectoriloque* (literally, a 'chest speaker'), but later settled on stethoscope, from the Greek *stethos*, meaning 'breast', and *skopein*, 'to examine'.

The advent of medical signs

Laennec used the instrument to produce detailed descriptions of lung and heart conditions, as reflected in the clicks and gurgles he heard through the process he called auscultation, or 'listening'. He published his findings in 1819 in *De l'auscultation mediate*, a basic text for modern heart and lung medicine. This marked the beginning of the era of signs in medical diagnosis – the gathering of objective data by physicians through physical examination to supplement the subjective accounts of symptoms from their patients.

Using both ears

Laennec died in 1826 from tuberculosis probably contracted while using his device on an infected patient. Others carried on improving his invention. In the 1850s an American named George Cammann came up with a flexible, binaural stethoscope that we would recognise today. He did not patent his device, believing the technology should be freely available to doctors.

THE PERCUSSION TECHNIQUE

In 1761 an Austrian physician named Leopold Auenbrugger published *Inventum Novum* ('A New Discovery') in which he described the medical technique of percussion – tapping a patient's chest to determine the condition of the internal organs and aid diagnosis. Although few doctors showed much interest at the time, Laennec was impressed. The combination of his stethoscope with the Austrian's method made medical examination a much more accurate process.

Examination aid
A simple, non-intrusive listening device, the stethoscope gives doctors insights into the functioning of a patient's heart, lungs and stomach.

The kaleidoscope 1816

Eyecatcher
The kaleidoscope was not the only optical toy to win favour in the 19th century. There was also the kinetoscope, a device for viewing moving-picture strips.

Why would a serious physicist like Scotland's Sir David Brewster invent something as seemingly frivolous as the kaleidoscope? Perhaps because he was not only a scientist conducting research into light, but also a writer, a philosopher and a man of wide intellectual curiosity. In 1816 he set a number of mirrors in a small tube equipped with an eye-hole. Fragmented and reflected, the light entering from the far end of the cylinder created patterns of a complex and ever-changing symmetry. The device had no purpose other than to create beautiful images, and its name said as much, being derived from the Greek *kalos* ('beautiful'), *eidos* ('image') and *skopein* ('to examine').

AN INSPIRATIONAL TOY

The kaleidoscope was seen as an educational plaything, a conjuror's tool, and became an instant international success. It even came to serve as an inspiration for writers and philosophers such as Marcel Proust and Arthur Schopenhauer, who saw in its images a metaphor for the world's endless mutability.

Hydrogen peroxide 1818

Today, hydrogen peroxide is mainly familiar as the bleaching agent used to lighten hair to the near-white colour known as peroxide blonde. But this chemical with bleaching and disinfectant properties has other uses. It was first discovered in 1818 by a French chemistry professor named Louis Jacques Thénard, who had already helped to reveal – either on his own or in collaboration with his equally distinguished colleague, Joseph Gay-Lussac – the properties of potassium, sodium, boron and silicon. In his laboratory at Paris's École Polytechnique, Thénard observed that by combining nitric acid with barium peroxide he obtained a blueish liquid with strong oxidising properties that discoloured everything it touched. This was hydrogen peroxide, sometimes misleadingly known as oxygenated water because of its chemical composition (H_2O_2). Thénard's laboratory curiosity soon turned out to have industrial applications, notably for bleaching the woodpulp used to make paper. Even now the greater part of the hydrogen peroxide produced in the world is destined for the paper-making industry, although it also has an entirely different use as a rocket propellant.

Essentially blonde
Hydrogen peroxide is used as a bleaching agent for delicate substances such as feathers, ivory and human hair.

Macadamisation 1818

As late as 1930, the hamlet of Sauchrie in the west of Scotland was linked to the main Alloway-to-Maybole road by a track laid in 1783 by John Loudun McAdam. It was McAdam's first attempt at road building, and he probably had little inkling at the time that he had found the vocation that would make him famous. He had recently returned from the newly founded USA, where he had lost much of his fortune in the course of the American War of Independence. Plunging back into business, he began manufacturing tar for the navy. In 1798, at the start of the Napoleonic Wars, the British government charged him with supervising the transport of men and materiel to the western ports. The wretched state of the region's roads drove him to seek a simple, economic way to construct highways that would remain usable in all weathers.

King of the roads

With the end of the Napoleonic wars in 1815, McAdam was appointed surveyor-general of the roads round Bristol. This gave him the opportunity to put his ideas into practice, supervising the building of some 30 highways. By 1818 he had perfected his technique. Macademised roads were made of several layers of graded crushed stone, with the lumpiest aggregate at the bottom and the finest gravel on top. They were built with a slight camber to allow rainwater to drain off to the sides.

McAdam set down his ideas on the subject in two works published in 1816 and 1819, which brought his method wide attention and spread his reputation beyond Britain to Europe and the USA, future heart of the motor industry. By the time of his death in 1836, aged 80, his fame was so widespread that the term 'macadamisation' had entered common usage.

Level surface
A steam-roller flattens and compacts a macadamised roadway in London's Hyde Park in the mid 1860s. The roller was built by Aveling and Porter, specialists in agricultural machinery.

TOLL ROADS AND TURNPIKES

Until the late 17th century the responsibility for highway maintenance in Britain devolved onto individual parishes. The system worked well enough for local traffic, but was inadequate to support the main roads linking cities. So tolls were introduced to pay for the upkeep of main roads, and from 1707 turnpike trusts were set up to coordinate their collection. By McAdam's day, the tollhouses – there were seven on the road from Bath to London – were increasingly seen as obstacles to the flow of people and goods. The last trusts disappeared in the late 19th century, and county and borough councils inherited the task and cost of keeping the highways in good repair.

JOHN DALTON – 1766 TO 1844
Pioneer of the atomic age

Long accepted implicitly by the scientific community, the atomic concept of matter became an established reality only after John Dalton revealed, in 1808, his theory that atomic weights could be calculated. An outstanding chemist, Dalton also did important work on meteorology and on colour blindness, a problem that affected him personally.

Teacher and scientist
John Dalton, the founder of atomic theory (above). As a young man he helped to run a Quaker school in Kendal in the Lake District, then taught in Manchester.

Colour blindness is still sometimes known as daltonism, a term that also found its way into the French language as *daltonisme*. John Dalton's own limited colour vision in no way affected his research in other fields, particularly not in chemistry. Self-taught and solitary, he took up and carried on the work of Antoine de Lavoisier, the brilliant French chemist executed in the Terror, and led science into the atomic era. It was thanks to Dalton that science and industry acquired the necessary tools to transform natural elements into a rich variety of synthetic compounds. His most important discovery was that every

different type of atom – in other words, those constituting each of the separate chemical elements – had a specific weight that was shared by every other atom of the same type but not by the atoms of other elements. The corollary was that the atomic weight of a compound molecule was that of the individual atoms making it up. From the publication of Dalton's theory in 1808, chemists have taken up the task of deconstructing molecules to determine the weight of the atoms of which they are composed, a field of research that has had world-shaking implications.

A modest Quaker

Throughout his life, Dalton had to struggle to fulfil his ambitions. As a student and beyond, he never enjoyed the support of the great universities. Born in 1766 in Eaglesfield, near Cockermouth in Cumbria, he was brought up a member of the Society of Friends at a time when Quakers were still socially disadvantaged. His first teacher was his own father, a weaver. Happily, the Quakers took a positive view of science, and before long the boy's education was entrusted to another member of the community known for his learning, one Elihu Robinson. Besides teaching Dalton maths, Robinson gave him an abiding interest in meteorology, a subject close to the teacher's own heart. Dalton's first book, published when he was 27, was entitled *Meteorological Observations and Essays*, and he subsequently acquired the habit of keeping a detailed diary of the weather. The close

Quaker meeting
A painting of a Quaker meeting made in 1839. At their regular meetings Quakers seek to commune with God directly, without any set rites or order of service.

attention he paid to atmospheric phenomena helped to hone the intuitions about the behaviour of gases that would be at the root of his later chemical discoveries.

From meteorology to chemistry

The year 1793 marked a turning point for Dalton. His scientific gifts and the support of prominent Quakers won him a position at Manchester's New College, an academy for religious dissenters who at that time were denied access to the universities. His job was to teach maths and natural philosophy – the term then used to describe the sciences – and he was working there when his meteorological essay was published. The book attracted little general attention but won him a certain local reputation, helping him to gain election to the Manchester Literary and Philosophical Society, the 'Lit & Phil', which gave him a platform to air his ideas. From then on he published a stream of studies, many under the Lit & Phil's own imprimatur, on subjects ranging from colour blindness to the behaviour of gases at different pressures and temperatures.

Between 1800 and 1805 chemistry replaced meteorology as the focus of Dalton's research. In 1800 he became secretary of the Lit & Phil and in that capacity he presented a series of 'experimental essays' describing the first results of his work on gases. His most important finding was that, if mass and volume are constant, the variation of pressure with temperature is the same for all gases. This law was established independently by the French scientist Joseph Louis Gay-Lussac in the same year – 1802.

An intuitive and mistrustful outsider

Despite his membership of the Lit & Phil, Dalton remained cut off from the mainstream of the British scientific establishment. He conducted his experiments in his own laboratory within the society's premises, and it was there that he arrived at the modern theory of atoms. His social isolation – he had no wife and few friends – was an integral part of his discoveries: not trusting results published by other scientists, he restaged all of their experiments, taking only his own findings into account. His first breakthrough came in 1803, when he formulated the law of partial pressures, also known as Dalton's law. This states that the total pressure of a combination

DALTON AND COLOUR BLINDNESS

In 1794 Dalton wrote an essay entitled *Extraordinary Facts Relating to the Vision of Colours* that was published by the Manchester Literary and Philosophical Society. In it he noted that 'that part of the image which others call red appears to me little more than a shade or defect of light ... the orange, yellow and green seem one colour which descends pretty uniformly from an intense to a rare yellow, making what I should call different shades of yellow.' Dalton's study was the first technical description of colour blindness, a condition he suffered from himself. Dalton gave instructions for his eyes to be left to science after his death. Two centuries later, in 1995, DNA analysis carried out on one of the eyeballs indicated that he suffered from deuteranopia, a condition in which the cones of the retina that distinguish medium-wavelength colours are missing.

Specimen colours
Sample colour swatches used by Dalton to test his own sight, establishing that he was indeed colour blind – an abnormality of the vision that is generally hereditary and primarily affects men.

AN ENDURING OBSESSION

Beginning in 1787, Dalton noted his daily meteorological observations in a diary that he kept for 57 years. In all, he made over 200,000 separate entries, the last one in June 1844, just a month before his death. Historians would subsequently note the germ of many of his later chemical insights in his first book, *Meteorological Observations and Essays*, which he published in 1793.

THE CRUCIAL EXPERIMENTS

In 1803 John Dalton promulgated his law of partial pressures. This stated that the total pressure exerted by a mixture of gases is equal to the sum of the partial pressures of each individual component. To demonstrate why each gas apparently acted as if no other was there, Dalton undertook a series of experiments. He put water in a receptacle containing a gaseous mixture and observed that the pressure of one gas diminished while the other remained constant. He deduced that the water must have absorbed the atoms of one gas in preference to the other, drawing from this the conclusion that every type of atom was separate from all other types and had its own distinctive weight. The proposition was to prove crucial in future science.

of gases is the sum of the (partial) pressures of all its constituents. So, for example, if oxygen and nitrogen are mixed in a sealed container, the total pressure of the mixture is equal to the sum of equivalent volumes of the oxygen and nitrogen alone. The discovery had important implications, which Dalton recognised. In his own words: 'I am nearly persuaded that the circumstance depends on the weight and number of the ultimate particles of the several gases' – that is, each particle or atom had a specific weight that affected its behaviour.

The law of multiple proportions

To confirm his intuition, Dalton had first to establish a methodology. To simplify the problem, he put forward the hypothesis that the compounds produced when elements combine consist of whole numbers, not fractions, of the constituent parts. So, when oxygen combines with hydrogen, the elements may do so in proportions of 1 to 1, say, or 1 to 2 or 3, but not in proportions of, for example, 1 to 1.2 or 1 to 2.3.

Between 1805 and 1808, Dalton set about evaluating the weight of oxygen, carbon, nitrogen, sulphur and phosphorus, by comparing them with hydrogen, to which he assigned the number 1. He calculated that an atom of oxygen is seven times heavier than one of hydrogen (the actual figure is 8). He first revealed his theory in 1807 in William Thomson's *A System of Chemistry*, before laying it out in greater length and detail in his own *A New System of Chemical Philosophy*, published the following year.

Fishing for gas
A mural (top) by the Pre-Raphaelite painter Ford Madox Brown depicts Dalton gathering natural gases from a marsh for use in his experiments. The painting is one of a series decorating Manchester Town Hall.

Gas lighter
Filled with inflammable gas under hydraulic pressure, this device was designed by French chemist Joseph Gay-Lussac. Initially used in his researches, it later came to serve as a model for modern cigarette lighters.

ELEMENTS

		wt			wt
⊙	Hydrogen.	1	⊕	Strontian	46
⊖	Azote	5	⊛	Barytes	68
◯	Carbon	54	Ⓘ	Iron	50
⊘	Oxygen	7	Ⓩ	Zinc	56
⊗	Phosphorus	9	Ⓒ	Copper	56
⊕	Sulphur	13	Ⓛ	Lead	90
⊗	Magnesia	20	Ⓢ	Silver	190
◒	Lime	24	Ⓖ	Gold	190
⊟	Soda	28	Ⓟ	Platina	190
⊜	Potash	42	⊛	Mercury	167

Dalton's table
Dalton drew up this table listing 20 elements with their atomic weights in 1808 (above). He used the wooden balls (above right) to represent atoms in public lectures. The sticks and holes served to attach the balls in different molecule combinations.

An incalculable legacy

Dalton's breakthrough opened new horizons for science. His atomic theory led 19th-century researchers to establish the system of chemical notation used to this day, as in the familiar formula of H_2O for water. Others, including Johannes van der Waals of the Netherlands, worked to determine the number of atoms contained in given volumes of gas, discovering many new chemical elements and compounds in the process.

In 1860 the Karlsruhe Congress, which drew chemists from all over Europe, provided official recognition for the concept of the atom and the molecule. Nine years later the Russian Dmitri Mendeleev drew up the periodic table, revealing underlying patterns in the distribution of the elements. As for Dalton, he continued with his researches until his death in 1844, but his later work added little to the breakthrough achievements that he had made in the first decade of the century.

Water molecule
A symbolic computer-generated image of water (H_2O) shows the two constituent hydrogen atoms in green, with the single oxygen atom in red.

GAY-LUSSAC'S LAW

This states that the pressure of a fixed volume of any gas is directly proportional to the gas's temperature. Dalton arrived at Gay-Lussac's law through his own work, contemporaneously and quite independently.

31

Giving divers mobility and time underwater

The helmeted diving suit was first developed by the German coppersmith Augustus Siebe. The key element of his device was that it enabled the diver to move in water while breathing through a tube linked to the surface.

In 1819 Augustus Siebe prepared to test his prototype diving-suit. The most important part of the contraption was a rigid copper helmet, fitted with three windows for vision, plus a tube which supplied compressed air fed down by a pump above the water's surface. The outfit was completed by a leather outer garment riveted to the helmet and lead-weighted shoes. At the time, Siebe was living in England. He had been approached by John and Charles Deane, who had earlier devised an iron helmet fixed to a cloth cape intended for use by firefighters in the holds of ships. Switching their interest to the recovery of lost anchors and fishing-nets, they wanted to adapt their invention for use underwater.

The first tests were not promising. The kit weighed 90kg and the diver had to stay upright to prevent water getting into the helmet – if he fell, he risked drowning. Even so, Siebe's design was to become the model for the modern diving suit.

Inventive predecessors

Siebe's device took its place in a long line of earlier subaqueous inventions. The English scientist Edmund Halley had devised the diving bell in 1690. Then 25 years later John Lethbridge, a West Country wool merchant who was a keen diver, constructed a diving outfit consisting of an iron-hooped oak barrel equipped with armholes and a glass window for viewing. At the end of the 18th century the German Karl Klingert adapted a design drawn up more than a hundred years before by the Italian physicist Giovanni Borelli. Klingert's device featured a metal cylinder covering the chest

THE DEANE BROTHERS

As young men Charles and John Deane spent seven years at sea before returning to their native Deptford, where Charles got work in a shipyard. It was there that he developed his idea for a 'smoke helmet', later adapted by Augustus Siebe into the diving helmet (right). Both brothers were keen divers; in 1836, while doing salvage work in the Solent, John discovered the sunken remains of the Tudor warship *Mary Rose*.

The wreck of the *Royal George*
Sunk in 1782 off Spithead, with the loss of 900 lives, the British warship was salvaged (above) from 1839 by divers equipped with suits designed by Siebe.

attached to an iron helmet fed with air through two tubes linked to a manually operated pump located above water. The problem was that the diver's body was unprotected; below a certain depth, the pressure of the water beneath the cylinder became so intense that it blocked circulation.

A new freedom

Siebe's experiments finally met with success in 1837, largely thanks to the work of an English engineer named George Edwards who had the idea of clamping Siebe's helmet to a waterproof suit that covered the entire body. Siebe duly developed an integral goatskin garment that was fixed to the helmet by 12 copper bolts. The

THE MYSTERY OF DECOMPRESSION SICKNESS

The upsurge in diving activity in the 19th century was accompanied by an increase in little-understood ailments such as the bends. It was only after 1878, when the French physiologist Paul Bert published a ground-breaking book on barometric pressure, that the damaging effects of pressurised oxygen on the central nervous system below a depth of about 7m were finally explained.

impermeable diving suit was born. From that time on the design of diving suits was steadily improved. In 1855 a Frenchman named Joseph Cabirol came up with a new model that he presented at the Paris Universal Exhibition. He used rubber in place of goatskin for the suit, while the helmet had four windows and a valve that could be turned on and off to discharge waste air.

Cabirol's version still relied on air pumped from the surface. Subsequent research concentrated on developing a system that permitted divers to carry their own air supply so they could move around freely without cables or tubes.

Two other Frenchmen, the engineer Benôit Rouquayrol and a naval lieutenant named Auguste Denayrouze, devised the first closed-circuit breathing apparatus in about 1865. But the amount of air that could be carried was limited, allowing the diver only about 30 minutes of free movement at a depth of 10m. The problem was only finally resolved in 1943 with the invention of the aqualung by Émile Gagnan and Jacques-Yves Cousteau.

Yet Siebe's helmeted suit continued to have an afterlife. Its successors are still used for laying underwater cables and for salvage missions. And astronaut's spacesuits are its distant descendants.

The Newtsuit
A rigid, self-contained diving suit (above), designed by the Canadian Phil Nuytten, allows a diver to work several hundred metres down at normal atmospheric pressure.

Articulated diving suit
Made by the Carmagnole brothers in the 1880s, this diving suit (left) had so many articulated joints, each one attached to a fabric backing, that it proved insufficiently waterproof for operational use.

ANDRÉ MARIE AMPÈRE – 1775 TO 1836

The Newton of electricity

A philosopher, poet and teacher as well as a scientist of exceptional talent, Ampère left a considerable legacy even though his life was marked by personal tragedy. Today he is best remembered for his breakthrough discoveries in the field of electricity.

Portrait of Ampère
By the age of 14, the future scientist (above) had already read all 35 volumes of the Encyclopédie, *the monumental 18th-century work of the French Enlightenment.*

It was the great Scottish physicist James Clark Maxwell who first called André Marie Ampère 'the Newton of electricity'. The epithet was praise indeed, but no more than the French scientist deserved. A precocious genius, he did much to create the science that he called electrodynamics and that is known today as electromagnetism, bringing together electricity and magnetism in a mathematical theory that explains the interactions between currents. An heir to the intellectual curiosity of the Enlightenment, Ampère made his major breakthroughs in a relatively short period, between 1820 and 1826. Posterity gave his name to the ampere or 'amp', the international unit of measurement of electric current.

Rousseau and the guillotine

André Ampère was born in Lyon, France, on 20 January, 1775. He spent his childhood in a village some 6 miles to the north of the city,

where his father had a substantial estate. Ampère senior was a wealthy silk merchant, a passionate lover of literature and by all accounts a strong personality. As a fervent disciple of Jean-Jacques Rousseau's back-to-nature philosophy, he decided that André should be taught at home, not at school, following the precepts that Rousseau had spelled out in his book *Émile, or Education*.

The last years of Ampère's youth were scarred by tragedy. His eldest sister, Antoinette, died. Then his father, for all his progressive sympathies, was arrested by revolutionaries; he died on the guillotine at the height of the Terror in 1793. Terribly affected by these losses, Ampère sank into depression for a year, and was only pulled out of his despondency by reading Rousseau's *Letters on Botany*, which kindled a passion for plants and science.

Soon he was thinking up new scientific instruments, as well as studying astronomy, throwing himself into the study of Latin and Greek, and even working on a project to create a universal language. He found time, too, to write a tragedy that was to remain unfinished, as well as a work called *L'Americide* ('America's Assassin'), in which he blamed Christopher Columbus for bringing corruption and decadence to previously innocent Native Americans.

A PRODIGIOUS MEMORY

Almost as soon as he could read, Ampère began to devour the books in his father's library. He learned entire tragedies of Racine by heart. He read Virgil in the original Latin and made his own translation of Horace's *Odes*. By the age of 13 he was so passionate about algebra that his father had to call on professors from Lyon to help satisfy his son's hunger for knowledge.

A scientist in love
In an unpublished manuscript, a piece of which is reproduced here (right), Ampère describes meeting Julie Carron, the love of his life, in April 1796.

THE ABSENT-MINDED PROFESSOR

Ampère is remembered for his penetrating intellect, but he also developed a reputation for absent-mindedness. The lexicographer Pierre Larousse recorded one telling anecdote: 'On his way to deliver a lecture in Paris one day, Ampère noticed a small, multi-coloured pebble on the path in front of him. Picking it up, he examined its veining with fascination. Then, remembering the lecture, he pulled a watch from his pocket to check the time. Redoubling his pace, he carefully placed the pebble back in his pocket and threw the watch from a bridge into the River Seine.'

Cartoon character
One of France's first strip cartoons – drawn in the 1890s by an artist named Georges Colomb, who signed himself Christophe – featured a brilliant but distracted professor, thought to have been partly inspired by Ampère.

Aged 20 and short of cash, Ampère took an apartment in Lyon and supported himself by offering tuition in maths, physics and chemistry. By this time he was engaged to a girl called Julie Carron, to whom he wrote passionate poetry. The two married in 1799 and a son, Jean-Jacques (in later life himself a distinguished writer), was born soon after. But in yet another tragedy for Ampère, Julie died after a long illness just four years later.

A theory of chance

By that time Ampère had been appointed to teach physics and chemistry at the École Centrale at Bourg-en-Bresse, a graduate institution. It was while employed there that he published his first important essay, *Considerations on the Mathematical Theory of Chance*, in which he calculated the probability a gambler runs of losing his stake over a given number of bets. The work won him a position teaching mathematics at the École Polytechnique in Paris, France's foremost engineering school.

Ampère owed his advancement to the recommendations of well-known intellectuals, such as the mathematician Louis Lagrange and the astronomer Jean-Baptiste Delambre. Starting as a lecturer, he was promoted to the rank of assistant professor three years later in 1807. By that time he had remarried and had a young daughter, but the marriage was not a success and he and his second wife soon

Prospecting for business
A leaflet advertising lessons in physics and chemistry (left), prepared and distributed by Ampère in 1801, when he was earning a precarious living as a private tutor in Lyon.

separated. (The daughter, Albine, would eventually marry an alcoholic officer and end up going insane.) Meanwhile, Ampère had flung himself into chemical research, where he played a part in the discovery of iodine and fluorine. He also established that the number of molecules in a given volume of gas is constant whatever the gas may be, confirming a finding made independently three years earlier by the Italian savant Amedeo Avogadro and still known as Avogadro's Law.

Paris and electromagnetism

From that time on, Ampère's reputation grew steadily. In 1809 he became a full professor at the École Polytechnique. In the years that followed honours rained down: he received the Légion d'Honneur, France's highest civic award, in 1814, and in the same year was also elected to the French Academy of Sciences.

He started his researches into electricity in 1820. A few months earlier the Danish physicist Hans Christian Œrsted had observed that each time a current passed through an electric wire, it slightly deflected the needle of a

Giving directions
In this 1820 sketch (right), Ampère indicated the flow of an electrical current from south to north. The stick figure is gesturing in the appropriate direction.

ranging from the solenoid – a coil of wire twined around a metallic core that produces a magnetic field when an electric current is passed through it – to the galvanometer, designed to detect and measure electric current. He also collaborated with François Arago on developing the electromagnet. This period of Ampère's work culminated in 1826 with the publication of his *Memoir on the Mathematical Theory of Electrodynamic Phenomena, deduced from Experiment Alone.*

A mystical Romantic

Ampère's great scientific preoccupations never quashed his more philosophical interests in fields ranging from psychology to ontology (the study of the nature of existence) and epistemology (the theory of knowledge). He was on friendly terms with leading lights of the French Romantic movement, notably the novelist and essayist Chateaubriand. Deeply religious by nature, he exhibited a tormented faith that came close to mysticism.

Worn out by his work, Ampère caught pneumonia in 1829 and temporarily moved to the Mediterranean port of Hyères to restore his health. In the years that followed he worked on an *Essay on the Philosophy of the*

magnetic compass placed close by. At the time, there was no scientific explanation for this phenomenon – scientists in the early 19th century still generally considered electricity and magnetism to be unconnected. That summer Œrsted's experiment was repeated across Europe, notably in Geneva, where a 34-year-old French mathematician named François Arago was one of the observers. He in turn restaged the experiment for two separate sessions of the Academy of Sciences, bringing it to Ampère's attention.

Fascinated by what he had seen, Ampère threw himself into researching the subject, spending long hours conducting experiments and writing up his findings. He came to the conclusion that electrical and magnetic phenomena are in essence one and the same, thereby clearing the way for a new field of study concerned with the interaction between currents. He called this new field electrodynamics.

Ampère was appointed to the chair of experimental physics at the Collège de France, where he turned his attention to developing industrial applications for the new science. He devised a variety of different instruments

Œrsted's experiment
Using this simple-looking apparatus (above), Danish scientist Hans Christian Œrsted was the first to show that an electric current could deflect a compass needle.

A BRITISH PIONEER OF ELECTROMAGNETISM

Self-taught William Sturgeon was a lecturer at the East India Company College at Addiscombe in Surrey when, in 1825, he demonstrated the world's first electromagnet. It was a horseshoe-shaped iron bar, wound around with copper wire and varnished to provide insulation for the metal. When a current was passed through the wire, the iron became sufficiently magnetised to lift a 4kg weight, even though the bar itself weighed just 200g.

Sciences that he was never to finish. He died six years later on a visit to Marseilles.

Over the course of his career Ampère made significant contributions to chemistry, optics, mechanics, the life sciences and mathematics (Monge-Ampère equations play a part in differential geometry to this day). But above all, at least in his own opinion, he had added to the theory of knowledge. In 1869 his remains were transferred to Paris and reburied in Montmartre Cemetery alongside his son Jean-Jacques, who had died four years earlier.

Ancient and modern
A 19th-century ammeter (right), used to measure the electric current in a circuit. The world's largest particle detector today is Atlas (below), part of the Large Hadron Collider project at CERN, the European Centre for Nuclear Research, near Geneva in Switzerland.

Electromagnetic pioneers
A 19th-century illustration shows Ampère (left) and François Arago (seated) demonstrating electro-magnetism at the French Academy of Sciences in 1820.

Fingerprinting 1823

As every enthusiast of detective stories knows, the tips of the fingers – like the toes, palms and soles of the feet – are lined with a complex pattern of friction ridges that are unique to an individual. When the fingers touch an object, they leave behind an imprint of this pattern: fingerprints. Various systems exist for classifying the elements of each print. Historically, these involved the visual identification of features in the pattern such as arches, loops and whorls; today, the work is mostly done by computer. Fingerprints stay the same throughout life, and the probability of two separate prints completely matching is virtually nil, even between identical twins.

The first person to attempt to classify fingerprints was a Czech physiologist, Jan Evangelista Purkyně, working at the University of Breslau (now Wroclaw in Poland). In 1823 he identified nine fingerprint patterns. No-one at the time imagined that this discovery might one day prove of use in criminal investigations.

A universal method

The next important development came in 1858 when William James Herschel, a son of the astronomer John Herschel, was acting as a magistrate in Bengal, India. To verify contracts he introduced a system in which people placed their inked fingerprint above their signature as a supplementary means of identification. In 1877 the practice was extended to the prison service as a way of identifying detainees.

At about the same time, a Scottish doctor named Henry Faulds, then working in a Tokyo hospital, wrote to Charles Darwin to describe an idea that had come to him while studying ancient pottery found in the bay of Edo. He noticed prints left by the long-dead craftsmen who had fashioned the pottery fragments, inspiring him to suggest that fingerprints might be a method for identifying both known recidivist criminals and unknown corpses. He published his ideas in *Nature* in 1880. In the ensuing years, the use of fingerprints in criminal investigations gradually spread across the world.

Modern scanning technology
A digitally scanned infrared print from an index finger (above). The tiny dotted marks help to highlight the print's unique features.

Recovering fingerprints
A crime scene investigator dusts a residue print with fine powder. The next step is to lift the print off the surface with an adhesive strip (right).

TELLTALE SIGNS

The first use of fingerprint evidence to solve a murder occurred in Argentina in 1892. A woman was found with neck injuries alongside the bodies of her two sons, both with their throats cut. She accused a neighbour of the crime, but police were able to identify a bloody print found on a door as belonging to the woman herself, who subsequently confessed to killing her children.

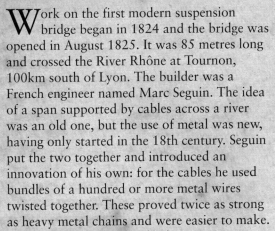

The suspension bridge 1824

Work on the first modern suspension bridge began in 1824 and the bridge was opened in August 1825. It was 85 metres long and crossed the River Rhône at Tournon, 100km south of Lyon. The builder was a French engineer named Marc Seguin. The idea of a span supported by cables across a river was an old one, but the use of metal was new, having only started in the 18th century. Seguin put the two together and introduced an innovation of his own: for the cables he used bundles of a hundred or more metal wires twisted together. These proved twice as strong as heavy metal chains and were easier to make.

Seguin reinforced the bridge supports, which had been regularly swept away by floods in the past, consolidating them with reinforced cement. He also introduced improved construction methods. Taking advantage of hydraulic flow, and aided by the capacity of the local lime mortar to harden underwater, he used diving bells that permitted work below the water's surface, enabling his workers to construct pillars with deep foundations to support the bridge.

The Clifton suspension bridge, spanning the Avon Gorge, is Britain's oldest suspension bridge, opened in 1864. The original design was created by Isambard Kingdom Brunel, but it was modified several times after Brunel's death in 1859. Modern computer analysis has revealed that in his design of the crucial joints between the 4,200 links that make up the bridge's chain, Brunel had made an almost perfect calculation of the minimal weight required to maintain maximum strength.

Three bridges
Marc Seguin's original suspension bridge over the River Rhône (inset, above left) was built too low over the water. In 1847 it was replaced by a higher structure (top). The collapse of the Tacoma Bridge in 1940 was caught on film by the owner of a local camera store (below).

THE TACOMA DISASTER

Until computer simulation finally solved the problem, suspension bridges suffered badly from vibration, and sometimes the consequences were dramatic. The collapse of the Tacoma Bridge in the US state of Washington in 1940 still remains fresh in some people's memories. The 2km bridge had only been open for a few months when, on the morning of 7 November, 1940, the span began to sway in 60km/h (40mph) winds. Soon the apron was swinging as much as 8m. After an hour the central span could take no more and collapsed, fortunately without loss of life. A replacement bridge was built in 1950.

The dawn of the consumer era

Perhaps it is not surprising that the dawn of shopping in style should have been in Paris. The opening of La Belle Jardinière, a huge clothing emporium, on 25 October, 1824, was big news even beyond France's borders. Other stores followed in its wake, with an ever wider range of goods and new marketing strategies. Before long department stores were influencing urban lifestyles.

La Belle Jardinière rose in the heart of Paris, on the Ile de la Cité not far from Nôtre-Dame Cathedral. It was the brainchild of Pierre Parissot, a merchant who had formerly run a haberdashery in the Faubourg Saint-Antoine district of the French capital. He named his new establishment after a painting by Raphael, the Renaissance master, that showed an elegantly and modestly dressed Virgin Mary.

Parissot's idea was to sell off-the-peg fashions to a middle-class clientele that was rapidly expanding thanks to the spread of industrialisation. The sewing machine, patented in France by Barthélemy Thimonnier in 1830, soon gave him the means to mass-produce garments, although his early machines were destroyed by rioting tailors fearful for their jobs. The store expanded and branches opened up in the provinces; there were 90 of them by 1840. Although Parissot died in 1843, his creation lived on. In 1867 the Paris store moved to larger premises on the Right Bank, where it stood until the 1970s.

The art of advertising *A 1902 poster (right) produced to promote the summer clothes collections at La Belle Jardinière in Paris.*

COMMERCIALISING CHRISTMAS

One effect of the rise of the department stores was the commercialisation of Christmas. Almost unobserved in the early 19th century, the festival enjoyed a revival following the publication of Charles Dickens's *A Christmas Carol* in 1843. From the 1860s, the illustrator Thomas Nast popularised the image of Santa Claus, the bringer of gifts, encouraging an increase in seasonal sales. By the 1960s the Christmas season had become the busiest time of the year for retailers in many Western lands.

Seasonal promotion *A Christmas poster for the Bazar de l'Hôtel de Ville, another 19th-century Parisian emporium.*

BRITISH PIONEERS

Several British department stores trace their roots back to the early 19th century. Some can even claim to predate the great Parisian emporia in offering a variety of goods under a single roof, although not on such a grand scale. Joplings of Sunderland opened as a drapery store in 1804, before branching out into other fields. Austins has occupied the same site in Londonderry, Northern Ireland, since 1830. The first of the great London stores was Whiteleys of Bayswater, which opened as a drapery shop in 1863.

The pride of Paris
La Belle Jardinière as it looked in the 1870s (left), after moving to new premises on the Right Bank of the Seine. It concentrated on selling clothes and was the first of the Parisian stores to develop a branch network in the provinces.

Set prices and sales

La Belle Jardinière concentrated on selling clothes, but other emporia that followed in its footsteps cast their nets wider. In 1852 Paul Videau, creator of the Videau Bon Marché shop, teamed up with Aristide Boucicaut, formerly head of the shawls department at another store on Paris's Left Bank. Sales soared, but Videau decided to retire after ten years at the helm, overwhelmed by the sheer size of the commercial revolution his partner was steering.

Boucicaut believed that building a successful business demanded not just attracting customers but also retaining them by winning their trust. He did away with variable prices and with purchases on credit, both of which sometimes left a residue of bad feeling. At Bon Marché all items would be sold over the counter at a fixed price that was clearly displayed. Boucicaut also introduced home delivery and offered to exchange or reimburse any customers for merchandise that failed to satisfy on closer examination when they got their goods home.

To ensure a rapid turnover Boucicaut introduced seasonal sales and special promotions. In 'white weeks' the entire store was draped in pristine linen spread over the counters and wrapped around pillars – the effect was magical to look at and the events proved to be big money-earners. Word of these innovative commercial tactics was spread by advertising, which was also rapidly expanding at the time. In addition to advertisements in

Latest fashions
An illustration from the 1873 catalogue for the Grands Magasins du Louvre department store.

'GIVE THE LADY WHAT SHE WANTS'

Marshall Field's of Chicago was one of the stores that rose to prominence in the USA in the late 19th century, taking as its slogan 'Give the Lady What She Wants'. Like La Belle Jardinière in Paris, it offered to reimburse customers unsatisfied with the goods they bought. The policy proved expensive after the visit of Prince Henry of Prussia to Chicago in 1902, which stimulated a temporary surge in demand for expensive lace collars among the prince's dinner guests. On his return home, most found their way back to the store as their new owners suddenly found them surplus to requirements.

Arresting display *Passers-by admire the goods on display at Marshall Field's in Chicago (above). The store burned down twice – in the Great Fire of 1871 and again in 1877.*

newspapers, stores emblazoned themselves on publicity hoardings and sent out catalogues, heavily illustrated and sometimes offering free samples on request. The way was opening to mail-order shopping, a market that would blossom in the 20th century.

Emancipating female shoppers

In the store itself, a huge variety of goods enticed shoppers to different departments specialising in everything from toiletries and knick-knacks to babyware and table displays. A department store not only offered women a single shop where they could buy all they needed to dress themselves and run their households, but also gave them a place to go outside the home, contributing to female emancipation. Some women found jobs in the new emporia, joining a burgeoning workforce with a hierarchical order in which the top layers were invariably occupied by men.

Department heads were responsible for the goods they bought in as well as for sales. They were assisted by a small army of sales assistants, supplemented by a supporting cast

of shop inspectors, store-keepers, delivery men, lift operators and bellboys. Motivated either by a spirit of philanthropy or a keen sense of what might now be called human resources management, Boucicaut secured the loyalty of his staff by offering generous fringe benefits of a kind that were new in their day, although his rivals, including Ernest Cognacq of Paris's Samaritaine store, soon copied them. Fines imposed on staff for misdemeanours were done away with and replaced instead with a system of incentives, rewarding employees who boosted sales with regular pay rises and the chance to win promotion on merit alone.

Bon Marché had a staff canteen and even housing for unmarried female workers – a perquisite that made it hard for them to quit their jobs. Before the law demanded it, Boucicaut was giving his employees Sundays off, and he also set up a contingency fund covering sickness and other mishaps financed out of the profits of the firm. After his death in 1877, his wife established a pension fund for the workers.

Planet Enterprise

In time Boucicaut felt the need to rehouse the business in new premises that reflected its soaring commercial ambitions. In 1869 he hired the architect Louis Auguste Boileau and the engineer Gustave Eiffel, the future builder of the Eiffel Tower, to design a vast structure that would be functional, attractive and filled with light from large bay windows. The aim, as always, was to attract customers, so the new store was provided with monumental staircases and giant stained-glass domes, setting a fashion that would be followed by other Parisian establishments such as the Magasins du Louvre, founded in 1855, and Au Tapis Rouge, originally set up in 1784 but magnificently relocated in 1871.

The great department stores built over the following decades in Berlin and Brussels, London and New York followed a similar pattern. Yet while the Parisian model spread widely, there were local variations in the manner of doing business. In the USA customers proved more ready to make purchases if they did not have to hand over cash on the spot, so buying on credit became

Food, glorious food
Harrods, with its famous Food Hall, dates from 1849 when the grocer Charles Henry Harrod moved from premises in Stepney to a shop on the store's present site in Knightsbridge. This image (right) shows the store's immaculate butcher's shop.

Guaranteed delivery
The new department stores made a point of offering free delivery to people's homes. The card below advertises the service in an exotic flight of fancy, but in practice it was more likely to involve a delivery man on foot (right)

Service des livraisons en l'an 2000

AU BON MARCHÉ

Au Bon Marché

popular. Employees in the USA tended to be less well-treated, without long-term contracts or workers' compensation insurance.

Alongside the 'proper' department stores, like Lord & Taylor which traced its origins back to 1826, new types of enterprise sprang up to exploit fresh commercial possibilities. These included the so-called 'dime stores', where everything cost 10 cents or less – Woolworths first opened in 1878 – and mail-order companies like Sears, Roebuck & Co, founded in the 1880s. Between them, companies like these helped to prepare the way for the development of the consumer society, whose 20th-century symbols would be the supermarket and the retail mall.

Secular cathedral
Installed in 1923, the stained-glass dome of the Printemps department store in Paris (left) is 20m across and 16m high. It was temporarily dismantled during World War II to protect it from bombs.

PALACES OF COMMERCE

Store proprietors in the USA employed some of the finest architects of the day to design their shops and offices. In 1909 Daniel Burnham, the chief architect of the 1893 Chicago World's Fair, was commissioned to plan new premises for Wanamaker's in Philadelphia, taking his inspiration from Italian Renaissance models. One year later Frank Woolworth hired Cass Gilbert, architect of the US Supreme Court building, to construct a new headquarters for his retail empire. The 57-storey building he designed was 240m high.

The Woolworth Building
This skyscraper in New York was the world's tallest building when it was completed in 1913.

Turning heat into energy

The cycle described by Sadi Carnot in 1824 marked a decisive step forward in the history of science and technology. Based on detailed study of the steam engine, his theory described the functioning of a hypothetically perfect engine and founded the science of thermodynamics. Cars, power stations and jet engines all operate according to its principles.

The full title of Sadi Carnot's pivotal 1824 work was *Reflections on the Motive Power of Fire and on Machines Fitted to Develop that Power*. In writing it he used the language of the engineers and industrialists of his day. The book spoke of pistons and of cylinders, of boilers, heat and 'work', the term he used to describe the energy that a machine could exert – for example, the amount of water a pump could extract per second from a well 10m deep. Yet in one sense the terminology now seems misleading, for Carnot's ideas were so potent that they extended well beyond their early 19th-century context, applying not just to heat transfer but to all forms of energy.

Simplified motion

Carnot described the motion of a simplified steam engine – or 'fire engine', as it was often called at the time – consisting of a gas-filled cylinder closed by a piston that, for the purposes of the argument, moved up and down without generating friction. He spelled out a straightforward operational cycle: the piston starts from a motionless state, then moves upward when the gas is heated (the expansion phase) before falling as it cools (contraction), finally returning to its original position. In the mental exercise Carnot sketched out, the heating and cooling of the gas are effected by the cylinder coming into contact first with a heat source then with a cooling medium. Then he went a step further, imagining an ideal machine with no heat source but a cylinder-piston system that functioned like a perfect Thermos flask, neither losing nor gaining heat.

A four-phase motion

To understand Carnot's reasoning, it is easiest to look at the cycle from the piston's point of view. To begin with, the piston and the machine are both at rest. The first movement occurs when the heat source warms the

THEORIST OF THE AGE OF STEAM

Steam engines had existed for well over a century when the young Sadi Carnot – full name Nicolas Léonard Sadi Carnot (1796–1832) – turned his attention to them in about 1820. But even though steam engines were widely used in factories, providing much of the energy that powered the early decades of the Industrial Revolution, the principles on which they worked were poorly understood. Mechanics was already an advanced science, being firmly based on mathematics. Yet heat – studied since the invention of the thermometer in the 17th century – had mostly fallen within the domains of medicine and chemistry. Physicists, mathematicians and meteorologists were just beginning to take an interest in the question of heat transference. Carnot's contribution lay in providing a theoretical framework to explain how heat transference operated – a theory that was to prove vital in enabling engineers to calculate the efficiency of engines, improving their design and performance. His research also proved to have wider applications, laying the groundwork for the laws of thermodynamics.

Travelling by steam
A steam-powered vehicle in a print of 1834.

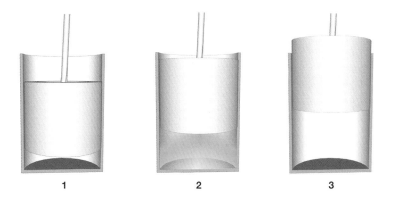

1 2 3 4 5

Demonstrating the Carnot cycle

*Moved successively by a cycle of heating and cooling, a piston moves up and down, driven by the expansion and contraction of gases. In stage **1**, the piston is at rest at the start of the cycle. Stage **2** shows the piston rising through the application of heat. In stage **3**, the heat source has been removed, but the piston has continued to rise, before plummeting with the application of coolant in stage **4**. Stage **5** shows the piston's final position in the cycle, a little below where it started. Carnot used steam engines as his models to show how the transfer of energy between warm and cool regions allows some of the energy to be converted into mechanical work.*

cylinder, causing the gas within it to expand and so driving the piston upward in the first phase of expansion. If the heat source is then removed, the piston will continue upward, but at a slowing pace until it finally stops, completing the second phase of the expansion.

If, hypothetically, the cylinder lost no heat, the piston would remain immobile until the cooling medium began to work on the cylinder. At that point the next step of the process begins, this time a two-phase process of contraction. The gas starts to contract, causing the piston to move back down. If the cooling medium is then removed, the piston will slow, eventually coming to rest a little below its original starting point, unless a little heat is applied to return it to the mark. That way the cycle is completed and the machine recovers its initial equilibrium.

Heat is not a fluid

Carnot described the process thus: 'Simply applying heat is not in itself sufficient to create a driving force; cold is also necessary; without it, the heat will be ineffective.' In other words, it is not simply the heat that produces the 'work', but rather the circulation between two sources, one hot and one cold. Carnot saw

Hydraulic energy in a water mill
Carnot wrongly conceived of heat as a fluid, rather like the water powering this water wheel (left).

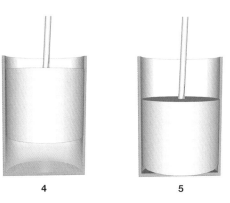

BASIC LAWS OF THERMODYNAMICS

The First Law of Thermodynamics states that the total energy contained within a self-contained system remains constant. The Second Law posits two separate bodies, one hotter and one colder than the other, and demonstrates that in a self-contained system heat will naturally and irreversibly flow from the hotter to the colder via the process of degradation of energy.

heat as a fluid; in his view, the motion of the piston resembled that of the wheel in a water mill. This was an error – we now know that heat is not a substance, it is rather a form of energy – but not for the first time in science a mistaken premise led to a correct conclusion. In effect, the comparison with water allowed the young scholar to grasp the crucial point that it is the transfer of heat between hot and cold sources that makes the machine work, helping him to arrive at the fundamental principle behind the Second Law of Thermodynamics (see box, below left).

Carnot reasoned that the heat lost from the heat source must all be transferred to the cold source. This was another mistake, for part of the thermal energy is actually transformed into work – another form of energy. At this point Carnot comes close to grasping the principle of the conservation of energy within a system that would eventually be spelled out in the First Law of Thermodynamics.

CARNOT'S ERROR

Like most scientists of his day, Carnot wrongly conceived of heat as a fluid, known at the time as 'caloric'. The notion was an offshoot of the theory of phlogiston, a hypothetical element supposedly released during combustion, which was favoured by such noted chemists as Joseph Priestley. Antoine Lavoisier had already called the theory into question in the course of his work on oxygen.

The ignition phase in a petrol engine
By igniting a mixture of air and petrol, the spark (above) heats gas that expands to drive the piston.

Carnot's legacy

Despite the errors in his thinking, Carnot's work proved as fertile in its influence as any comparable text in the history of physics. He established that heat and work are two aspects of a single entity – energy – and thereby launched the theoretical study of the transformations of energy. Not just steam engines but all machines – petrol-fuelled cars, battery-powered radios, solar panels turning light into electric current – transform energy following the principles that Carnot sketched out. Today these have come to affect every branch of science – chemistry, biology, meteorology and even computer science, as well as physics and mechanics.

As for Carnot's ideal machine, it would become a metaphor for every physical system that transforms one form of energy into another, from disintegrating atoms (which transform the energy of mass into that of light) to helium-burning stars, from biological organisms that respire and/or digest to microprocessors running calculations. Even more extraordinarily, this exercise in pure thought took place at a time when many of the fundamental concepts of the physical sciences had still to be defined. That in itself is a measure of the intellectual force behind Carnot's *Reflections*.

Exploding star
The explosion of a supernova, seen in a computer-generated image (above), can release energy equivalent to almost 10 per cent of that emitted by our entire galaxy. The scientific quest to understand the supernova phenomenon involves particle physics, fluid dynamics and thermodynamics.

LAZARE AND SADI CARNOT
A scientific dynasty

Sadi Carnot's *Reflections on the Motive Power of Fire* reverberated around the world and won its author a unique place in the history of modern science. Yet he could easily have been overshadowed by his father, Lazare Carnot, who was a revolutionary politician and general, as well as an engineer and mathematician. The influence that Lazare exerted on his son's career was both beneficial and lasting.

'The wise man is ahead of his own time, and what he has to say can only be understood by posterity.' So claimed Lazare Carnot (1753–1823), an internationally known scholar who was also a key player in the French Revolution and France's minister of war under Napoleon Bonaparte. His remark eerily foretold the tragic destiny of his eldest son, Sadi.

Portrait of Sadi
Lazare Carnot named his son (right) after the mystical Persian poet Sadi, or Saadi, whose Gulistan *('Rose Garden') had been translated into French as early as 1634.*

Sadi Carnot (1796–1832) is now remembered for a single work, the *Reflections on the Motive Power of Fire*, running to just 118 pages and printed in an edition of 600 copies. It was presented to the French Academy of Sciences in June 1824 and was well received, but then disappeared almost totally from view. Thirty years later, long after the premature death of its author, the work re-emerged from oblivion, rescued and revived by the French physicist Benoît Clapeyron. Only then was it seen for what it was: the founding text of thermodynamics – the study of the transfer of energy in physical systems – and one of the most important scientific theories of all time. The book was nothing less than revolutionary in its implications.

A radical father

Revolution seemed to run in the Carnot family. The father, Lazare Nicolas Marguerite Carnot, was a hero of the early days of the French Revolution. Called the 'organiser of victory' for his role in rallying the nation against its foreign enemies, he was one of the few men to hold onto power in France (with some interruptions) for most of the three chaotic decades that followed the storming of the Bastille. He was finally driven into exile with the return of the monarchy after Napoleon's fall. Other, later Carnots would also leave their mark, notably Sadi's nephew Marie François Sadi Carnot, who would be elected fifth president of the Third Republic in 1887 and was assassinated by an anarchist seven years later.

The Carnots owed their revolutionary sympathies at least in part to the fact that they could never have aspired to the highest ranks of science and the state without the events of 1789. Lazare Carnot came from a lower-middle-class background in the Burgundy region. At the age of 18 he was accepted into an army engineering college in northern France. At first his advancement was held back by his plebeian origins, leading him to throw

SADI'S LEGACY

The man responsible for rescuing Sadi Carnot's *Reflections* from obscurity was physicist Benoît Clapeyron (left), who came across it in 1834 while presenting a series of lectures on steam engines. His enthusiasm roused the interest of other scientists. By about 1850 William Thomson, later Lord Kelvin, and the German physicist Rudolf Clausius had established a mathematical basis for Carnot's work and had coined the term 'thermodynamics'.

his energies into science. In 1784 he published an *Essay on Machines* in which he spelled out the laws of conservation of mechanical energy – a work that would later significantly influence his son's thinking (see box, right).

As captain of a garrison at Arras in northern France, Lazare met Robespierre and travelled with him to Paris to foment revolution. From that point on, his life was subject to the ups and downs of political fortune, until his exile from France in the 'White Terror' following the restoration of the Bourbon monarchs in 1815. In the intervening years he had been elected to the French Academy of Sciences (in 1796) and had worked alongside the mathematician Gaspard Monge to found the science of descriptive geometry. He had also married Sophie Dupont, mother of Sadi and of another son, Hippolyte, who would later become France's minister of education. Lazare died in Prussia in 1823.

An Enlightenment education

Through all the twists and turns of his career Lazare never neglected his sons' education, instructing them in the arts and sciences and inculcating them with the ideals of the Enlightenment. When Sadi entered France's elite École Polytechnique at the age of 16, he already shared his father's ideas, although not the older man's robust health nor his military enthusiasms. After graduating, Sadi briefly served in the military before concentrating on science. His father's fall from favour in 1815 also no doubt inclined him in this direction, for he now had little to hope for in the way of political advancement. Eager for knowledge, he haunted Paris's most prestigious centres of scientific and industrial research, from the Collège de France to the School of Mines.

A career cut tragically short

Even so, it was his father, whom he visited in Germany in June 1821, who encouraged him to turn his thoughts to the steam engine. Sadi published his *Reflections* three years later. In the remaining eight years of his life he continued to work on heat transferral but produced little of scientific value, mainly due to his fragile health. His mental and physical condition deteriorated significantly in 1831, and he died a year later in a clinic on the outskirts of Paris. His medical records recount that 'having recovered from his delirium, he died on August 24, 1832, of cholera'.

His father's final resting place was in the Pantheon in Paris, home to France's heroes. As for Sadi, he found his lasting memorial in the annals of contemporary physics.

LIKE FATHER, LIKE SON

In 1784 Lazare Carnot published his *Essay on Machines*, which contained ground-breaking studies of the physics of falling weights and kinetic energy. Forty years later his son Sadi addressed similar themes. In the 1970s researchers demonstrated structural similarities between the ideas of father and son, touching on such common themes as geometric movement and the continual transmission of energy. These propositions, which made little impact at the time, were to prove fundamental for future generations of scientists.

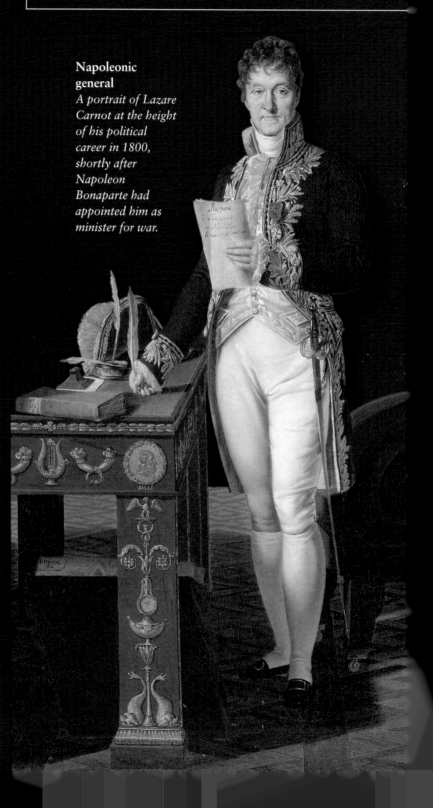

Napoleonic general
A portrait of Lazare Carnot at the height of his political career in 1800, shortly after Napoleon Bonaparte had appointed him as minister for war.

The dawn of the railway age

The early progress of rail transport owed as much to the growing iron and steel industry as to advances in steam engines. With the coming of locomotives capable of hauling heavy loads and the rapid spread of tracks, the age of the long-distance horse-drawn vehicle was over.

Historic journey *George Stephenson's* Locomotion No.1 *made its first journey on the Stockton-to-Darlington Railway line on 27 September, 1825 (right). Local dignitaries were among the passengers in the open wagons, some of which were loaded with coal and flour.*

Steam circus
Richard Trevithick exhibited his steam locomotive on a circular track in London in 1804 (above). Customers paid 1 shilling (5p) to have a ride.

On 27 September, 1825, the world's first passenger railway was inaugurated on a 9-mile stretch of the track linking Darlington in County Durham with the North Sea port of Stockton. The driving force behind the achievement was the engineer George Stephenson. Four years earlier he had persuaded Edward Pease, a wealthy merchant in northeast England, to allow him to redesign part of a proposed 26-mile horse-drawn track to allow the trains to be powered by steam. Two years later, his proposal was approved by Parliament and work got underway.

The engine Stephenson designed to pull the train, *Locomotion No.1*, was one of the first to have wheels linked by coupling rods rather than chains. It weighed 8 tonnes and was capable of pulling a load of 50 tonnes. Stephenson himself was at the controls on the day, cheered on by spectators and by 533 passengers. The train was not fast: for most of the journey it was preceded by a horse at just 5mph (8km/h), although Stephenson did get an opportunity to open up to full steam on the final stretch, reaching 15mph (24km/h). He was greeted on arrival in Stockport with a 21-gun salute. The railway age had begun.

Trevithick's experiments

Horse-drawn railways had existed for several centuries; in 1720 some 20,000 horses were employed in the Newcastle region alone to haul coal. Each wagon was pulled by a horse with a man leading it and the load could not exceed 1 tonne. By the 19th century expanding industrial production and the growing demand

In 1814 William Hedley – like Stephenson, an engineer from northeast England – had the idea of coupling the two wheels on the same side of an engine to overcome the problem of slipping. Until then, railways had been used exclusively for the transport of coal, iron or textiles in mines and factories, but now the prospect of carrying passengers opened up and Stephenson stepped up to make history.

Stephenson's engines

Following the success of the Stockton-to-Darlington Railway, Parliament authorised the construction of a line linking Manchester, a centre of the textile industry, to Liverpool, the main entry-point for the importation of raw cotton from the United States. Stephenson's company, with his son Robert as a director, joined the competition to provide locomotives for the new line. Over the next two decades Robert Stephenson & Co, as it became known, would emerge as the nerve centre of locomotive design and construction as well as a training ground for engineers. *Locomotion No.1* was followed in 1828 by the *Lancashire Witch*, a 7-tonne engine with a simplified design that was capable of hauling a 50-tonne load up a slope at 8mph (12km/h).

Better known still was the *Rocket*, which triumphed over four rivals in trials held in 1829 at Rainhill, near Liverpool, by the Manchester-to-Liverpool Railway's directors to find the most efficient engine for their line. The *Rocket* weighed just 4.25 tonnes but could pull three times its weight at an average speed of 12mph (19km/h); it had a top speed of 29mph (47 km/h). A tender conveniently

SETTING STANDARDS

Britain's role in the invention of rail travel meant that its authorities established many of the standards that came to apply around the world. Early trains in Japan and elsewhere, for example, ran on the left following British practice, and the 4ft 8½in gauge used by George Stephenson on the Stockton-to-Darlington line was adopted as the international norm.

Stephenson's Rocket
The Rocket *(below) was the fastest locomotive of its day. It was powered by two cylinders inclined at an angle of 35°, one on each side of the tubular central boiler.*

for coal were providing the impetus for a transport revolution. The Cornishman Richard Trevithick, a passionate proponent of high-pressure steam engines, built the first full-scale railway locomotive in 1804. Meanwhile, iron was replacing wood in the manufacture of rails, itself to be replaced by steel from the 1850s on.

In its first trial on 24 February, 1804, Trevithick's locomotive pulled five wagons containing 60 passengers and 20 tonnes of iron for 6 miles at a speed of 5mph. The engine, which weighed 8 tonnes including its load of water, was powered by a high-pressure steam engine and had a chimney to increase the draw on the firebox and hence the performance of the boiler. But there was a problem of adhesion between the engine wheels and the rails, and the weight of the locomotive proved too much for the cast-iron tramway, which fractured in places. Despite his huge contribution to the railways and many other inventions, Trevithick died in poverty in 1833.

A FAMILY BUSINESS

George Stephenson (1781–1848) was born the son of an illiterate mineworker at Wylam on the banks of the River Tyne in Northumberland. As a teenager he put himself through night school with earnings made working in a nearby colliery. He first became involved with steam engines when a pumping engine broke down at the pit where he was working and he fixed it. In 1814 he designed his first locomotive, the *Blucher*, to haul coal on a pit wagonway; six years later he constructed a railway 8 miles (13km) long connecting Hetton colliery to Sunderland. So he already had experience when work began soon after on the Stockton-to-Darlington railway, originally planned to connect local collieries to the River Tees. He set up a company to produce engines for the line, bringing in his son Robert (1803–1859) to help run it. The firm, operating as Robert Stephenson & Co, soon became an established leader in the field of locomotive engineering, remaining so until Robert's death. Both men died rich and famous; Robert was buried in Westminster Abbey.

French and British rail engineering
A steam engine (above) designed by the French engineer Mark Seguin for the Lyon–St Etienne Railway, which he helped to set up. The railway station (above right) is Tunbridge Wells in Kent, which opened in 1845. It was connected via a branch line to the main London–Hastings railway. Fast rail links made it easier to transport freshly grown produce to the capital, while this particular line also encouraged Londoners to visit the Kentish spa.

The great leveller
Passengers from all walks of life could afford the fare in third class. This engraving (right) is from a sketch by the French caricaturist Honoré Daumier.

Metropolitan hub
The Gare de l'Est (far right) opened in 1849 as the Parisian terminus for lines from eastern France. Within five years it had to be extended to handle extra traffic.

placed immediately behind the engine carried the water and coal needed to heat it. Other factors contributing to the *Rocket*'s superiority were its big front driving wheels and above all its multi-tubular boiler, invented by French engineer Marc Seguin in 1828. Inside the boiler 25 separate copper tubes carried the heated gases from the firebox, greatly increasing the capacity to heat the surrounding water and so increasing the amount of steam produced. The Sequin-type boiler would be the model for locomotives for more than a century.

The line between Manchester and Liverpool was completed in 1830 and the *Rocket* was an immediate success; early predictions of 400 passengers a day soon rose to more than 1,000, and new engines and carriages had to be bought in to cope with the demand. The first railway station opened at Liverpool Road, Manchester, in 1830, complete with a waiting room and separate booking halls for first and second-class. From here on, railway expansion in Britain was rapid: by 1851 there were more than 6,000 miles of track and in that year trains carried almost 6 million people from all over the country to visit the Great Exhibition in London. Railway mania spread from Britain to the rest of Europe, then to the entire world.

The quest for speed

The Stephensons had continued to improve upon the *Rocket*, which had proved unstable at high speed. In 1833 they introduced the *Patentee*, which had extra wheels at the back as well as a reinforced chassis and horizontal cylinders set low down. With its increased

DEATH OF A POLITICIAN

William Huskisson was one of the first casualties of the railway age. He was a well-respected politician and a prominent supporter of free trade, who had served in three cabinets, latterly as Secretary of State for War and the Colonies from 1827 to 1828. As the serving MP for Liverpool, he was invited in September 1830 to attend the grand opening of the Liverpool and Manchester Railway, the second line to be opened in England after the Stockton-to-Darlington line. Huskisson rode in the *Northumbrian*, the same train as the Duke of Wellington, then Prime Minister, and during a temporary halt he descended from his carriage. While standing on the opposite track he was greeted by the Duke, and tragically did not see that the *Rocket* was fast approaching. Alerted to the danger by spectators, he tried to get round the carriage door, which opened outwards, to remount the train, but he was too late. The *Rocket* struck the open door, knocking Huskisson under the train's wheels. Still alive but with a badly crushed leg, he was taken aboard the *Northumbrian* and George Stephenson himself drove as fast as he could to Eccles, but Huskisson died in the vicarage there before effective medical help could reach him. He was not the first railway casualty (a blind woman had earlier been killed on the Stockton-to-Darlington line), but his death attracted huge publicity, stoking suspicions that rail travel was dangerous.

stability the *Patentee* was able to pull seven or eight carriages, weighing up to 40 tonnes, at speeds of over 40mph. It became the model for locomotives in many European countries. Yet it, too, was soon surpassed. In 1843 an engineer from Kent named Thomas Crampton took out a patent on a revolutionary new engine, the Crampton, which won a reputation as the greyhound of the tracks. It had two huge driving wheels, located at the rear of the engine so as not to raise the boiler, which allowed for a lower piston speed and faster forward motion. Crampton's locomotives proved more popular on the Continent than in Britain, notably in France where in 1853 Napoleon III authorised a service that would average an astonishing 75mph (120km/h).

Train crash in France (right) *On 6 May, 1842, a train travelling from Versaille to Paris derailed; 55 passengers died, trapped in locked wooden carriages.*

Express service
The Crampton locomotive, pictured on the Paris–Strasbourg line in 1852 (top), was twice as fast as its competitors and also cheap to run. Their golden age lasted for about half a century, during which time the phrase 'prendre le Crampton' came to mean 'take the express'.

THE FIRST RAIL DISASTERS

On 24 December, 1841, at Sonning Cutting on the Paddington to Bristol line, a train ran into a landslide: 9 passengers were killed and 17 injured. The dead were stone masons who had been in open wagons and the accident called into question mixing passengers and freight. Casualties in the French crash recorded in the painting below were made worse as carriage doors were locked.

EVOLUTION OF BRITAIN'S RAIL NETWORK

From haphazard beginnings, rail services in Britain developed into a national network in the course of the 1840s railway boom. There were dozens of competing operators, but over the ensuing decades a series of amalgamations put the system in the hands of a few major companies. After a brief interruption in World War I, when the railways were taken under government control, the network returned to private management in the shape of the 'big four' operators, which between them had come to dominate the sector: Great Western; London and North Eastern; London, Midland and Scottish; and Southern Railways. Following World War II, all four were nationalised by the postwar Labour government, jointly forming British Rail in early 1948. After an initial rise in passengers, numbers began to fall away as car ownership surged in the 1950s. By the early 1960s the network was deeply unprofitable and the Conservative government commissioned Dr Richard Beeching to mastermind cuts. He proposed a major contraction that led eventually to the closure of half of Britain's stations and a quarter of its track. High-speed intercity services were introduced in the 1970s. British Rail was privatised in the years after 1994, with lines run by private companies and Railtrack taking responsibility for track and infrastructure.

Brakes and bogies

Crampton engines were perfect for swift, light trains, but they did not have enough traction to respond to the rising demand for locomotives that could pull heavier loads. In particular, they were never very successful in the USA, where from the start the preference was for slower, heavier trains. In the land of wide-open spaces, economy and security won out over speed. Partly as a result, American inventors were responsible for two innovations in the late 19th century. One was compressed-air brakes, developed by the engineer and industrialist George Westinghouse in 1869. The other was the bogie – a trolley-like device supporting two or three sets of wheels attached by a swivel to the underside of the carriage. The use of bogies paved the way for the construction of longer coaches that provided more seating and also a smoother passage around bends.

New power for trains

The invention of electric trains, pioneered by the German engineer Werner von Siemens in 1879, and then diesel locomotives, named for Rudolf Diesel who patented his compression ignition engine in 1892, signalled the approaching end of the age of steam. In the event, the switchover took place gradually in the course of the 20th century at a rhythm dictated by economic conditions, passenger numbers, geography and government policy. In the second half of the 20th century airlines replaced railways as the principal symbols of national prestige. Today, amid rising concerns about fuel prices and pollution, railways are regaining something of their former status.

Into the 20th century
A diesel train being assembled at a factory in Preston in 1956 (above). By the 1950s diesel had largely replaced steam on the railways, but it in turn lost ground to electrification from the 1960s onwards. The New York–Chicago Express (below) crossing the Allegheny Mountains in the 1930s.

The train

Railways were invented before the locomotive, which eventually saw the light of day thanks to steam power. Diesel engines and electrification both stimulated fresh rail expansion. In recent years high-speed trains have opened up new horizons for rail travel.

A first-class carriage in 1842 (below)

CARRIAGES
FROM COACHES TO SLEEPING CARS

In 1830 the earliest first-class railway carriages resembled stagecoaches, adapted to run on rails and topped by roof-racks for luggage. The second-class equivalents were open to the elements and had only bare wooden benches to sit on; most third-class passengers did not even have that basic comfort. The first wagons designed specifically with trains in mind appeared around 1840. Ten years later the seats in first class were upholstered, and a decade after that gas lighting was introduced. The first sleeping cars came into service in 1859 in the USA. By 1870 the carriages were heated by steam and also provided with toilets and lounge cars. Luxury travel had arrived.

SIGNALS
FROM FLAGS TO TRACK CIRCUITS

From the start, railways needed signals to warn train drivers when to stop and when it was safe to proceed. The earliest manual arrangements involved flags or beacons. These were soon replaced by lights or mechanical semaphore arms, first patented in the 1840s. Today's systems employ track circuits that electronically detect the presence of trains and control traffic automatically.

Semaphore signal gantry, 1992

POWER TRANSMISSION
CONNECTING RODS AND CRANKSHAFTS

Connecting rods and crankshafts had been used to transform horizontal into rotary motion since the 15th century. In 1814 William Hedley adapted the system to give wheeled locomotives sufficient adhesion to travel on smooth rails. George Stephenson's *Locomotion No.1*, built in 1825, had wheels linked by rods. Four years later Stephenson built the *Rocket* with obliquely inclined cylinders linked by short rods to driving wheels on either side of the central boiler. In 1884 Anatole Mallet introduced the articulated locomotive, featuring two bogies, each with a set of cylinders driving axles attached to coupled wheels; the foremost wheel was attached to the fixed rear wheel by a hinge, which allowed it to swivel.

The wheel arrangement of a locomotive on the Paris–Orléans line, 1910

BRAKES
FROM BLOCKS TO COMPRESSED AIR

In the 16th century the wagons used in coal mines had brakes of simple wooden blocks that pressed against the wheels. These were adapted for the first trains, which had brakemen who, at a given signal, moved along the tops of the carriages turning a wheel to operate the brake-blocks on each coach. The system was slow and poorly synchronised, leading to accidents. In 1869 American engineer George Westinghouse invented compressed-air brakes, which arestill in use on trains to this day.

Maglev train in Germany, 2001

A race between a horse-drawn cab and a steam train, 1830

The City of Miami *diesel locomotive on the Chicago–Miami run, 1947*

The Mayflower *(below), a steam locomotive built in 1948 by the North British Locomotive Co.*

MOTIVE POWER
FROM HORSES TO ELECTRICITY

As early as the 14th century, horses were pulling coal wagons along rails in mines in Europe. In 1804 Richard Trevithick showed that steam locomotives could pull heavier loads than draft animals. George Stephenson introduced passenger steam services with *Locomotion No.1* in 1825, followed four years later by the *Rocket* which had a multi-tubular boiler. Electrified trains first appeared on underground railways at the end of the 19th century; electrification spread widely on overground services after World War II. By then steam was also giving way to diesel. By the 1970s steam engines had all but disappeared except in countries like China, with plenty of coal but little petrol.

IDEAS WHOSE TIME HAS YET TO COME
EXPERIMENTAL SYSTEMS

Several experimental rail systems have been invented but not yet gone into widespread use. The aerotrain, developed in France in the 1960s, employed the hovercraft principle to travel along a single rail shaped like an inverted T. Probably the best-known is the Maglev (magnetic levitation) system, tested in Germany in 1979, but with limited applications to date.

HIGH-SPEED TRAINS
FASTER, EVER FASTER

In 1964 Japan opened a new era in railway technology with the first of its high-speed electric *Shinkansen* lines, with 'bullet trains' reaching speeds of up to 130mph (210km/h). In 1981 the bar was raised again when France opened its first TGV (*Train à Grande Vitesse*, or 'high-speed train') line from Paris to Lyon, with trains travelling at up to 160mph (260km/h). Germany launched its Inter-City Express in 1985, and set a new world record of 253mph (406.9km/h). The current record is held by a modified TGV that touched 357mph (574.8 km/h) in a test run in 2007.

RAILS
FROM WOOD TO STEEL

Wagonways in mines were made of wood. Until 1840 the first trains travelled on cast-iron tracks that had a tendency to break. Then wrought iron was used, but it too was unsatisfactory. From the 1850s on, steel gradually came to replace iron, providing a firmer track, but the risk of breakages did not finally disappear until after 1930 with the introduction of more resilient tempered steel.

A Shinkansen '700 series' high-speed train in Japan

Work in the fields gets mechanised

The first harvester was invented in Scotland, but it was the machine devised in America by Cyrus McCormick that brought riches in its wake. McCormick was tireless in improving and promoting his device and did more than anyone to bring mechanisation to the farm.

The original mechanical harvester
Patrick Bell's reaper (above) was pushed along by two horses walking behind it. The device was attached by a pole to the horses' collars.

In 1826 a Scottish clergyman named Patrick Bell invented a horse-powered mechanical harvester. At the time, crops were still being cut in much the same way that they had been since antiquity, but there had been some advances in machinery. Forty years before another Scot, Andrew Meikle, had built a threshing machine with mechanical beaters, which did in 12 hours as much work as had previously taken labourers a whole week.

The first patent for a mechanical reaper was issued to Joseph Boyce, an Englishman, in 1799, but agriculture was not yet ready to enter the machine age. Instead, people continued to harvest the fields by hand, cutting the crops with scythes or sickles. The work was time-consuming and this limited the amount of land that any one family or community could exploit. Bell's machine represented a step change. It had a rotating drum at the front to gather the cereals for cutting, then a set of blades to shear them in a scissorlike side-to-side motion.

The McCormick years

Not many of Bell's machines were ever made. Instead most of the credit for inventing the harvester went to an American, Cyrus Hall McCormick, who was following in the

AN AMERICAN SAGA

McCormick's reaper played a significant part in the conquest of the American West. It was said at the time that because of his harvesting machine 'the line of civilisation moves westward 30 miles each year'. From 1832 on, McCormick spread word of his invention among the farmers opening up the Midwest. He chose Chicago as the headquarters of his operation, as the city had easy access to the prairie states that were the breadbasket of the USA. He also benefited from other contemporary developments, such as the 1849 California gold rush which caused an exodus of farm workers, creating extra demand for his machines. The American Civil War had a similar effect as northern farmers were called up for military service. Some people even claimed that McCormick's reapers won the war for the Yankees.

Shaping the farmlands of America
McCormick demonstrates his reaper (above) in a painting by N C Wyeth (1882–1945), a popular US artist of the early 20th century.

Horse-drawn harvester
A photograph taken in Oregon in 1934 shows the huge team of horses needed to pull a combine harvester.

footsteps of his father. McCormick senior was the owner of the vast Walnut Grove estate in Virginia and had been working on a harvester design of his own for some years. In 1831 Cyrus took up where his father left off, perfecting the device and organising demonstrations. Three years later he took out a patent on the invention, and thanks to his shrewd business sense and constant desire to improve the device, it soon became a commercial success.

Taking the world by storm

The arrival of the McCormick harvester was timely, for the demand for agricultural machinery was growing, first in the USA and then across the rest of the world. Steel ploughs soon followed, then threshing machines, combine harvesters, binders and mechanical rakes, all still pulled by horses or mules.

Steam power made its presence felt from the 1870s on, gradually replacing animals where it could, but the machines were cumbersome. In the early 20th century steam power was rapidly supplanted by petrol and diesel engines. McCormick took much of the credit for getting the process under way. He was awarded a gold medal at the Great Exhibition in London in 1851, and was also elected a corresponding member of the French Academy of Sciences for having done 'more for the cause of agriculture worldwide than any other man alive'.

Machinery takes over
A modern combine harvester cuts, threshes and cleans a crop of wheat in Minnesota (right).

BUSINESSMAN INVENTOR

Pioneer of industrialisation that he was, McCormick showed quite as much talent and enthusiasm for making money as he did for building machines. He produced his first reapers in the blacksmiths' forge on the family estate. As the demand for the devices increased, he built up a network of farmers licensed to sell his products. In 1847 he and his brothers set up the McCormick Harvesting Machine Co, with its own factory in Chicago. Competition grew, but he kept ahead of his rivals thanks to innovative marketing methods such as sale on credit, with teams of salesmen trained to demonstrate the devices. Other advantages were easy availability of spare parts (the machines were sold in kit form) and constant technical improvements including a sheaving system for the cut corn. By 1860 70 per cent of all cultivated land in the USA was being harvested mechanically, and with 60 per cent of the market McCormick had realised his dream of becoming a millionaire.

On the move in cities

The buses and trams that criss-cross cities around the world make up a significant part of the rhythm of urban daily life. It is hard to imagine towns and cities without them, yet most forms of public transport date back no further than the first half of the 19th century.

In 1826, in the city of Nantes in western France, Stanislas Baudry had the idea of putting into regular service two large coaches, each capable of seating 16 people. His plan was to provide transport for people wishing to visit the steam-baths that he had established in an outlying suburb. In doing so, he created a horse-drawn public omnibus service that is now acknowledged as the first in the world. Punctual and cheaper than cabs, the coaches were an immediate success and soon could barely keep up with the demand.

Baudry's idea was not entirely new. In France alone, the inventor–philosopher Blaise Pascal had briefly established a public carriage service in Paris in 1662 (see box, below). By that time, the French capital already had cabs, known from their yellow livery as 'cuckoos', that stopped to pick up passengers on demand, carrying up to eight people.

Early omnibuses
Sebastian Baudry's innovative bus service in Nantes issued tokens like this (above left) to show that passengers had paid for their ride. Horse-drawn public coaches like the one above (right) were operating in central Paris in the mid 19th century.

Baudry's innovation caught on in a way that its predecessors had not, reflecting a worldwide phenomenon. Cities were getting bigger all around the globe, and private transport was a luxury that few could afford. The time was right for public transport.

Paris pioneer

Baudry was so impressed by the success of his coaches, he decided to try out the idea on a bigger stage. In April 1828 he founded the Entreprise Genérale des Omnibus, Paris's first regular bus service. Fares were fixed at 25 centimes, a fifth of the cost of travelling in a horse-drawn cab, although still a substantial sum for poorer citizens. The coaches carried from 12 to 20 passengers and were drawn by two or three horses. They set off every 15 minutes from the Place de la Bastille on two separate crosstown routes. They proved popular and quickly attracted rivals – before long a hundred or more conveyances were working eight other routes. In six months they carried 2.5 million fares between them, revolutionising public transport in Paris.

In the years that followed the influx of workers seeking employment in the French capital further boosted demand, stimulating fresh competition: by 1836 there were 17 separate omnibus companies, between them operating 378 coaches. Business flourished for the rest of the century, declining only from 1900 on with the arrival first of the Metro underground railway and then of the motor bus. The last horse-drawn omnibus in Paris was taken out of service in January 1913.

BLAISE PASCAL'S PUBLIC CARRIAGES

In 1662 the philosopher Blaise Pascal obtained permission from Louis XIV to launch five public coach lines across Paris. The terms of the concession specified that Pascal's carriages should operate between 7 in the morning and 8 at night, should depart on schedule regardless of whether or not they were full and should follow fixed routes to their destinations. The scheme was initially very successful, but some members of Paris's city council took exception to the inclusive nature of the service in regard to its clientele. Seeking to protect 'honest citizens' from having to rub shoulders with 'drunkards and people of little account', they banned 'soldiers, page-boys, lackeys and other manual labourers' from the conveyances, which consequently lost an important part of their trade and their popularity. The company went into decline, finally going out of business in 1677.

Horse-drawn tram
Passengers alight at a stop near the Pont St Michel in Paris.

A BRITISH PRECURSOR?

In 1824, two years before Stanislas Baudry began his experiment in Nantes, a 36-year-old Englishman had a similar idea. John Greenwood kept a tollgate at Pendleton, now an inner-city area of Manchester. Buying a horse and cart, he installed seating and started to run a stop-on-demand omnibus service to the city centre 2 miles away. Although the vehicle was described as 'little more than a box on wheels', his initiative was a success. By the time of his death in 1851, the business he had founded owned almost 200 horses.

A worldwide phenomenon

An English coachmaker named George Shillibeer supplied some of the vehicles for the French operators, and he recognised that a similar enterprise must be welcomed in London. The first London omnibus came into service on 4 July, 1829, from Paddington to Bank by way of the Marylebone and City roads, for a fare of 1 shilling (5 pence). Shillibeer's vehicles each had space for 20 passengers. The first bus conductors, friends of Shillibeer from the Navy, were dressed in blue cloth uniforms in the style of a midshipman. To pass the journey, passengers were offered free newspapers and magazines.

Two years later the public transport concept reached New York City, where the New York & Harlem Railroad Company had the idea of running omnibuses on rails for a faster, smoother ride. Their first horse-drawn trams entered service in November 1832. Other US cities followed suit from the 1850s on: by 1890 more than 6,000 miles of tramway in the USA were used by 28,000 vehicles drawn by 105,000 horses and mules.

Trams were taken to France by an entrepreneur named Alphonse Loubat, who had seen them in America. In 1852 he patented

Rush for seats
A sketch by the French illustrator Gustave Doré shows passengers fighting for places on a Paris omnibus in 1860.

POLITE TRANSPORT

At first, the word 'omnibus' was considered vulgar, so coaches were known as 'Shillibeers'. To distinguish his own service, Shillibeer coined the phrase 'Shillibeer's Original Omnibuses', and the term soon became accepted vocabulary.

London Bridge
By the 1880s the bridge linking Southwark and the City of London was being used by some 22,000 vehicles and 11,000 pedestrians each day.

BEYOND CITY LIMITS

Set up in 1840, the General Steam Carriage Company aimed to popularise steam omnibuses in Britain. Demonstration runs from London to the south coast and back proved the vehicles could cover the 130 miles (205km) in daylight hours, but the initiative came too late – railways were already spreading across the country.

Steam machine
Put into service in London by Walter Hancock in 1833, the steam-powered Enterprise *omnibus operated on a scheduled route between Paddington and the City.*

a sunken-rail design, unlike that used in the USA where the rails projected above the road surface. The Parisian example was later taken up in Berlin, Geneva, Copenhagen and other cities. An eccentric American entrepreneur named George Train established Britain's first horse-drawn tram services in 1860, with one line in Birkenhead and three in London.

Experiments with steam

Horse-drawn trams had their limitations. They were hard on the horses, which could cover no more than about 10 miles a day and had a

working life of just five years. To some, steam power seemed to offer the answer. As early as 1829 an English engineer named Walter Hancock invented a steam-powered omnibus that he christened the *Infant*. In 1831 he inaugurated a regular service between his works in Stratford and central London, but the bus's boiler blew up after just six days. A new *Infant* was rapidly brought into service, then an enclosed omnibus called the *Enterprise*, which operated a route between Paddington and London Wall in the City.

Soon Hancock had competition: two fellow entrepreneurs established rival services, one along Oxford Street to Edgware Road, the other from Piccadilly Circus to Uxbridge. In response Hancock relaunched his Paddington–London

LONDON PADDINGTON STEAM CARRIAGE COMP.Y

ENTERPRISE

PADDINGTON

To the

CITY

car ownership became common, a social divide opened up, with only the middling and poorer sections of the community using public transport. Yet by the end of the 20th century, growing concerns about the environment, combined with worsening traffic congestion in major cities, had brought about something of a change of heart. Public transport regained at least some of its earlier appeal.

Electric trams
Boston was the first city in the world to introduce electric trams, starting a transformation of US cities. The trams below are in Washington in 1895.

Wall service with three vehicles; by his own later calculation, his buses carried more than 12,000 passengers and made 366 separate return journeys. But by 1840 these early experiments had, as it were, run out of steam, largely because successive Turnpike Acts placed heavy tolls on the ponderous steam-powered vehicles which quickly damaged road surfaces. Steam was to have a glorious future on the railways, but not on the roads.

New methods of propulsion

The hills of San Francisco were a particular problem for horses, so in 1873, at the instigation of an engineer named Andrew Smith Hallidie, the city installed its first cable car line. The cars were propelled by a continuously moving cable, with grips to prevent backsliding. They were a great success and the system rapidly grew, but a new source of power was about to be exploited.

The first electric tramway was opened in the city of Boston in 1889. All the major cities of the USA, then of Europe, soon followed its example. After various initiatives involving live rails proved impractical, overhead cables became the norm, with trams drawing power via 'trolley' poles. The German firm of Siemens was soon a leading producer of equipment.

Fom the start of the 20th century trams in their turn gave way to underground railways and to petrol-driven buses, which left less of an imprint on city roadways.

A profound change

Urban transport had a profound impact on city life and the viable size of cities. Before 1830 most people walked to work, but first omnibuses, then trams, made it possible for people to live further away. Later, as private

New generation
The Flexity (below) is a modern, air-conditioned, articulated electric tram built for the city of Berlin by the Canadian conglomerate Bombardier.

THE FIRST TURBINE-POWERED STEAMSHIP

The first boat to be equipped with a steam turbine was the *Turbinia* (below), built in 1894 to a design by the English engineer Charles Parsons. Powered by three turbines driving three separate propellers, *Turbinia* quickly proved to be the fastest ship of its day, with a top speed of 34.5 knots (64km/h). It demonstrated its prowess by arriving uninvited at a navy review at Spithead, organised in honour of Queen Victoria's Diamond Jubilee in 1897, where it easily outpaced the naval dispatch vessel sent in pursuit. Impressed by the display, the Admiralty entrusted Parsons with the task of constructing two destroyers. From 1905 on, all Royal Navy ships were turbine-powered, among them the celebrated battleship HMS *Dreadnought*.

the paper-making industry. In the second half of the 19th century, when electricity was first being used to facilitate transport and communications, turbines found a new role in the development of early generators and in factories where electric motors were introduced to drive machinery. Powerful and compact as they were, steam turbines were also put to use in ships, where they quickly proved more adaptable and efficient than piston engines, which they replaced altogether in the years after World War I. In the later decades of the 19th century, steam turbines themselves took on something like their modern form thanks to the work of the American engineer Charles Gordon Curtis and France's Auguste Rateau.

A profound transformation was under way that would bring a whole new generation of turbines into operation. These would perform not so much as simple converters of energy derived from steam, but more as internal combustion engines. In 1872 the German physicist Franz Stolze designed a 'fire turbine', which he finally assembled in Berlin in 1904. The prototype performed poorly, largely because the materials used did not stand up well to the high temperature required – 400°C (750°F). The American George Brayton and Norway's Ægidius Elling came up with similar ideas, in 1870 and 1903 respectively. Also in 1903, French inventors René Armengaud and Charles Lemale developed an operational gas turbine.

By the 1930s, with the benefit of stronger materials and improved compressors, many different applications were being found for gas turbines, not just in industry but also in the military field,

Laval's turbine

The Swedish engineer Gustaf de Laval had the idea of adding a nozzle to boost the speed of the steam as it entered the turbine, thus accelerating the rotor.

where they were used to provide warships with vastly increased powers of acceleration. But it was in the aviation industry that turbines showed their true potential. Aeroplane constructors were attracted by the low weight-to-power ratio, and whole new technologies were developed to put them to use either to turn propellers or, in jet engines, to create thrust from exhaust gases. In 1930 Britain's Frank Whittle patented his design for a gas turbine for jet propulsion. The first jet-propelled plane to fly was a German Heinkel in 1939, employing an engine designed by Hans Pabst von Ohain. Frank Whittle's design was flight-tested two years later. Their work in turn stimulated research into turbojets, opening up new horizons for air travel.

TURBINES POWERED BY COMBUSTION

In a heat engine, the steps in the four-stroke firing cycle – consisting respectively of fuel intake, compression, power and exhaust – take place in succession within a single location. In a gas turbine, the four steps take place simultaneously in different spots. Air is continuously admitted and compressed at the front of the engine. The compressed air is mixed with fuel and ignited in the combustion chamber, escaping in the form of exhaust gases vented through the turbine's rotor blades.

ENERGY FROM NUCLEAR REACTORS

In nuclear power plants today, the biggest steam turbines drive 1,750-megawatt alternators.

Kaplan turbine
A water-driven propeller turbine developed in 1912 by the Austrian Viktor Kaplan (left).

Hydroelectric power
The giant turbines driving this power station's generator are fed by four steel tubes 160m (525ft) long, linked to an outside reservoir.

Fixing the real world in images

First invented by Nicéphore Niépce, photography would in time, after a long series of technical advances, come to change people's view of the world. The end result was the birth of both a new art form and a thriving industry.

Early reproduction
Nicéphore Niépce produced this copy of a 17th-century Flemish engraving in 1825, using a photographic process he called heliography.

Joseph, known as Nicéphore, Niépce was a keen amateur print-maker and a tireless inventor. In company with his brother Claude he carried out researches in various fields from 1798 on, notably taking out a patent in 1807 on an internal combustion engine, the world's first, which he called the pyreolophore. In 1816 he sought a means of fixing the images formed by a camera obscura, a device used by artists as a drawing aid. Niépce already knew that silver chloride darkened when exposed to light, so he experimented by coating a leaf of paper with the substance and placing it at the back of the camera obscura box.

The first prints

Pointing the camera's 'lens' – in a camera obscura, actually just a hole admitting light – at a window of his house, Niépce effectively obtained a negative image, but one that continued to darken until it was lost entirely. He tried again, this time with a petroleum derivative known as bitumen of Judaea, which the academic painters of the day used as a paste to give works a patina or to create the effect of ageing. The substance was known to harden in the presence of light, making it resistant to most solvents then in use, including lavender oil. This fortunate inspiration enabled him to discover the principle of what would be called the contact print. In 1822 he succeeded in capturing ghostly reproductions of drawings by applying varnish to copper or pewter plates coated with bitumen. He exposed these rudimentary light-sensitive plates to sunlight for several hours, then rinsed them in lavender oil, which dissolved only the bitumen in areas protected from the light by the dark strokes of the drawing. The clear, denuded backing formed a fixed, upside-down image on the brown bitumen.

The invention of photogravure

By inserting a similar plate into a camera obscura, Niépce produced the first fixed image of a landscape. He called the process heliography – literally, drawn by the sun. In order to capture the images he had created on paper, he used etching techniques, thereby laying the foundations of the photogravure process. Finally, in 1828, Niépce succeeded in creating positive images by employing silver plates polished with iodine vapour; the silver, badly protected by the varnish, oxidised into silver iodide which darkened in the presence of light when the protective varnish was removed. These were the very first black-and-white photographs.

Niépce's heir

Meanwhile, in Paris, a painter by the name of Louis Jacques Daguerre was creating dioramas, dramatic public spectacles featuring landscapes animated by special lighting effects. To prepare the paintings, he was in the habit of using a camera obscura. Niépce teamed up with him in 1829, hoping that the two of them might between them create a device that would produce a more luminous image. Niépce died four years later without having improved on his previous heliographic techniques.

Daguerre took up the baton, building on Niépce's discoveries. In particular he became interested in the idea of a latent image – an image that, in some light-sensitive materials exposed to light, becomes visible after subsequent chemical treatment. In 1835 he covered a copper plate in silver iodide using Niépce's method, which had proved more effective than bitumen, then exposed the plate

---

A HELPING HAND

In 1819 the English scientist John Herschel first noted the action of sodium thiosulphate on silver halides. He passed on news of his discovery to Niépce and also to his friend William Fox Talbot, to whom he suggested the word 'photography'. Derived from the Greek *photos* ('light') and *graphein* ('to draw'), the term had been in use in Europe since 1839, pioneered either by the Brazilian Hercules Florence or the German Johann von Mädler. Herschel himself introduced the terms 'positive' and 'negative' to describe photographic images with tones either corresponding to or reversing those of the original subject.

THE FIRST PHOTOGRAPH

The earliest known photograph is this view of the Niépce family home (above) in the village of Saint-Loup-de-Varennes in France's Burgundy region. It was taken by Nicéphore Niépce himself on a pewter plate in the summer of 1827. The image has faded badly, but it is still possible to make out patches of wall and roof made to look unreal by the shadows the sun cast as it moved across the sky in the course of an eight-hour exposure.

in a camera obscura and finally treated it with mercury fumes to reveal the image. By 1837 he was using table salt to fix the image. Subsequently, he settled instead on sodium thiosulphate, which proved more effective at eliminating the non-exposed silver salts. The result was the daguerreotype, a positive image that could be produced in less than an hour. Demonstrated to the French Academy of Sciences and Fine Arts in August 1839, it was the first photographic procedure to be put to commercial use. Studios opened all over Paris, and people flocked to have their portraits taken in the new medium. From there the mania for daguerreotypes spread out across Europe and to the USA.

Tools of a new trade
The equipment (left) required to produce a daguerreotype image, like this one of its inventor, Louis Daguerre (right).

The English pioneer

While Niépce and Daguerre were at work in France, an English gentleman scholar was pursuing his own researches at a great house in Wiltshire to which he was heir. William Fox Talbot of Lacock Abbey had been seeking to fix images formed with the aid of a camera lucida since 1833. This optical device, patented by William Wollaston in 1807, combined a prism with a lens attached to a supporting rod. It enabled artists to see at the same time both the scene they were sketching and its image superimposed on the drawing surface.

In 1835 Fox Talbot succeeded in exposing vegetables and transferring their silhouettes onto paper coated with silver iodide. He then placed the sheet in a housing he had designed and produced through a window a negative image about the size of a postage stamp that he called a 'photogenic drawing'. He gradually improved the procedure, using the principle of the latent image and its development to reduce the exposure time from 30 minutes to 30 seconds. Like Daguerre, he began by using table salt and then switched to sodium thiosulphate to halt the effects of exposure. The advent of the daguerreotype persuaded Fox Talbot to go public with his own work in 1839. Two years later, in 1841, he patented what came to be known as the talbotype or calotype (from the Greek *kalos*, 'beautiful').

Rival systems

For a time, Talbot's patent acted as a brake on further progress in Britain, in contrast to the situation in France, where daguerreotypes were

Fox Talbot at work

An 1853 calotype (top) shows Fox Talbot (on far right in the photo) taking an outdoor portrait while his assistant (on the left) makes a copy of an existing print. The wooden camera obscura (above) belonged to Fox Talbot in the 1820s. The simple device had no lens.

FAMILY ALBUMS

In 1854 a French photographer named André Disdéri invented the photographic visiting card. He used a camera with four lenses and a sliding plate holder to create eight separate images of his subject, all printed on a single sheet. The photos, measuring roughly 5cm by 9cm, were then mounted on card. Cheap to produce and easy to send, they became an international craze and gave rise to a new phenomenon: family photograph albums.

not similarly protected. Daguerreotypes were fragile images, which had to be displayed behind glass, but the process did have one important advantage over calotypes – it produced a cleaner, more accurate image. In contrast, calotypes were affected by the texture of the paper on which they were printed. On the other hand, a decisive factor in favour of calotypes was that, as negatives, they could be reproduced mechanically in the form of contact prints, whereas daguerreotypes required a separate engraving process.

The result was that most subsequent enthusiasts of photography chose to follow in Fox Talbot's footsteps. In 1847 Abel Niépce de Saint-Victor, Nicéphore's nephew, achieved prints of daguerreotype quality by using the calotype process, substituting glass plates coated with albumin (egg white) for the paper Fox Talbot had used. Three years later, William Scott Archer replaced the albumin with recently discovered collodion, reducing exposure times to just seconds. From that point on, daguerreotypes fell into disuse in favour of the negative–positive model, the steady progress of which was to make up a good part of the technical history of photography.

A new way of seeing the world

Despite the best efforts of Daguerre, with his artistically composed still lifes, and of Fox Talbot, who aimed at Rembrandtesque effects of light and shade, photography had trouble establishing itself as an art form. From an early stage, painters used the new technique to record their works and even used photographs as creative tools: the Scottish artists David Octavius Hill and

Robert Adamson, for instance, took reference shots as aids for a panoramic painting recording the founding of the Free Church of Scotland in 1843. From the early days there was a market for photographic portraits because they were cheaper than the painted equivalent, but the length of time for which subjects had to pose in direct sunlight still proved off-putting. Some portrait photographers insisted on cluttering their work with antique columns and similar props, but

Leading lady
The French photographer Félix Nadar took this portrait of the actress Sarah Bernhardt in 1865 (above).

The first war photography
British soldiers in the Crimean War (1854-55) captured by Roger Fenton, the world's first official war photographer, commissioned at the suggestion of Prince Albert.

73

STEREOSCOPIC VIEWS

Invented by the English scientist Charles Wheatstone in 1832, the stereoscope used mirrors to allow the viewer to observe two marginally different images placed side by side, one produced as if seen by the right eye and the other by the left, resulting in a 3-D effect. In 1849 the Scottish physicist David Brewster adapted the device to permit viewing through two lenses. Photographers carrying stereoscopic cameras soon set out around the world to capture views both in the daguerreotype format and on glass plates or mounted on paper. The results of their efforts were a popular attraction at the Great Exhibition in London in 1851, creating a fashion for pictures of famous monuments, landscapes and even risqué bedroom scenes.

Wheatstone's stereoscope
Stereoscopy attracted so much attention at the Great Exhibition of 1851 that some 250,000 images were sold in just three months.

Double vision
A stereoscopic view of the Great Pyramid of Giza, part of a series issued in 1905 under the title Egypt Seen through a Stereoscope.

Natural wonder
Between 1844 and 1846 Fox Talbot published 24 varied calotypes, pasted in by hand, including this image of a leaf (right). They were issued in six instalments that made up the first photographically illustrated book.

others preferred to concentrate on the psychological essence of their subjects by posing them against plain backgrounds.

In the long run it was photography's role as a faithful recorder of the real world that established its position. Documentary photographs made their appearance as early as 1842 with pictures of Hamburg taken by Hermann Biow and Alfred Stelzner following the city's great fire. The ensuing decade saw Roger Fenton's images of the Crimean War.

A revolution in knowledge

Scientists were quick to take advantage of the new medium. Daguerre himself took photographs of the Moon in 1839, opening a new avenue for astronomy. He was soon followed by William Draper in the USA and by pupils of the French scientist François Arago, who trained their lenses on sunspots in 1845. Fox Talbot was interested in botany, producing images of leaves. In 1844 he began publishing the first book in the world to be illustrated

SOLVING THE PROBLEM OF LENGTHY EXPOSURES

In the mid 19th century the collodion process reduced exposure time to a few seconds, but that was still too long to take action shots. The problem was finally resolved with the development of glass plates coated with a gelatin containing light-sensitive cadmium bromide, an idea suggested by Richard Leach Maddox in 1871. Thanks to work by two other British scientists, John Burgess and Richard Kennett, dry plates – more versatile than the wet plates that had preceded them – appeared on the market from 1878 on, introducing a whole new era in the history of photography.

Dangerous business *A photographer perches precariously on the 18th floor of an apartment block under construction on Fifth Avenue to capture a view of New York in 1905.*

with photographs; his leaf image was included in the second instalment. Two French scientists, Léon Foucault and Alfred Donné, pioneered microphotography; in 1845 they displayed a number of daguerreotypes taken through microscopes. By the 1850s France's National Museum of Natural History had installed a glass roof to make it easier to photograph the objects on display, and the British Museum was employing Roger Fenton to make a record of its collections and statues.

Photography was also making inroads into other areas. Mentally disturbed patients in a Surrey asylum posed for the camera, while enthusiasts set about recording ancient monuments. In 1849 the writer Maxime Du Camp took some 200 archaeological views in the course of a visit to Egypt and the Middle East in the company of the novelist Gustave Flaubert. Two years later, the French government commissioned the Mission Héliographique to establish a photographic archive of landmark buildings, designed to help in future restoration.

By the 1850s photography had acquired an unstoppable momentum. Photographic lantern slides, used to project narrative sequences, were first produced in 1850 by the brothers William and Frederick Langenheim in Philadelphia. In later years the invention of the X-ray would even enable it to reveal the insides of people's bodies, while new printing techniques would lead to photographs being printed in newspapers and books and on street hoardings. By the end of the 19th century the appearance of inexpensive and portable box cameras employing strips of film brought photography into daily life. By then the new art was already changing the way that people viewed the world around them.

Testing the boundaries *A camera and photographic plates that once belonged to Alexander Wollaston, who took them on an expedition to Everest in 1921.*

PHOTOGRAPHIC SOCIETIES

In 1853 the Photographic Society was founded at the suggestion of Roger Fenton, with the aim of promoting 'the art and science of photography', and 20 years later became the Royal Photographic Society endorsed by Queen Victoria. The French Society of Photography followed in 1854, set up in Paris under the presidency of the physicist Henri Victor Regnault. From the start, members built up collections and exchanged the fruits of their expertise. Today the two societies remain active, rewarding those who have made significant contributions to the field and also preserving important historical collections of photographs and cameras.

Braille 1829

As early as the 16th century, the Italian mathematician Girolamo Cardo was teaching the blind to read by tracing letters, engraved onto metal, with a stylus. In Madrid, Francesco Lucas engraved letters in wood for a similar purpose. But such efforts were limited. When Louis Braille, blind from the age of 3, was admitted to the Royal Institution for Young Blind People in Paris in 1819, it was the only school in the world teaching the unsighted to read and write, and he found the work difficult. The school's founder, Valentin Haüy, had texts printed in a raised relief version of the standard Roman script, but this did not lend itself easily to tactile decipherment.

In 1821 an army officer named Charles Barbier de La Serre visited the school to demonstrate what he called sonographie, known in the English-speaking world as night writing. Barbier had devised the system for use by soldiers in the Napoleonic Wars.

It involved transcribing 36 different sounds – the letters of the alphabet, plus diphthongs and trigraphs (combinations of three letters) – in the form of raised dots. Barbier's system had drawbacks: it employed too many dots, it was phonetic rather than alphabetic and it lacked punctuation. But even so, the dots proved far simpler for the blind to interpret than embossed letters. They could be taken down from dictation with a stylus, then read by turning over the sheet of paper and running a fingertip over the indentations.

Improving the system

Louis Braille, who was 12 years old at the time, quickly mastered night writing. He then set about attempting to improve on it. Having tried out various arrangements of dashes and dots, in 1829 he put forward his 'procedure for reading words', which took its definitive form by 1837. The system, which soon became known by his own name, used arrangements of up to six dots to create 64 characters to transcribe not just the letters of the alphabet but also punctuation and musical notation. In 1839 Louis introduced another process, called décapoint, designed to enable blind people to communicate with the sighted by means of embossed Roman letters shaped with the aid of a grill and stylus. In 1841 François-Pierre Foucault, one of Braille's blind friends, mechanised the system by inventing a device called the raphigraphe, an ancestor of the typewriter. In the 1950s, Braille was adapted to all languages and scripts. Today, reading machines, computers and GPS navigation devices are all available using the Braille system.

BRAILLE IN BRITAIN

The Royal National Institute of Blind People traces its origins back to a society founded in 1868 for the purpose of 'improving embossed literature for the blind'. Two years later, following tests, this group opted for Braille as the best system to go forward with in Britain.

Braille script
Each of the 64 Braille characters consists of up to six dots. The meaning is determined by the number and position of the dots.

The lawnmower 1830

In 1830 an engineer named Edwin Budding, from Stroud in Gloucestershire, took out a patent on the first lawnmower known to history. The device had a large roller at the rear connected by a system of gears to a bladed cylinder at the front. When the mower was pushed forward, the roller's revolutions drove the cutting blades to trim the grass the machine passed over. Made mostly of cast iron, the device was so heavy that it took several people or a horse to handle it.

The following year Budding teamed up with an industrialist called John Ferrabee, who financed production of the first models for sale. Manufacturing licences were also sold to other firms, including Ransomes, which brought out designs of its own from 1832 on. Many improvements were made over the following decades. The first motor mower came onto the market in 1893, driven by steam created by burning kerosene. Rotary mowers were introduced in the 1930s, powered by gasoline.

Cutting and rolling
One of Budding's early mowers (above). He got the inspiration for his lawnmower from observing a rotary cutter in a Gloucestershire cloth mill, where it was used to trim the nap off woollen cloth.

The safety pin c1830

An American inventor named Walter Hunt took out a patent on the safety pin in 1849, but the invention itself already dated back about 20 years. The device that Hunt came up with was very similar to the safety pin familiar today. It consisted of a length of bent metal wire, coiled at one end into a spring. At the other end the metal was flattened out to form a clasp, which shielded the pin's pointed end when fastened, thus preventing accidental pricking.

Safety pins were initially used to fasten women's clothing, but they were soon also put to other uses. By the late 19th century they were famously in demand as fastenings for babies' nappies – they still are, although in disposable nappies their function has been taken over by Velcro. Safety pins are still widely used for a variety of medical purposes and also by launderers and dry cleaners.

DISTANT ANCESTORS

The safety pin principle was originally developed in the ancient world in the form of brooches with catch plates to hold the pins that fastened them. Known as fibulae, they dated back as far as the late Bronze Age, when they were made in Mycenaean Greece.

Nappy fastener
For generations of families, safety pins played a crucial role in the home by holding babies' nappies in place.

THE SEWING MACHINE – 1830
A tool for tailoring

The sewing machine received a lukewarm reception when it was first introduced. Yet it opened the door to ready-to-wear clothing, putting fashion within the reach of modest purses and raising clothes manufacture to an industrial level.

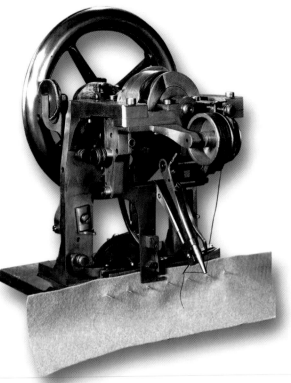

PERFECT PATTERNS

Paper patterns for home-sewers were the brainwave of Ebenezer Butterick, an American tailor. His first – for a shirt – was in 1863. Millions of patterns, for all kinds of garments, soon followed.

The sewing machine inherited the concept of small, quick, regular stitches from an 18th-century embroidery technique. This was chain stitching, employing a crochet hook in the form of a double-pointed needle with an eye at one end, which a German immigrant to England named Charles Frederick Wiesenthal invented in 1755. Because only the point of the needle passed through the material, its other end could be fixed to a machine. The first patent for such a machine was issued in 1790 to Thomas Saint, a London cabinet-maker who planned to use the device for sewing boots, but he failed to follow up the idea. Another 40 years would pass before a practical sewing machine was invented by a Parisian tailor called Barthélemy Thimonnier.

An early difficulty …

The machine that Thimonnier built in 1830 was operated by turning a handle connected to a rod whose shuttling motion made the needle

American competitor
A sewing machine built by the Boston mechanic Elias Howe in 1845 (above). He developed the machine after watching the movements of his wife's arm while sewing.

move. By 1841 he was running a clothing factory equipped with 80 separate machines, each working at the rate of 200 stitches a minute, making military uniforms in an early form of mass production. Thimonnier showed off an improved version of his invention at London's Great Exhibition of 1851, but with little success, for the machine still had one major drawback: the chain stitching it produced was easily unravelled.

… and its solution

The solution turned out to lie in lockstitching. The first machine capable of performing this manoeuvre was built in 1833 by the American inventor Walter Hunt (also responsible for the safety pin – see page 79). It employed a curved needle with an eye in the point, fixed to a moving arm; this formed a buckle of thread on the lower surface of the material, where a second moving needle secured the stitch with a second thread.

From the mid 1850s on Isaac Merritt Singer, a single-minded entrepreneur, started mass-producing sewing devices based on a design by Elias Howe, which had been patented in 1846. Howe sued Singer for infringement of his patent, but the two eventually agreed to work together in one of the first ever 'patent pools'. Singer forged ahead, building the first machine in which the

French prototype
Thimonnier's original 1830 machine (right) was turned by hand with the aid of a driving wheel. This feature disappeared from later models.

needle moved up and down, rather than side to side. He also introduced the treadle, allowing the needle to be powered by foot, leaving both hands free to control the cloth being stitched. In the ensuing decades, amid a flurry of technical improvements and new patents, the modern sewing machine gradually evolved.

By the turn of the 20th century more than 2,000 separate models were available. There were specialised machines for sewing buttons and buttonholes, for making stockings, for putting felt backings on leather. One model had seven needles simultaneously sewing seven rows of stitches at a rate of more than 20,000 stitches a minute.

The golden age

Singer's success changed attitudes toward sewing machines. In England it encouraged the development of cloth-cutting machinery, which became a speciality of the Greenwood & Batley engineering works in Leeds. Invented in 1860, these devices could handle up to 50 layers of material at a time, leaving them all ready for sewing. The clothing industry had a golden age in the late 19th and early 20th centuries. First water, then steam drove the machines in factories, followed from the 1920s on by electricity. The engine block became integral to the design of a piece of machinery. Cams came to replace driving belts and chains, allowing the needles to move from side to side and paving the way for fancy stitching.

Manufactured on production lines, sewing machines became affordable home appliances. From 1910 on, amateur dressmakers had the necessary equipment to make their own clothes. The introduction of electric machines in the 1920s did not entirely displace the older, treadle-operated devices. Today the Singer Corporation, long the market leader, has lost its dominant market position. The latest electronic models perform a wide range of stitches, including elaborate embroidery, and also employ step motors that direct the needle to match the requirements of the material being sewn.

FROM DIVERSITY TO UNIFORMITY

Sewing-machine design has changed over the years. The early machines were ornately decorated as individual manufacturers competed to produce a look considered suitable for 19th-century homes. More recently, rival products have come increasingly to resemble one another, largely as a result of the long-lasting commercial dominance of the Singer machines.

UNJUSTIFIED FEARS

Treadle, or pedal-driven, machines were an instant success in the USA, rapidly replacing hand-cranked models, but they encountered initial resistance in Britain, where the operation of the pedal was considered unfeminine and dangerous for the ankles. In France there were even worries that the vibrations might be harmful to women's fertility.

Happy housewife
The illustration (below) shows a woman delighted with her Mine d'Or sewing machine, claimed at the time to be 'the best in the world'. The needle (inset) passes down through the foot to make a stitch.

A generous genius

François Arago was one of the great scientific figures of the first half of the 19th century. In an age that saw the birth of photography, electricity and thermodynamics, he always took care to put science at the service of human progress.

Man of action

Arago – seen here (right) in a portrait made in 1842 by Ari Scheffer – was kidnapped by brigands while on a mission to Spain in 1806 (below).

François Arago was born on 26 February, 1786, at Estragel, a small town in the French Pyrenees where his father was the mayor. A precocious scholar, François obtained admission to the recently founded yet already prestigious École Polytechnique in Paris, taking up his place there in 1803. He quickly attracted attention. Within a year he obtained an appointment as secretary to the Paris Observatory, with a salary of 1,800 francs, as well as rooms in the Observatory that would be his home for the rest of his life. In 1806 he set off on a geographical expedition to Spain, only to fall into the hands of brigands. It was 1809 before he finally found his way back to France, where most people had given him up for dead. His reappearance was rewarded with the offer of the position of secretary to the French Academy of Sciences at the age of just 23, and he was also appointed a professor at the École Polytechnique.

A man of wide interests

Arago owes his place in the history of science as much as anything else to the breadth of his intellectual concerns. As an astronomer he made ground-breaking observations of comets, double stars and planets and also contributed to the development of efficient measuring instruments. In the field of optics he supported the pioneering views on the wave theory of light put forward by Augustin-Jean Fresnel, Étienne-Louis Malus and Thomas Young, lining up with them against Laplace, Poisson and Biot, the champions of emission theory. Charged by the Academy, in company with the German Alexander von Humboldt, to draw up a report on Fresnel's work, Arago undertook his own experiments to establish the speed of light through air, glass and water.

If light consisted of particles, as Laplace and Biot believed, then it should travel faster when passing through a denser medium; if Fresnel's wave theory was correct, it would move more slowly. Arago's attempt to resolve the problem was delayed by the complexity of the equipment needed for the experiment, which he first envisaged in 1838, then by the 1848 revolution in France. Two years later, with everything finally in place, Arago lost his eyesight. The work went on without him, but he had the satisfaction of learning before he died that his reasoning had been correct.

A pioneer of electromagnetism, Arago collaborated with André-Marie Ampère on constructing an early electromagnet, and also discovered the phenomenon of induction, subsequently explained by Michael Faraday.

KEEPING A PERMANENT RECORD

As secretary of the French Academy of Sciences, Arago instituted the practice of publishing the society's proceedings, making them available to all who were interested. He also opened some Academy sessions to the public and press.

COMETE DE 1843.

Détails curieux et exacts sur cette Planète, sa forme, sa longueur, sa largeur, et son apparition dans toute l'Europe.

The Paris Observatory
As director of the observatory from 1843 on, Arago took the decision in 1846 to commission the observatory dome (below). A 38cm (15in) telescope with a focal length of 9m (30ft) was subsequently installed and came into service in 1854, the year after Arago's death.

THE LESSONS OF ASTRONOMY

From 1812 on Arago delivered a series of public lectures on astronomy at the Paris Observatory. Although they were aimed primarily at seafarers, Arago proved such a popular and eloquent speaker that he was soon attracting audiences that overflowed the lecture hall. He published a version of the talks, written up from his notes, in 1835, and these came out in an English translation four years later.

Observing the Great Comet of 1843
In the same year that Arago was appointed director of the Paris Observatory, an extraordinarily bright comet attracted worldwide attention. It passed closer to the Sun than any previously recorded object and had a tail 250 million km (155 million miles) in length – the longest ever known.

As a meteorologist he made observations that would later prove of service to weather forecasting bureaux around the world.

A political progressive

A lifelong republican, Arago entered politics in 1830, when he was at the summit of his scientific career. In an age when public opinion held science in high prestige, he soon became a member of France's Chamber of Deputies, a position he retained until Napoleon III created the Second Empire with his *coup d'état* of December 1851. As a deputy Arago championed the cause of progress, putting the case for the construction of railway lines and steam engines, and introducing a measure to reward Daguerre for his contribution to the invention of photography. Appointed minister of war and of the colonies in the course of the 1848 republican revolution, Arago brought distinction to his brief tenure of office by ordering the abolition of slavery in the French colonies. He subsequently served as president of the executive power commission in May and June of that year: for 46 days, he was effectively France's head of state.

Badly afflicted by diabetes, François Arago died on 2 October, 1853. Sixty thousand people followed his funeral procession to the Père-Lachaise cemetery in Paris.

Turning plant fibres into paper

French chemist Anselme Payen was researching the chemical composition of wood when he isolated a substance extracted from the cell walls of plants. Like starch, it could be broken down chemically into its glucose units. He called the substance cellulose, and it opened the way for the fabrication of a whole range of fibre-based products, from paper and textiles to explosives.

Cellulose is everywhere. The main constituent of vegetable fibre, it is by far the most common organic compound on Earth. People have been exploiting it on a trial-and-error basis for more than 2,000 years: paper-making in China dates back to the 2nd century BC and perhaps even earlier. Yet no-one knew what the fibres were composed of until a chemist called Anselme Payen began to research the structure of wood in 1834.

In the beginning was sugar

Early in his career Payen became interested in sugar. In 1820, the year his father died, he became the director of a sugar beet refinery. The sugar beet industry had taken off in France as a side effect of Napoleon's Continental System. This banned British goods from mainland Europe and as a result sugar cane from Britain's Caribbean colonies was soon in short supply. The ban came to an end when the Napoleonic Wars ended in 1815. From here on, sugar beet had to compete with sugar cane, making it necessary to find more efficient processing methods.

Payen came up with a new refining method using activated charcoal to whiten the sugar, a process that is still used to this day.

THE MOLECULES OF LIFE

In a living cell, thousands of chemical reactions take place every instant, at moderate temperatures and with results that only register on a microscopic scale. That they happen at all is only possible because of the presence of natural catalysts – molecules that facilitate chemical reactions without themselves forming part of them. These are the enzymes. In fact, most of the proteins fabricated by cells are enzymes, without which the proteins could not survive.

Making paper
Workers in an Indian paper-making factory (below). Individual sheets are pegged out to dry, then stacked in piles ready for the export market.

Pulping process
An illustration of a 19th-century paper factory (left), built near a river so the machinery could be driven by hydraulic power. A modern pulping machine (above) strips the bark from logs, which are then cut into shavings and reduced into the pulp needed for paper-making.

The charcoal was found to be efficient at absorbing dangerous gases (which later led to it being used in gas masks). Payen turned his attention to starch and in 1833 isolated a natural ingredient in malt that catalysed starch into glucose. He called his discovery diastase, from the Greek *diastasis* meaning 'separation'.

What Payen had come to realise was that starch is made up of a chain of glucose units and the new substance he had discovered effectively separated one glucose unit from another. Diastase was in fact an enzyme, although the word had yet to be coined. Without knowing it, Payen had also started a convention that would be followed by later scientists – he had initiated ending the names of enzymes with '-ase', a practice maintained for all enzymes subsequently discovered.

Similar to starch

In 1834 Payen turned his attention to wood and a few years later, through the French Academy of Sciences, he published an article that would in time become a classic. In it he described a 'resistant fibrous solid that remains after various vegetal tissues have been treated with acid and ammonia'. Whatever type of wood he used, he got the same result, as he did

AN INDUSTRIALIST TURNED ACADEMIC

Anselme Payen (1795–1871) was introduced to chemistry by his father, the founder of a chain of factories producing chemical products, before going on to study the subject at Paris's elite École Polytechnique. Anselme was only 20 years old when his father put him in charge of a factory that refined borax, which was used in metallurgy and to whiten porcelain. At the time the market in borax was dominated by the Dutch, who imported it in its natural state from their East Indian colonies. Payen set about finding a way to synthesise the mineral from soda and boric acid, which he eventually achieved at one third the cost of the natural substance. He went on to devise various artificial colourings, but he remains best known for his discovery of diastase and cellulose. He gave up his business interests in 1835 to concentrate on further research and teaching. He died, laden with honours, in 1871.

when he repeated the experiment using cotton. The substance, which was odourless and tasteless, was composed of white fibres, light in weight and hydrophilic – that is, it attracted water. What he was describing would now be called loose-fill cellulose, as used for insulation.

In its chemical composition the substance resembled starch, which could similarly be broken down into glucose, at least if treated with acids at a high temperature. He called his discovery 'cellulose', because it came primarily from the cell walls of plants, thereby starting off another naming tradition – that of giving '-ose' endings to sugars. At the same time he revealed that wood (but not cotton) contained another, very different substance: lignite, also known as brown coal because it keeps the colour of the wood from which it was originally derived.

Rayon sample
Sometimes known as artificial silk, rayon (above), like cellophane, is derived from viscose, a thick liquid made from cellulose and caustic soda.

The white stuff
An illustration (right) from a 19th-century edition of Jules Verne's fantasy novel, From the Earth to the Moon. *In Verne's tale, the rocket is launched using guncotton, an explosive derived from the cellulose of the cotton plant.*

The road to man-made fibres

Cellulose had far more to offer than curiosity value. Today it is the main component of paper, produced industrially since the early 19th century. As the demand for paper rose, the supply of rags and scraps of hemp rope, the original raw materials of paper, proved insufficient. Manufacturers looked to wood instead. In 1844 a German inventor named Friedrich Gottlob Keller took out a patent on a wood-pulping machine, but the lignite in the pulp prevented it from producing a high-quality product. Payen's work gave fresh momentum to the search for chemical ways of extracting cellulose, helping to establish its current predominance in the paper industry.

Payen could hardly have dreamed of the uses that future chemists would find for his discovery. In the 1860s celluloid, one of the earliest plastics, was synthesised from cellulose nitrate. From the early 20th century, viscose (made by treating cellulose with chemicals) was used to create the first artificial fibres and also to make cellophane, patented by the Swiss chemist Jaques Brandenbergen in 1912. And as the raw material of nitrocellulose (see box), cellulose even produced new types of explosive.

JULES VERNE AND GUNCOTTON

By getting cellulose from wood to react with nitric acid, the French chemist Henri Bracconot first created nitrocellulose, a powerful explosive, in 1832. Then in 1846 Christian Friedrich Schönbein accidentally produced the same effect using cotton: he mopped up some spilled acid with a cotton apron which, as it dried, exploded. France's Paul Vieille found a way of using it to make so-called 'white powder', which came to replace the black gunpowder long used in firearms; it had the advantage of not creating the telltale puffs of smoke that had previously revealed the position of marksmen to the enemy. The new explosive was sometimes known as guncotton, because the cellulose used in its production usually came from the cotton plant. The name caught the attention of Jules Verne, who made guncotton the explosive used to fire the *Columbiad*, the huge gun that launched the rocket in his 1865 fantasy novel, *From the Earth to the Moon*.

THE SCREW PROPELLER –1836

Putting Archimedes' screw to work in ships

The Archimedes' screw dates back more than 2,000 years, but the principle underlying it gained new relevance in the 19th century with the invention of the screw propeller. As a means of propulsion the screw would come to supplant sails and paddle wheels in all kinds of ships, from small pleasure boats to giant tankers.

Many people have a claim to have invented the screw propeller. The earliest, perhaps, was the Greek Archimedes, whose famous screw, designed to draw up water for irrigation, established the principle on which the much later screw propeller worked. The first person to produce a durable working model of a maritime propeller was a Swedish-born mechanical engineer named John Ericsson.

The original Archimedes' screw. *As the spiral shaft turns (above), it draws the water upwards. These early water-lifting devices are still in use in some unindustrialised countries for irrigation.*

Troubled beginnings

A former lieutenant in the Swedish navy, Ericsson moved to England in 1826, where he ended up working for John Braithwaite, a prosperous manufacturer of steam engines. The two men collaborated on a variety of innovative projects, constructing the first steam-powered fire engine and building a locomotive, the *Novelty*, that competed unsuccessfully against Stephenson's *Rocket* in the Rainhill Trials of 1829 (see page 51).

In the wake of that disappointment Ericsson turned his attention to propellers and in 1836 took out a patent on a propulsion unit powered by twin screws designed for use on steamboats. Steam propulsion rapidly proved to be more powerful and reliable than the wind power on which sailing ships depended. The sturdy little steamer that Ericsson developed proved its worth by towing an American packet steamer, the *Toronto*, along the River Thames at a speed of 8 knots (15km/h). Sadly, the demonstration failed to impress the Admiralty.

By chance Ericsson crossed paths in London with a wealthy American by the name of Robert F Stockton, who commissioned him to build a propeller-driven steamship. Launched in mid 1839, the 22m (72ft) long boat set off for the USA, where Ericsson took up residence that same year. There, in 1841, he was commissioned by the US Department

AN INVENTOR AHEAD OF HIS TIME

Charles Dallery was born into a French family long known for making organs. Breaking with parental tradition, he determined instead to devote himself to designing better steamships. In 1803 he took out a patent on a propeller-driven vessel (below), but he failed to interest the French government in his invention. With no more credit available, he was overwhelmed by debt. In despair, he destroyed the boat and tore up his patent. Ten years after his death, the French Academy of Sciences belatedly recognised his achievement, awarding him a posthumous honour for devising boilers with vertical tubes linked to a steam reservoir and employing submerged propellers to drive and steer the craft.

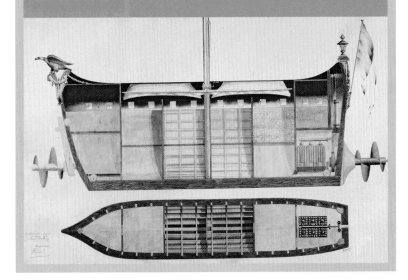

SCREW VERSUS PADDLEWHEEL

In 1845 the Admiralty organised a competition, setting two steamships with similar engine capacities against one another in a tug-of-war. The screw-driven HMS *Rattler* (on the left) was easily the stronger, towing the paddlewheel-powered *Alecto* backward through the water. The contest conclusively demonstrated the superiority of the propeller.

Naval pioneer
Launched in 1850, the Napoleon *(below right) was the world's first steam-powered battleship. It was also the first French naval vessel to employ a screw propeller.*

and the *President*, which sank without trace in the Atlantic in 1841 with 136 crew and passengers aboard, auguring badly for the propeller's future.

Brunel himself stayed faithful to the concept, although when he started work on the *Great Eastern* in 1852 he decided to hedge his bets by providing it with two paddle wheels, each 17m (55ft) across, as well as a 36-tonne propeller with a 7.2m (24ft) diameter. When

the ship was launched in 1858 it dwarfed even the *Great Britain*; its total length was 211m (692ft), and in addition to its steam-driven engines it carried 5,400m² – more than an acre – of sail. Unfortunately, the ship's boiler exploded on its maiden voyage, bringing down one of the funnels. Although the vessel was repaired and sailed again, it was evident that even the greatest ship-builders of the age still had lessons to learn.

SCREW PROPELLERS AND ARMOUR PLATING

In the mid 19th century, Emperor Napoleon III of France was an early proponent of the value of armour plating, both on sea and land, and an enthusiast for the mechanical propulsion of ships. At sea the two ideas were linked, for the masts on sailing ships were vulnerable to enemy fire. The Emperor's support was vindicated by French success at the battle of Kinburn in 1855 in the final stages of the Crimean War, when five 1,500-tonne ironclads, each powered by a single propeller, destroyed Russian shore forts in a four-hour onslaught. The ships emerged relatively unscathed, even though they took 189 direct hits from the defenders' cannons. Inspired by this victory, in 1858 the 34-gun *Gloire* was laid down; this screw-driven ironclad was the prototype of the modern warship. The British Navy, worried by the threat to its naval supremacy, responded by building two screw-propelled ironclads of its own, the *Black Prince* and the *Warrior*. The propeller had finally established itself in the military domain.

HOW SCREW PROPULSION WORKS

Originally invented in about 250 BC, Archimedes' screw was designed to draw water upward, typically from a river to an irrigation channel on its bank. The marine propeller applied the same principle but instead of raising water forced it horizontally backwards, creating forward thrust.

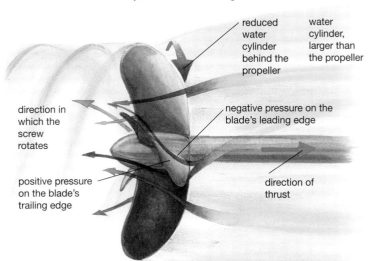

reduced water cylinder behind the propeller

water cylinder, larger than the propeller

direction in which the screw rotates

negative pressure on the blade's leading edge

positive pressure on the blade's trailing edge

direction of thrust

Creating and using pressure differential

When the motor turns the screw, each blade draws water toward the rear of the vessel, establishing a positive pressure. A vacuum of negative pressure forms immediately in front of the blades. The pressure differential thus created sucks in the water cylinder coming from the front of the boat and pushes it back toward the stern, at the same time narrowing it down. This contraction increases the water's speed, helping to drive the boat forward.

Driving force

One of the propellers is manoeuvred into position on the icebreaker Manhattan, *originally designed to carry oil from Alaska. The screw measures more than 8m (26ft) across.*

Success at last

Between 1842 and 1857 there were 29 transatlantic shipping lines and all opted for sail rather than steam. With the development of the great clipper sailing ships, wind power was in the ascendant. But from the 1860s, economic factors began to favour steam. Wooden sailing ships were becoming expensive to construct, given that they had a working life of just 15 years as against 25 for metal-hulled equivalents, and they were limited in size: the hull of a metal vessel accounted for just 18 per cent of a ship's displacement, compared with 46 per cent for wood. From 1880 on propeller-driven vessels were once again the norm.

In the years leading up to the First World War, the giant British liners *Olympic* and *Titanic* were both propeller-driven, as were their later, even larger German rivals, the *Imperator* and *Vaterland*. New speed records were set as shipping companies competed for the coveted Blue Riband awarded for the fastest transatlantic crossing. By then, propeller design had been taken into the air in the development of powered flight.

An intuitive genius

From humble origins and largely self-taught, Michael Faraday carved himself a place in history as one of the world's great physicists. His work was inspired by experiment and intuition, as he paved the way for the linkage of the sciences of electricity and magnetism that would culminate in the 1860s in James Clerk Maxwell's formulation of electromagnetic theory.

Portrait of a prize-winning physicist
Michael Faraday (above) twice won the Copley Medal, the Royal Society's oldest and most prestigious award.

Michael Faraday was 'a mathematician of a very high order – one from whom the mathematicians of the future may derive valuable and fertile methods'. This posthumous compliment from James Clerk Maxwell would have thrilled its subject. Before becoming one of Britain's most prolific scientists, Faraday had little in the way of formal education. His father was a Cumbrian village blacksmith who moved to the outskirts of London in the year that Michael was born. As a child, he learned only the rudiments of reading, writing and arithmetic, and had no background at all in higher mathematics. Yet he would pass on to posterity the laws of

Practical chemistry
A device used by Humphry Davy, the inventor of the miners' safety lamp, in experiments with electrolysis. Davy was a pioneer in the field, studying the effects of electric currents on chemical compounds.

electrolysis, which became the basis of electrochemistry, and of electromagnetic induction, essential for the working of electrical motors and generators. In addition he left behind the concepts of magnetic fields and field theory, fundamental tools in almost all aspects of modern physics. For later generations, Faraday's extraordinary career came to symbolise the triumph of natural genius, sewing the seeds from which contemporary physics would blossom.

A passion for books

Books played a key part in Faraday's advancement. As a 14-year-old he had the good fortune to be taken on as an apprentice by a London bookbinder named George Riebau, and the seven years of his apprenticeship served as his 'university of life'. He claimed that he first became passionate about electricity while binding a copy of the *Encyclopaedia Britannica*, when his eye happened to fall on an article on the subject.

He subsequently started attending lectures at the Royal Institution and the Royal Society by Sir Humphry Davy, one of the scientific luminaries of the day. The two men were 20 years apart in age and separated by a wide social divide, but Faraday was inexhaustible on the subject of chemistry. In 1812 a client of the bookshop who knew Davy decided to introduce the extraordinary young man to the great scientist. Faraday took the opportunity to present Davy with the notes he had taken at his lectures, neatly bound in a 300-page book. Fate then intervened. Having recently damaged his eyesight while conducting an experiment, Davy engaged Faraday as his secretary and laboratory assistant. When a vacancy arose, he had him appointed chemical assistant at the Royal Institution.

From 1813 to 1815 Faraday accompanied Davy and his wife on a journey around the Continent. The trip gave him the chance to meet the scientific elite of Europe, but he almost resigned his position because Lady Davy insisted on treating him as a servant.

Faraday's career as a chemical researcher truly got under way on his return home. By that time he was 24 years old. For the next seven years he devoted himself to research, always under the guidance of his eminent patron. He liquefied gases, synthesised optical glass with the aid of alloys, studied compounds of chlorine, finding two new ones, and showed a growing interest in electrical phenomena and the effects they had on matter.

The year 1821 proved pivotal in his life and career. In its course he married Sarah Barnard, a woman nine years his junior, and he made his first forays into the almost unexplored world of electromagnetism, constructing a low-voltage electric motor.

Falling out with Sir Humphry

Faraday's device represented a fundamental breakthrough for electromagnetic technology, and it came as a logical consequence of the work he had been doing on the links between electricity and magnetism. The connection between the two forces was already estabished by 1821, but no-one had yet made much sense of it. The Danish physicist Hans Christian Ørsted had made an important discovery two years earlier by noting that an electric current passing through a wire deflected a compass needle from magnetic north. While other scientists strove to explain the connection in terms of static electricity, Faraday had the sense to associate it with the current itself. Picking up on Ørsted's findings, he created a rudimentary electric motor using current to rotate a magnetised metal rod around a magnet set in a pool of mercury.

Important though it was, the invention got Faraday into trouble, for he published his results without acknowledging the

THE ANCESTOR OF THE ELECTRIC MOTOR

When he first discovered electromagnetic induction in 1821, Michael Faraday could hardly have imagined that legions of engineers would soon be following in his footsteps. Using the modest laboratory assembly shown below, he revealed that an electric current could rotate a magnetised rod around a magnet set in a mercury bath. A few months later, in 1822, the physicist Peter Barlow followed up on Faraday's work by using an electric circuit to turn a toothed wheel whose serrations similarly passed through mercury. Other inventors took up the baton in the ensuing years.

Makeshift arrangement
In Faraday's prototype electric motor, a rod attached to an electric wire protruded into a mercury bath containing a magnet. When current was passed through the wire, the rod revolved around the magnet.

THE ROOTS OF ELECTROLYSIS

From his researches into the influence of electric currents on matter, in 1834 Faraday deduced and set down the laws of electrolysis: that matter subjected to an electrical charge tends to break down through a separation of the atoms of which it is composed; that the transformation is marked by the appearance of new substances around the electrodes; and that the amount of matter transformed is proportional to the quantity of electric charge passed through the circuit.

contribution that Davy and other scientists had made to the work. His patron took umbrage, and for a time Faraday felt obliged to abandon his researches on electricity. He turned instead to the optical properties of glass, which remained his main focus of interest until Davy's death in 1829.

The miracle years

The 1830s saw Faraday's genius in full bloom. On 29 August, 1831, he discovered electromagnetic induction, observing that a

Faraday's electromagnet
Faraday used the large electromagnet visible under the worktable (left) to establish that an electromagnetic field could generate an electrical current. This reversed an experiment conducted by his Danish contemporary, Hans Christian Ørsted, who had shown that an electric current could create a magnetic field.

THE GENERATOR – PRECURSOR OF THE DYNAMO

In 1831 Faraday invented the so-called homopolar motor, which generated electric current by mechanical movement. It consisted of a copper disc rotating between the poles of a magnet (above). Just one year later, the French instrument-maker Hippolyte Pixii built on Faraday's idea to devise a prototype generator, featuring a hand-cranked rotating magnet that created an alternating current as it turned under a solenoid (wire coil).

magnetic field passing through a conductor produces an electric current. Ørsted had shown that electric currents had magnetic properties; now Faraday demonstrated that magnetism could generate those currents. Between 1832 and 1834 he established the laws of electrolysis, using currents to create chemical reactions. Over the next five years he developed the concept of magnetic and electrical fields to explain the effects the two forces could exert on one another from a distance. Above all, he sought a unitary explanation that would cover all of his discoveries – and he found one.

Inspired to the last
For Faraday, electricity, magnetism and chemical reactions were all the result of a subtle game of electromagnetic attraction and repulsion played out between atoms. His insight was not so much an inspired guess as a prophecy – one that would first be confirmed in the 1860s by the electromagnetic laws spelled out by James Clerk Maxwell, and then by 20th-century atomic theory.

Faraday continued to make important discoveries in the later decades of his life. In 1845 he constructed a glass that polarised light under the influence of a magnetic field – the so-called Faraday effect. In 1847 he observed the behaviour of nanoparticles less than a millionth of a centimetre in size, a development often considered the first step on the road to nanoscience. In 1862 he used a spectroscope in an attempt to show that magnetism acts directly on the visible spectrum, but the equipment proved inadequate to the task and it was 1897 before the Dutch physicist Pieter Zeeman was finally able to observe the effect.

The great scientist died on 25 August, 1867, at Faraday House, a grace-and-favour residence in Hampton Court offered to him in perpetuity 19 years earlier on the initiative of Prince Albert, consort to Queen Victoria. It was only 12 miles from his birthplace, but the blacksmith's son had come a long way.

Prototype lightbulb

In 1857 Faraday used a device like this one (above) to study electrical discharges. When the two metallic balls inside the bulb were linked to an electric current and the air pressure (which could be controlled by the tap at the top) was reduced, light was created.

Safe from static

While researching conductivity, Faraday noted that an enclosure made of conducting metal serves to block out external static electricity (right). The term 'Faraday's cage' is still used today to describe the phenomenon.

THE CONCEPT OF FIELDS

Thanks to a famous experiment involving iron filings and a magnet, Faraday gradually succeeded in establishing a crucial concept for physics: that empty space containing no matter can have physical properties – stable or changing – even if those properties only become apparent in the form of forces when matter is present. Electrical and magnetic fields are prime examples of the principle.

95

FORENSIC MEDICINE
Experts enter the crime scene

In the 19th century, following breakthrough discoveries in medicine, chemistry and biology, forensic pathology established its place in the law courts. The universities provided the necessary expertise, and a cast of colourful characters contributed to its progress.

On May 22, 1810, Sweden's crown prince fell dead from his horse while reviewing troops. His physician, Dr Rossi, conducted an autopsy within 24 hours of the death, but he failed to carry out a chemical analysis of the contents of the prince's stomach, a procedure that would have proved or ruled out the possibility of poisoning. Accused of negligence, Rossi was subsequently put on trial then banished from the kingdom.

Such stories were not uncommon at the time. Physicians were often called on to examine the dead, but their responsibilities were ill-defined and their expertise was questionable: some overlooked obvious signs like strangulation marks, others forgot to return corpses. Despite such failings, forensic medicine gradually became an accepted discipline, notably in France, where a decree of September 1795 gave it official recognition.

A role model from fiction
Sherlock Holmes, Arthur Conan Doyle's forensically minded detective, performs a chemical analysis as his assistant Dr Watson looks on admiringly. This illustration, for the story entitled The Naval Treaty, *appeared in the* Strand Magazine *in 1893.*

A PRECURSOR

As personal physician to Pope Innocent X, the Italian doctor Paolo Zacchia was required to give evidence in witchcraft trials. His Latin work *Quaestiones Medico-Legales*, published in 1651, dealt with such matters as pregnancies and abortions, poisonings and other unnatural deaths. He also described cases of real or simulated madness, raising questions of criminal responsibility.

Between medicine and the law

During Napoleon's years in power in France, new medical schools were established in the cities of Montpellier, Strasbourg and Paris, each endowed with a chair of forensic medicine. In the 19th century medical discoveries would outnumber by far those of previous eras and forensic science benefited enormously from developments, especially in the fields of anatomy, biology and chemistry.

Napoleon also reorganised the French criminal justice system. The new criminal code introduced in 1808 spelled out for the first time the principles on which forensics should be based. In the years that followed a first generation of experts sketched out procedures to be followed in a succession of scientific papers. Research into the causes of death was carried out in several countries, from Britain and Italy to the USA. In Germany in 1808 Theodor Rose published a *Manual of Autopsy*, filling a need noted by one French reviewer: 'Forensic practitioners previously lacked a

AN 18TH-CENTURY PRECEDENT

An early English example of the use of forensic techniques occurred in Lancaster in 1794, when John Toms was found guilty of shooting dead one Edward Culshaw. Traces of the wad of paper used to secure the bullet were found in the fatal wound, and they exactly matched a torn-off corner of a ballad sheet found in Toms' pocket.

FORGOTTEN PIONEERS

An important early contribution to the progress of forensic medicine came from 17th-century Germany, where in 1689 Johannes Michaelis and Johannes Bohn published an important treatise on wounds. In the following century Michael Valentini, Frank, Plenck, Metzger and others produced systematic case studies of incidents of poisoning and wounds that had been purposely inflicted. In 1722 Valentini, professor of medicine at the University of Giessen, produced a comprehensive study of the state of knowledge in his day.

work spelling out the precautions needed in dissecting corpses and the scrupulous procedures required to properly inform magistrates.' In France in 1813 François-Emmanuel Fodéré published details of the requisite examinations in his *Treatise on Forensic Medicine and Public Hygiene* of 1813: 'One must examine the colour of the skin, the body temperature, the rigidity or flexibility of the limbs, the state of the eyes and of the jaws, swellings, bloatedness … wounds, ulcers, fractures … anything that departs from the body's normal condition.' His descriptions covered the effects of extreme cold, lightning strikes, brute force, poisoning and suffocation.

Lesions and poisons

With professional standards set, soon no abnormality was escaping attention. Experts provide increasingly detailed anatomical descriptions of the corpses they examined and

learned to distinguish posthumous wounds from injuries inflicted when a victim was alive. Forensic medicine gradually lost its subjective quality, at the same time turning up celebrities like Ambroise Tardieu, the author of the first work on child abuse, who became president of the French Academy of Medicine in 1867.

Advances were also made in toxicology. One pioneer was Mathieu Orfila, whose *Treatise on Poisons* (see box, page 108) listed the protocol that experts should follow when removing and analysing organs. He stated his goals in ringing terms: 'Revolted by the hideous crime of homicide, the chemist must constantly improve the procedures necessary to prove poisoning, in order to cast light on the crime and to properly inform the magistrate who must punish the perpetrator.' His suggestions often no longer stand up to scrutiny. He paid little attention to the relationship between the amount of poison ingested and the damage done; he described the effects of poisons on animals without allowing for the weight difference with humans; and he wrote of mysterious 'fly powders' without providing details. Even so, he was an influential figure, helping to establish a discipline that later scientists would make more rigorous.

Deathly investigations
An autopsy photographed at the turn of the 20th century (above). In England and Wales today, autopsies are conducted in about one in five deaths.

THE MARSH TEST

In 1832 a man named John Bodle was accused of having poisoned his grandfather's coffee. James Marsh, a chemist, was called to give evidence at the trial. He had detected traces of arsenic, but the test he employed proved inadequate: the precipitate obtained deteriorated, and Bodle was acquitted. Marsh set about devising a more reliable test, which he perfected by 1836. The test is still used to this day.

Poison of choice
Arsenic has been known since antiquity, but not just as a poison – in small doses it is used as a medicament. The most common medicinal form is arsenic trioxide, used in the treatment of various maladies, mostly of the blood and skin.

Checking for arsenic
The Marsh Test involves adding zinc and acid to the suspect substance in a ceramic bowl, then holding it over an open flame. If arsenic is present, a black deposit will form on the bowl.

Influential cases

Poisoning trials involving arsenic regularly made headlines. The British chemist James Marsh developed a method for arsenic detection – a substance often untraceable because it is metabolised by the liver into naturally occurring chemicals. In 1832 a man named John Bodle was brought to trial accused of poisoning his grandfather by putting arsenic in his coffee. Marsh, then working at the Royal Arsenal in Woolwich, was called by the prosecution to try to detect its presence. He performed the standard test, which involved passing hydrogen sulphide through the suspect fluid. A tell-tale yellow precipitate formed, confirming the presence of arsenic, but by the time the evidence was presented to the jury it had deterioriated and Bodle was acquitted.

Frustrated by his failure – especially when Bodle later confessed to the killing – Marsh decided to devise a better test. He discovered that by adding a sample of tissue or body fluid to a glass vessel with zinc and acid, if arsenic was present it would produce arsine gas and hydrogen. Igniting this gas mixture oxidised the arsine into arsenic and water vapour which, when put into a cold ceramic bowl and held in the jet of the flame, would create an arsenic deposit. As little as 0.02mgs of arsenic could be detected in this way.

By now the medical witness had become an essential part of most major murder trials, although the reliability of the evidence was sometimes suspect. The case of Pierre Rivière, a mentally disturbed youth accused in 1835 of killing several members of his family, showed up the inadequacies of contemporary psychiatry. Even though the principle of attenuating circumstances was made part of France's legal code in 1832, a conflict of opinion between the expert witnesses led to

A 19TH-CENTURY PHARMACOPAEIA OF POISONS

In 1813 Mathieu Orfila, a Spanish chemist and physician, drew up the first comprehensive work on poisons. He divided the known poisons of the day into six classes: *corrosives*, including acids, caustic soda and preparations based on mercury or arsenic; *astringents*, among them foodstuffs contaminated with lead; *acrid substances*, such as ricin, autumn crocus bulbs and certain toxic seafoods; *narcotics*, like those in the opium poppy and yew; *acrid narcotics*, under which he listed carbon dioxide, poisonous mushrooms and the fungus responsible for ergotism; and *septics*, which stretched from viper venom to 'contagious miasmas' and exhalations from cesspools and burial grounds.

Rivière being condemned to death, a sentence later commuted to life imprisonment.

An ongoing fascination

Expert witnesses carried increasing weight with prosecutors, judges and juries, who were impressed by their scientific aura and apparent ability to make the dead speak. Forensic examiners could reconstruct the circumstances of a crime, identify unknown victims, even work out the timing of a murder by studying the condition of the corpse. They also came to play a significant part in police enquiries by examining trace evidence left at a crime scene.

By the latter part of the 19th century, forensic medicine was well enough established for the world's first laboratory devoted to the struggle against crime to be set up: the Medico-Legal Institute was founded in Paris in 1868. Others soon followed around the globe. Today forensic scientists continue to enjoy celebrity status, although mostly in fictional television series like *CSI* and *Silent Witness*.

Poisoner at work
In Charlie Chaplin's black comedy Monsieur Verdoux *(above), released in 1947, the anti-hero makes a career out of murdering rich widows.*

Splitting hairs
A scientist carries out tests on a hair sample in a forensic laboratory. Chemical traces in hair can reveal, among other things, the presence of drugs or alcohol.

Cigarettes 1843

Although the Maya of Central America had enjoyed 'smoking tubes' of tobacco from the 9th century, it was another thousand years before cigarette smoking became a western habit. On 23 February, 1843, France's Queen Marie-Amélie organised a charity gala to raise funds for the Caribbean island of Guadeloupe, lately ravaged by a hurricane. Among the lots up for auction were 20,000 cigarettes, rolled in decorated papers and provided with wooden filters. These novelties were well received, giving a kick start to the nascent cigarette industry, which got under way that very year in a factory in Paris.

The development was encouraged by Marie-Amélie's husband King Louis Philippe, who was eager to make cigarette manufacturing a state monopoly. The habit of smoking had made its appearance in European society circles a couple of decades earlier, imported from South America. The first known use of the word *cigarette* has been traced to 1833 and the writings of Petrus Borel, a Romantic of Bohemian tendencies.

The roll-up years

Cigarette smoking first became popular in the English-speaking world during and after the Crimean War (1853-56). At first cigarettes were hand-rolled by the working men and soldiers who provided most of the market for them. The first rolling machine arrived in 1844. An improved version, said to be capable of turning out 3,600 cigarettes an hour, went on display at the Paris Universal Exhibition in 1878. By that time smoking had caught on; the main Paris factory was producing 400 million cigarettes annually, up from just 10 million a decade earlier.

Looking at you
Hollywood actor Humphrey Bogart (1899–1957) was rarely seen without a cigarette dangling from his mouth.

ISOLATING NICOTINE

An alkaloid present in tobacco leaves, nicotine was first isolated in 1809 by Louis Nicolas Vauquelin, a French chemist. It got its name from Jean Nicot, a diplomat who sent tobacco seeds from Brazil to the French court in 1561. In limited doses, nicotine is a stimulant, speeding up the heart rate and releasing adrenaline into the bloodstream, but its toxic properties in higher amounts were also demonstrated from early on.

FATAL ATTRACTION

The link between cigarette-smoking and cancer was first clearly established in the 1950s as a result of extensive epidemiological research in Britain and the USA.

The rotary press 1845

The 19th century saw the arrival of new models of printing press to accompany the growing demand for newspapers. In 1812 Friedrich Koenig, a German inventor working in England, patented a steam-driven design featuring an impression cylinder, introducing a new level of mechanisation. In place of the old flatbed presses, Koenig's machine featured curved printing surfaces, held in place by wedges on a continually turning cylinder. The device printed only one side of each page at a time and 10 men were needed to operate it, but despite these limitations it was still faster than existing presses. In London, *The Times* newspaper adopted the system in 1814, using it to turn out 1,100 sheets an hour.

Faster and more efficient

In 1845 an American inventor named Richard Hoe patented a high-yield rotary press that speeded up the process further. Again, it only printed one side of the paper at a time, but it employed a huge cylinder with space to set up six to eight printing formes concurrently. By printing several pages simultaneously, it pushed total output up to around 8,000 pages an hour. Once more *The Times* was quick to take advantage of the innovation, installing the new machines from 1848 on.

More sophisticated devices followed that could feed huge reels of paper continuously between twin cylinders that printed both sides of a page at once. In 1866 Bullock printing presses in the USA reached 20,000 an hour, then in 1872 a French-made Marinoni press hit 50,000. Today, descendants of these machines dry and fold the pages as well as printing them, turning out daily newspapers in a matter of hours.

THE BIRTH OF THE SERIAL

In March 1836, the first of 20 instalments of *The Pickwick Papers* by Charles Dickens went on sale for 1 shilling (5p). Bound in a green paper cover, it consisted of 32 pages of text, two engraved illustrations and 16 pages of advertisements. A new instalment was published each month, each one ending on a cliff-hanger, until the final, more extensive episode. This new method of serial publishing caught on with readers and other authors, such as Wilkie Collins and Arthur Conan Doyle. After the last instalment, wealthier readers could take their monthly numbers to a bookbinder, where the paper covers and advertisements would be discarded and the pages bound into a single volume.

Page turner The Three Musketeers *first appeared as a serial in a French daily in 1844.*

Rolling news *It took ten employees to feed paper into this rotary press, installed in a New York printing works in 1846.*

Putting patients to sleep to beat pain

An American dentist named William Morton was the first person to successfully demonstrate the administration of ether as a general anaesthetic, rather than the laughing gas that had previously been used to kill pain. The discovery marked the start of surgery without suffering.

Anaesthesia through inhalation
An early device for the administration of anaesthetic (right) consisted of a flask containing sponges soaked in narcotic substances, which the patient inhaled through the mask attached by a tube.

Historic moment
Morton with his team on 16 October, 1846 (below).

On 16 October, 1846, a packed crowd had gathered in the amphitheatre of the Massachusetts General Hospital in Boston. Medical students seated on the benches rubbed shoulders with surgeons and curious members of the public; all had come to see William Morton verify his claim to be able to perform surgery without the patient feeling any discomfort. For some months past Morton had been extracting teeth painlessly with the aid of a substance whose composition he kept a closely guarded secret. That day, though, he was taking on an altogether more demanding challenge. He was preparing for a public operation on a young printer suffering from a tumour in a blood vessel on the back of his neck. He would be assisted by the surgeons Henry Bigelow and John Collins Warren.

The preparations duly got under way. Morton lifted a retort containing a sponge soaked in ether to the patient's face, telling him to breathe in deeply. The young man did as he was asked, as the audience watched each move intently. Once the ether had taken effect, Morton handed over the conduct of the operation itself to Bigelow, who later reported that the patient seemed totally insensible to what was happening, showing no signs of discomfort although he remained conscious throughout. At the time the surgeon limited himself to observing to the auditorium at large, 'Gentlemen, this is no humbug!'.

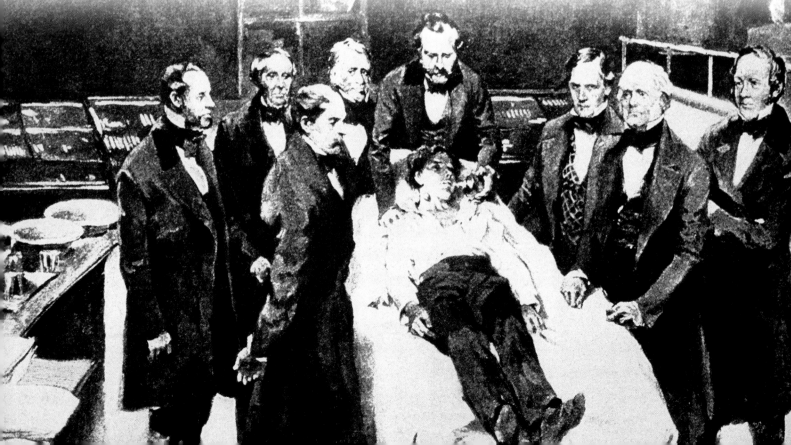

The astonished spectators had in fact just witnessed the first surgical operation performed under general anaesthetic. One of the principal obstacles in the way of surgery – namely, the suffering it caused to those undergoing it – had just been removed.

Mysterious Letheon

Eager to profit from the procedure he had demonstrated, Morton at first refused to divulge the nature of the anaesthetic, choosing to refer to it mysteriously as 'Letheon'. He applied for a patent four weeks later, revealing discreetly in the accompanying documentation that the substance was in fact ether and claiming 10 per cent royalties on all revenues from its future use for anaesthetic purposes.

The demand was audacious, for knowledge of the anaesthetic properties of ether dated back at least a century, to the work of the German chemist Frobenius who had given the substance its name. In fact Morton's self-serving shocked the medical world, which demanded that he should reveal for free the exact composition of the formula used. Six days after he put in his patent application, his colleague Henry Bigelow went public in the *Boston Medical and Surgical Journal*, revealing that the substance had indeed been ether, a liquid chemical compound first synthesised in 1540 and frequently used as an analgesic across both Europe and America in the intervening centuries.

The laughing gas years

Morton's demonstration of the power of anaesthesia had been spectacular, but many people before him would have had a better right to be considered the inventor of the process if their work had not been impeded in a variety of ways. In 1799, for instance, Humphry Davy, the inventor of the miners' safety lamp, described the analgesic effects of nitrous oxide (laughing gas). He tested the substance on himself when facing treatment for a tooth abscess in what was history's first recorded use of an anaesthetic gas. Davy, who was just 21 at the time, was a passionate chemist and physicist, but had little thought of applying his discovery to general medicine.

Then, in the 1820s, a Shropshire-born country doctor named Henry Hickman carried out a series of disturbing experiments involving vivisection, amputating limbs from animals after making them unconscious with heavy doses of carbon dioxide to see if they showed signs of suffering. Eager to test his theories on human patients, in 1823 he applied for authorisation from the Royal Society in London and then, when that request was turned down, to

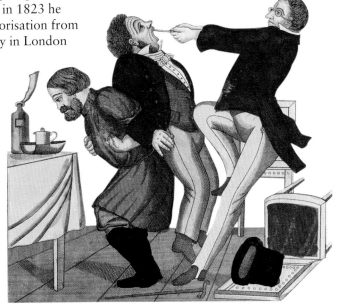

Dentist at work
In the absence of anaesthetics, patients having dental treatment sometimes had to be restrained by physical force, as this 1857 Russian engraving shows.

117

INDUSTRIALISATION
A social revolution triggered by science

In the 19th century the Western world went through an unprecedented economic upsurge. There were many strands to the Industrial Revolution that transformed society at the time: mechanisation, urbanisation, steam power, the rising use of metals, increased flow of capital and the improved transport links of the railway age all played a part.

In 1776 the Scottish economist Adam Smith published his masterwork *The Wealth of Nations*. The book, which was an immediate success, was a hymn to free enterprise. Smith argued that free enterprise encouraged private entrepreneurship and that the self-interest involved also served the greater public good by triggering growth. A few decades later Britain became the first nation to embrace the Industrial Revolution and free trade, taking pride in being the most liberal country in the world, both economically and politically.

Textiles and steam

Textiles played a crucial part in the nation's industrial take-off. Mechanisation of the weaving process reduced the size of the workforce and led to a marked drop in the cost of clothing, followed in turn by an increase in demand and distribution. The result was a previously unknown level of material well-being and a growing market for luxury goods. Workers were needed to operate the new machines, so the first factories came into being.

The machines were mostly powered by steam. When the wood needed to generate this became scarce, the factory-owners turned instead to coal, and the mining regions became centres of industry. Over the decades the rise in output was staggering: by the 1870s steam-operated machinery was doing the work of 40 million people in Britain alone. Steam power also revolutionised agriculture and sea and rail transport, which in turn provided a further stimulus for industry, with train and ship-building offering major new markets for the burgeoning iron and steel trades.

Spinning-mill in Brittany
An illustration from a French magazine in 1849 shows workers at the Landerneau spinning-mill in Finistère. In the mid 19th century the mill was the most modern in the region, processing local flax.

THE LUDDITES

Industrialisation meant job losses for many skilled craftsmen, and some were not prepared to take the situation lying down. The Luddites took their name from a semi-legendary machine-breaker, Ned Ludd. The movement broke out in 1811, spreading north from Nottingham to Yorkshire and Lancashire, and was marked by attacks on mechanised looms. The courts reacted savagely by hanging or transporting the perpetrators.

Europe gets richer

Other nations followed suit. Development in France was initially slowed by several factors: the relative lack of coal, protectionist economic traditions, conservative banks and the unwillingness of investors to buy shares in private companies. Changes slowly followed the Napoleonic Wars, but it was the 1870s before growth took off. By that time Germany, which had been even slower off the mark, had become the world's second industrial power after Britain. Europe's economy flourished, with 46 per cent of global industrial production in the years leading up to the First World War. By then Britain and Europe controlled two-thirds of world trade and provided 90 per cent of capital investment.

The spectacular economic growth was accompanied by profound changes in the way people lived. The coming of the railways brought a new mobility, allowing people to travel rapidly from one region to another. In 1750 it took six bone-shaking days for the stagecoach journey from London to York. The first rail link opened in 1840 and by 1852 the time from the capital to the city that was to become the centre of the railway industry had been reduced to a mere five hours. Besides narrowing the gap between cities, railways contributed to the economic boom by ensuring

A REVOLUTION IN SEVERAL STAGES

Britain was the first country to experience the Industrial Revolution, from the last years of the 18th century on, soon followed by Belgium then by early stirrings in France. A second wave of industrialisation got under way in the 1850s, in particular in Germany and the USA, with Russia and Japan following towards the end of the century.

Murton colliery
Located south of Sunderland in County Durham, the village of Murton saw its population rise from less than 100 people before 1838, when the pit (above) came into operation, to almost 1,400 by 1851. The colliery was finally closed in 1991.

Hexham station
Dominated then as now by its great medieval abbey, the Northumberland market town of Hexham (below) was an important stop on the Newcastle-to-Carlisle line, built between 1830 and 1838.

quarter of a million inhabitants. A member of a government commission said of it: 'I did not believe, until I visited the wynds of Glasgow, that so large an amount of filth, crime, misery and disease existed in one spot in any civilised country.' The story was the same everywhere. Manchester, home to 10,000 people in 1717, had 2.3 million by 1911. The town of St Etienne in France saw its population double in just seven years, reaching 40,000 in 1827.

The sudden arrival of large numbers of men and women looking for jobs provided the cities with a cheap and abundant workforce, but it also meant a shortage of housing and a rapid rise in slum dwellings, street urchins, beggars and epidemics. A French writer, Alexis de Tocqueville, toured the slums of Coventry, Birmingham, Manchester and Liverpool in 1835, recording a shocking account of what he found: 'Who could begin to describe the inner workings of these segregated quarters,

prompt delivery of raw materials. The amount of goods carried by rail increased ninefold between 1825 and 1875.

Transforming the landscape

Wherever coal and metal deposits were found, huge iron and steelworks soon rose up, flanked by rows of tiny, identical houses for the workers. Thick smoke rose from the chimneys of factories and dwellings alike, transforming whole districts into 'black countries'. Other industries flourished near the mines and around the big industrial conurbations, which drew in people from the countryside in search of jobs. The British census of 1851 showed that half the population was already urban; this was probably a first in world history. As the historian G M Trevelyan pointed out: 'John Bull was ceasing to be a countryman and a farmer … except in the cartoons of *Punch*.'

Cities experienced explosive demographic growth. Glasgow, with just 42,000 inhabitants in 1780, was described by a local historian as 'clean and well-paved'. By 1839 it had almost a

Industrialisation
A 19th-century engraving (below) shows a typical scene in a working-class district.

The Magnitogorsk steelworks
This gigantic complex in western Siberia (left), one of the oldest industrial sites in Russia, employed almost half a million people at its peak. Now privately owned, the works are still the nation's third largest.

WORKERS OF THE WORLD

Trade unions were a by-product of the exploitation of workers in the Industrial Revolution. From the 1840s on they were influenced by the 'scientific socialism' put forward by Karl Marx and Friedrich Engels.

receptacles as they are of vice and of misery, which surround the vast palaces of industry, clutching them in a hideous embrace?' Governments grew worried, coming to view the working classes as a potential threat.

Wretched working conditions

Conditions in the factories were poor, above all for child labour. Like their elders, many children worked 16 or 17 hours a day; in the textile industry they were put to work as young as five. Children worked in shipyards, match factories and as chimney sweeps – the appalling conditions of the latter were revealed by Charles Kingsley in *The Water Babies*. The pace in factories was set by machines, which had no need of food or sleep. Adam Smith, who had foreseen the possible ill effects of the division of labour, wrote that it risked making workers 'as stupid and ignorant as it is possible for a human creature to become'.

By 1850 manual labourers made up 90 per cent of the workforce, and in the years that followed the advent of time and motion studies and 'scientific' management techniques piled on added pressure. The only recourse available to workers lay in collective bargaining through trade unions, legalised in Britain in 1824 by the repeal of the Combination Acts, which had previously outlawed workers' associations.

The breaker boys
Teams of young boys (right) were employed in plants where coal was washed, broken up and sorted by size. Their job was to sit astride chutes fed by the sorting machines, removing stones, slate and other impurities. This photograph was taken at a mine at Pittston, Pennsylvania, in 1908.

The Fourth Estate
The Italian artist Guiseppe Pellizza da Volpedo took this term for the working classes as the title for his 1901 painting of striking workers in Turin (detail above).

THE FACTORY ACTS

Conditions in Britain's factories attracted the attention of social reformers, who were appalled by the long hours worked in dreadful conditions. The first attempts to improve matters dated back to the late 18th century, but it was 1833 before a comprehensive measure passed through Parliament. This was the Factory Act, which outlawed the employment of children under 9 years of age in the textile industry and set maximum working hours for those aged up to 18. Another act a decade later specified that machines must have guards to reduce the risk of accidents and that all workplace deaths must be reported and investigated. The 10 Hour Act, passed in 1847, limited the working week for women and children under 18 to 58 hours.

Neptune 1846

E xcitement mounted in the Berlin observatory on 23 September, 1846. The astronomer Johann Gottfried Galle and his assistant Heinrich d'Arrest were hunched over a map of the sky. They were searching for a celestial object they had just observed through their telescope. Some hours earlier Galle had received a letter from a French colleague, Urbain Le Verrier, asking him to scrutinise a particular corner of the sky where, according to Le Verrier's calculations, a previously unknown planet lay awaiting discovery.

At the time, Berlin was the only city to possess a sufficiently detailed sky map to show the dimmest stars known in that part of the heavens. Galle and d'Arrest were using their charts to work out whether the dot of light they had just observed could possibly be the suggested planet, or if it was a star that had yet to appear on the map. Unable to come to a conclusion that night, the two waited until dark the following evening. When they trained the telescope onto the same spot, they had their answer. The dot had moved, so it could not be a star, which would have remained in the same place. Le Verrier must be right: it was a new planet.

In France the news created a sensation. Victor Hugo wrote of the discovery in his journals. François Arago, director of the Royal Observatory, noted proudly: 'Monsieur Le Verrier has found the new heavenly body without even needing to look at the sky. He has discovered it at the tip of a pen.' On 1 October, 1846, the planet was named Neptune by the Paris Bureau of Longitudes.

Confirming Galileo

In fact, Neptune was not so much discovered as rediscovered, for Galileo had observed it twice, in 1612 and 1613, when it lay close to Jupiter. But the great Italian scientist had taken it for a star. The path towards correct identification had begun in 1821, when the French astronomer Alexis Bouvard noticed anomalies in the orbit of Uranus.

In the 1830s the idea that the gravitational pull of some unknown body must be disrupting Uranus's orbit gradually took hold. In September 1845 Bouvard's nephew posthumously published his uncle's remarkably precise tables charting the movements of

The Blue Planet
This photograph of Neptune (above) was taken from a distance of 30,000 miles (48,000km) by the Voyager 2 *space probe in 1989.*

Distant body
Neptune is the eighth planet in our Solar System, two beyond the ringed planet Saturn. It lies about 2.8 billion miles (4.5 billion km) from the Sun.

Mercury

Venus

Moon

Earth

Mars

Jupiter

Neptune

Saturn

Uranus

Uranus over the previous 30 years or more. The gap between the planet's predicted and actual position in the sky was at its greatest in 1822, after which it decreased. The figures reinforced the suspicion that another planet must be responsible for the irregularities.

At that point Arago entrusted the task of keeping track of the 'Uranus anomaly' to Le Verrier, a recognised authority on the movements of the heavenly bodies. He presented his findings to Arago on 31 August, 1846, and they were confirmed by the Berlin observatory just three weeks later.

August institution
Founded in Paris in 1667, the Royal Observatory (above) was tasked with drawing up sky maps for use by navigators on ships. Competition with England was fierce. A French cartoon (below) pokes fun at English astronomers for seeing only the calculations and not the planet in the hunt for Neptune.

AN AUTOCRAT AT THE OBSERVATORY

On Arago's death in 1853, Le Verrier took over as director of the Paris Observatory. It proved an unhappy choice. Le Verrier showed himself overbearingly authoritarian in his management style, having no qualms about dismissing employees who displeased him. Despite stirring up discontent, Le Verrier held onto the position until January 1870, when he was forced out by the threatened resignation of 14 of his colleagues. Nothing if not tenacious, he was reappointed to the job three years later, holding it until his death on 23 September, 1877, 31 years to the day after the discovery of Neptune.

ENGLISH INITIATIVES

In 1841 a Cambridge student named John Couch Adams used Bouvard's Uranus data to work out the orbit of the unknown planet affecting its motion. No-one paid much attention to his findings until word spread that Le Verrier was at work on the same problem in Paris. James Challis, director of the Cambridge observatory, then set to work, but was pipped at the post by the Frenchman. Only after the discovery of Neptune was announced did Challis discover, on going back over his notes, that he had twice observed it a couple of months before the Berlin astronomers, but had failed to identify it as a planet for want of an adequate star map.

LÉON FOUCAULT – 1819 to 1868

A scientific Jack-of-all-trades

Léon Foucault (right) was a wide-ranging inventor and unrivalled experimenter. His discoveries enriched the fields of astronomy, optics and electromagnetism. He is best remembered today for Foucault's pendulum, a device that he set up beneath the dome of the Pantheon in Paris in 1851 to demonstrate that the Earth rotates.

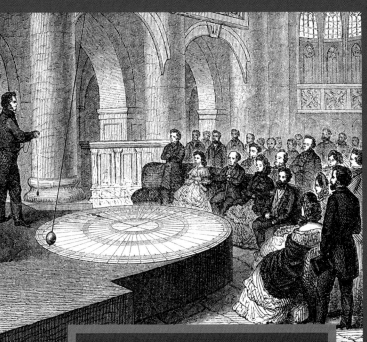

Foucault's experiment
The Pantheon demonstration attracted attention worldwide. In the USA alone, 39 similar displays were set up between May and June 1851.

Restitution
In 1995 the original iron sphere was reinstalled in the Pantheon as it had appeared in 1851 (below).

Léon Foucault had finally got what he wanted to stage his dramatic public experiment. In order to get it, he had gone to the very top – to the president of the Second Republic of France, the future Emperor Napoleon III. 'In the Pantheon', Foucault announced, 'we have found a wonderfully appropriate setting in which to install a gigantic pendulum.' The result was that on 31 March, 1851, the 31-year-old scientist was able to invite the public to one of the most splendid buildings in Paris to 'see the Earth turning'.

What they actually saw was a metal globe, 18cm across and weighing 28kg, suspended from the roof of the Pantheon's famous dome on a cord 67m long. The globe was extended by a fine tip that brushed against a layer of sand spread over a platform located directly beneath the point at which the pendulum was attached to the roof. To begin the experiment, the globe was pulled 50m back from its resting point, then released.

THE GENESIS OF AN EXPERIMENT

Early in 1851 Foucault tried out his experiment in the cellar of his home, using a pendulum just 2m long. It was there on 8 January that he made the discovery that the plane of oscillation of the pendulum remained constant while the Earth rotates. On 3 February he repeated the experiment for an audience of scientists at the Paris Observatory, using an 11m pendulum.

Demonstrating the Earth's rotation

It did not take long for the result to become apparent. 'After a double swing [there and back] that took 16 seconds in all,' Foucault later noted, 'the pendulum returned approximately 2.5mm to the left of its starting point. The same result was repeated with each swing, with the displacement steadily increasing with the passage of time.' The spectators could see for themselves that the marks the globe made in the sand with each swing did not coincide exactly with the ones that had gone before. After an hour, the marks had moved like the hands of a watch by more than 11° from their starting point – 11°19', to be precise – as though the watch's minute hand had moved from 12.00 to 12.02.

THE CORIOLIS FORCE

In 1835 a French mathematician named Gaspard-Gustave de Coriolis described the local effects of the Earth's rotation. He wrote of a force that deflects all movement to the right in the Northern Hemisphere and to the left in the Southern Hemisphere. Foucault does not seem to have been aware of this discovery, and it was only later that the pendulum's deviation was explained in terms of this force.

Six hours later, when the pendulum came to a halt as a result of air resistance and the braking effect of the sand, the final trace equated to 12.12. In other words, the pendulum's plane of oscillation had pivoted, offering visible proof that the Earth rotates.

A mysterious direction

It was already well established by Foucault's day that the Earth turned on its own axis, but up to that time all attempts to demonstrate the planet's rotation had failed. Scholars in Florence had noted a pendulum's deviation as early as 1660, but had failed to interpret the meaning correctly. Foucault understood that the movement of the pendulum is independent of the motion of the Earth, and that its plane of oscillation does not change while the Earth rotates daily on its axis and annually around

Exhibition piece
Another version of Foucault's experiment was staged at the Paris Universal Exhibition of 1855. The equipment (above) is preserved in the Musée des Arts et Métiers.

Whirling winds
The Coriolis force determines the direction in which winds rotate. This image (left) shows hurricane Chanchu, which struck China in 2006.

the Sun. But people watching the experiment are themselves firmly attached to the turning Earth, and so for them it is the pendulum's swing that seems to be moving.

The experiment begged the question of what the pendulum's plane of oscillation is oriented to. Initially people assumed that it was fixed in relation to the Sun, but that idea has since been shown to be wrong. Other suggestions have included nearby stars or the centre of the galaxy, but today the favoured view is that the pendulum's orientation is fixed in relation to the centre of gravity of the entire universe – a theory yet to be proved.

From photography to physics

Foucault was justly proud of his experiment, and of himself too, for he was not a man to hide himself away in some scientific ivory tower. Born in 1819, the son of a Parisian publisher, Léon was a sickly child who received most of his education at home from a tutor. He subsequently studied medicine, only to give the subject up through a fear of blood. Instead, he turned to photography, while also instructing himself in physics. This chequered

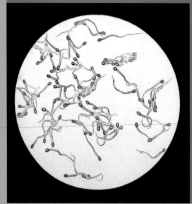

Foucault's gyroscope *A model of a device constructed for Foucault by the Parisian instrument-makers Dumoulin–Froment in 1852. It illustrates the same principle as the pendulum: whatever oscillations it undergoes, the axis of the swing is independent of the Earth's rotation.*

background may explain why Foucault became such an outstanding experimenter, seeking thereby to compensate for the gaps in his formal education by a combination of observation and intuition.

In time Foucault achieved the honours he craved – membership of the French Bureau of Longitudes in 1862, the Royal Society in London in 1864 and the French Academy of Sciences in 1865. He did so as a result of the experiments and instruments he devised, for the publicity coup of 1851 was far from his only success. From 1845 on, his work in the new field of photography attracted the attention of François Arago, at the time France's most influential scientist. Arago introduced Foucault to Hippolyte Fizeau, with whom he took ground-breaking images of the Sun in April 1845. The two men subsequently collaborated on research into the speed of light, inventing in 1848 an ingenious machine designed to trap a beam of light between mirrors so its speed could be measured.

Indices and currents

In 1850 Foucault had the idea of inserting a tube containing water inside the device. He thereby demonstrated that light travels more slowly through water than through air, drawing from the observation a fundamental law linking the speed of light in a transparent

Photographing the Sun *Foucault and Fizeau's first image of the Sun's surface (right) was reproduced in François Arago's* Astronomie Populaire *in 1855.*

medium, whether gaseous, liquid or solid, to its refractive index (associated with the degree to which the medium deflects light rays entering it).

In September 1851 – the same year as the pendulum experiment – Foucault chanced upon a significant electromagnetic phenomenon. By using a handle to turn a copper disc placed between the poles of an electromagnet, he discovered not only that the temperature of the disc increased, but also that some mysterious force seemed to be slowing the disc's motion. This odd phenomenon – which would not be fully explained until the end of the 19th century – is caused by eddy currents (sometimes known as Foucault currents)

PRECESSIONAL AXIS

This is the imaginary line around which the axis of a slowing spinning top revolves.

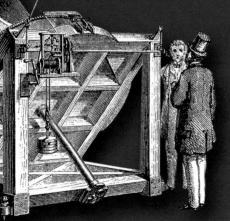

Foucault's telescope
Foucault built this device (above), which employs glass mirrors, in collaboration with a Swiss optician named Marc Secrétan. After he was appointed physicist to the Imperial Observatory in Paris, Foucault became one of the first telescope-makers to apply a thin layer of silver to his mirrors, reducing the need for constant polishing.

that circulate in the opposite direction to the one in which the disc is turning. Electro-magnetic brakes work on the same principle.

Gyroscopes, polarisers, mirrors …

Foucault showed great ingenuity in devising and improving instruments. In 1852 he adapted the gyroscope, invented in Germany 35 years earlier, to complement his experiment with the pendulum. His device featured a top spinning inside a frame, unaffected by the Earth's or any local movement. Modern guidance devices, whether stabilising camcorder images or steering intercontinental ballistic missiles, depend on this principle.

Foucault also did important work on the polarisation of light and on the binocular vision that permits people to see flat images in relief. He devised the Foucault test, still used to check whether the surfaces of mirrors are perfectly spherical. He died in 1868 at the age of 48, relatively young but laden with honours.

A SCATHING PEN

Between 1845 and 1862 Foucault wrote hundreds of articles for the *Journal des Débats*, an influential weekly newspaper founded in 1789. His column appeared once or twice a month, usually printed at the bottom of the front page in a slot at other times given over to serialised fiction by such novelists as Balzac or Alexandre Dumas, or to musical reviews by the composer Hector Berlioz. Foucault's articles were most often concerned with the doings of France's Academy of Sciences, and over the years his critical views on some of its proceedings made him a number of enemies.

Absolute zero 1848

In 1848 William Thomson, the future Lord Kelvin, accomplished a remarkable feat. He established an absolute scale of temperatures that depended not on the readings of thermometers, which could vary, but rather on the abstract, unchanging principles of physics. The Kelvin scale, recognised today as an international unit of measurement, defined absolute zero as 0°K (nought degrees Kelvin), which equates to −273.15°C. Absolute zero remains a theoretical temperature: it does not exist in nature and although it has been closely approached in a laboratory, it has never been reached. Needless to say, it has nothing to do with the 0°C (32°F), our everyday concept of zero, representing the freezing point of water, which registers on thermometers in cold weather.

Thomson's thermometers
Pieces of equipment (above) used in experiments on absolute zero conducted at the Kew Observatory in southwest London.

Responding to a need

Ever since thermometers were invented in the 17th century, competing temperature scales had emerged as individual scientists proposed their own preferred measure. Some coincided with one another but others did not, until eventually researchers started looking beyond the scales to the physical principles involved. The French physicist Sadi Carnot (see page 48) set the ball rolling in 1824 by suggesting that there must be a physical link between the heat generated by a machine and the mechanical energy, or 'work', it produced. In 1847 James Joule expressed the relationship between heat and work as a postulate: the amount of mechanical work required to heat 1lb (0.45kg) of water by 1°F (0.55°C) is constant, whether the water is at boiling point or freezing point. This remained true for all bodies.

Approaching zero

The question then became whether there was always enough heat in any body to generate some work, or if there was a state of such extreme cold that not even the slightest amount of energy could be extracted from it. Kelvin found the answer through theoretical calculations. Laboratory scientists have since used cryocoolers to reach within 0.45 billionth of a degree of the figure Kelvin gave.

The world's biggest experiment
The Large Hadron Collider is the world's largest particle accelerator, installed in a specially designed underground site by CERN (the European Centre for Nuclear Research) on the Franco-Swiss border near Geneva. The collider is at the forefront of experimental research into theoretical physics.

WHY PHYSICISTS LOVE LOW TEMPERATURES

Very low temperatures reduce or annul the electrical resistance of bodies. Some substances develop interesting new properties as a result, such as superconductivity or superfluidity. Unsurprisingly, then, much research work in physics is now carried out at temperatures approaching absolute zero.

The speed of light 1849

On 22 January, 1849, the French physicist Hippolyte Fizeau conducted an experiment intended to measure the speed of light. From his house in Suresnes, a suburb of Paris, he directed a beam of light at a mirror on the hill of Montmartre, 8.633km away (5.36 miles). He then turned a wheel with a serrated edge in front of the beam, so the beam projected through the serrations, in an attempt to link the speed at which the wheel rotated to that of light itself. The wheel had 720 teeth and the same number of similarly sized indentations. By turning the wheel at a rate of one revolution a second, Fizeau interrupted the beam every 0.69 thousandth of a second. At that speed, he could no longer see the reflected beam.

Beam or no beam

In effect what was happening was that the pulse of light, having managed to pass through an indentation on the outward journey, ran up against a tooth blocking its passage on its return. The same thing continued to occur as he speeded up the wheel to turn 10 then 20 times faster. It was only when he reached 25 revolutions a second that the pulse managed to travel from Suresnes to Montmartre and back – a total of 17.266km (10.73 miles) – in less time than it took for the tooth adjoining the indentation to move sufficiently to block it. Fizeau refined the figure to 25.2 revolutions, at which speed the teeth were passing across the beam of light at a rate of one every 55 millionth of a second. Deducing that that was the time it took for light to travel 17.266km, he was able to work out an absolute figure of 313,350km/s. It was a good approximation, only about 5 per cent off the actual figure. Today, thanks to a process called laser interferometry, we know that the precise speed of light is 299,792.458km/s or 186,287.48 miles a second.

THE ASTRONOMER'S METHOD

Galileo was the first person to suspect that the speed of light might not be infinite. In 1610 he tried unsuccessfully to time it by arranging for two people to unveil beams of light from adjoining hilltops. In 1876 the Danish astronomer Ole Römer calculated that Io, a moon of Jupiter, completed its orbit in 42.5 hours – a figure extended by 22 minutes when Jupiter and the Earth were furthest apart from one another. He deduced that the delay was due to the extra distance the light had to travel. Knowing the diameter of the Earth's orbit, he estimated the speed of light at 210,000km/s or 130,500 miles a second.

Ingenious equipment
Devices used by Fizeau in his speed-of-light experiment (above and top left). The photograph (centre) records a green laser beam projected between the Paris Observatory and Montmartre during a restaging of the experiment in 2005.

Fire at one's fingertips

Nothing seems simpler than striking a light on the strip attached to the side of a box of matches. Yet this straightforward response to the age-old need to make fire did not come about easily. A long succession of advances and setbacks preceded the emergence of the safety match.

Made in Sweden
Thanks to Johan Edvard Lundström and a plentiful supply of wood, Sweden long dominated the market for matches (right).

Safety matches were long known as Swedish matches, for it was a Swede named Johan Edvard Lundström who invented them. In 1852 he had the idea of making them less liable to accidental ignition by separating the combustible elements in the match head from the phosphorus, which he set on a friction strip. Inventors over the centuries had lavished much ingenuity and effort on other, less satisfactory arrangements, before this simple solution settled matters once and for all.

Candles and pocket lamps

The father of the match was undoubtedly the great Irish scientist Robert Boyle, who in 1680 discovered that wooden sticks that had been dipped in sulphur caught fire when they were rubbed against rough paper that had been soaked in phosphorus. Boyle dreamed of commercialising his discovery – at the time, the only easy way to make fire in the home was to keep embers smouldering – but phosphorus was prohibitively expensive.

A century later, in Paris, a first generation of chemical lighters came into use, although the name of their inventor has been lost to history. The devices took the form of small glass phials with narrow necks containing twists of wax paper, the tips of which were impregnated with combustible phosphorus that caught fire when exposed to the air. To strike a light, it was necessary only to break open a phial. But these, too, were costly, which restricted their use.

Then in 1785 an alternative became available in the form of small wooden sticks tipped with sulphur that were plunged into a flask of partially oxidised phosphorus. Like previous attempts, they failed to catch on commercially, but the idea of making fire by means other than striking two flints together was gradually becoming established in the public imagination. Inventors kept searching for a better solution.

Early effort
John Walker, a chemist from Stockton-on-Tees, used a mixture of antimony sulphide, potassium chlorate, gum and starch to produce his early matches (below).

CONGREVES AND LUCIFERS

In 1827, the English chemist and apothecary John Walker of Stockon-on-Tees discovered that if he coated the end of a stick with a mixture of antimony sulphide, potassium chlorate, gum and starch and let the chemicals dry, he could start a fire by striking the stick. These were the first practical friction matches. Walker called his matches 'Congreves' in honour of Congreve's rocket, a weapon invented in 1808. He did not take out a patent on them and they inspired imitations known as lucifers.

Before matches
Various devices were used to make fire before the invention of matches. These examples from the early 19th century include an urn filled with highly flammable phosphorus (above centre) and boxes housing chemically treated sticks that caught light when dipped in vitriol.

THE MATCHGIRLS' STRIKE

Safety matches had an unexpected impact on British social history when workers at the Bryant and May factory in Bow, East London, went on strike in 1888. Social campaigners like Annie Besant had already drawn attention to the dangers of working with yellow phosphorus, substituted for the red phosphorus used by Lundström because it was cheaper. The strikers stayed out for almost a month before winning better working conditions. Yellow phosphorus itself was not banned until 1910.

Long and dangerous

Two French innovators – Jérôme Cagnard de la Tour in 1810 and François Desrosne six years later – tried reversing the earlier procedure, so matches tipped with oxidised phosphorus were rubbed against a sulphur-coated tube. The path toward modern safety matches was gradually opening up, but several decades had still to pass before they finally took their familiar modern form. The trouble with most of the early matches was that they were extremely long, too expensive and also dangerous, for the phosphorus tended to flare up unexpectedly, emitting evil-smelling vapours that were said to cause abscesses of the jaw bone – a condition that would later affect employees in match factories and become known as 'phossy jaw'.

No real progress was made until an Austrian chemist named Anton Schrötter discovered less flammable red phosphorus in 1845. Seven years later Lundström devised his first safety matches, which only caught light when rubbed against a friction strip coated with this substance. In 1892 an American lawyer, Joshua Pusey, started producing books of 20 or more matches, but concerns about the health effects of phosphorus restricted sales.

The next step was taken in 1898 by two French chemists, E D Cahen and H Savène, who replaced the phosphorus with non-toxic phosphorus sesquisulphide. Subsequently a mixture of antimony trisulphide, potassium chlorate and sulphur or carbon with phosphorus by-products became the norm. Meanwhile matches got smaller and cheaper, eventually ending up as everyday household objects.

Street vendor
A young boy (right) photographed selling matches in the streets of London in 1884.

BRYANT & MAY'S
LONDON

137

The hypodermic syringe 1853

Drug dispenser
A modern syringe being prepared for an injection (below). The overall design has changed little since the syringe was invented.

In the early 1840s, while working at Dublin's Meath Hospital, an institution that cared for the poor, Dublin-born Dr Francis Rynd developed a hollow needle with a pointed tip that could pierce the skin and provide a conduit into a vein. In May 1844 Rynd became the first doctor to use this hypodermic needle to inject drugs into a patient.

A year later Dr Rynd published an article in the *Dublin Medical Press* describing his use of a 'hypodermic syringe', but he made no further attempts to publicise his invention until 1860,

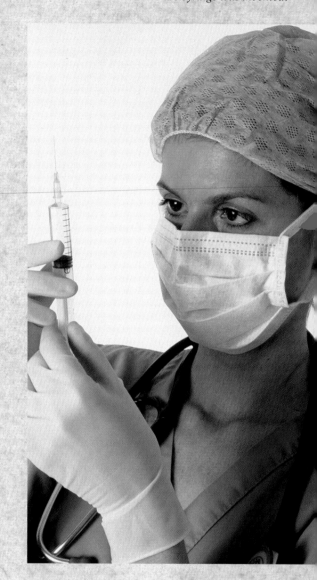

A RANGE OF POSSIBILITIES

By definition all injections are hypodermic – a word derived from the Greek *hypo-*, 'below', and *epidermis* (also used in English to denote the surface layer of the flesh) since the needle pierces the skin. Injections are intravenous if the point of the needle penetrates a blood vessel; subcutaneous if it stops immediately below the epidermis; and intramuscular if it travels farther into the flesh.

by which time others had come up with similar solutions to the problem of administering drugs. So it was that two doctors – Charles Gabriel Pravaz in the French city of Lyon and Alexander Wood in Edinburgh – came to be credited with independently inventing the hypodermic syringe in 1853.

Pravaz had taken his first step in 1841, when he commissioned a firm of instrument-makers to make a miniaturised version of the old clyster syringes used in the 17th and 18th centuries to deliver enemas. The instrument – 3cm long and 0.5cm in diameter – was made of silver, with a screw-on plunger made watertight by a leather seal. It foreshadowed modern syringes, for it enabled the clinician to control precisely the dosage of the drug he was injecting. Wood developed a glass syringe.

Pravaz's syringe
An orthopaedic surgeon, Pravaz made relatively little use of his invention (above), although he was a pioneer of scleropathy – a procedure to treat varicose veins by injecting medicines into the blood vessels to make them shrink.

A humane invention

Before the hypodermic syringe, the only way to introduce liquids directly into a patient's body was to make a cut in the flesh to insert a tube,

then close up the wound afterwards. The new method did away with the need for an incision, and so the patient suffered less discomfort and lost far less blood. From here on medicine became a much less bloody business.

The need to sterilise syringes was not generally understood until later in the century, after Louis Pasteur demonstrated the threat of germs. From 1894 on, syringes were usually made of glass and could be disassembled. Single-use syringes appeared after the Second World War, made out of glass from 1954 on and from plastic the following year.

The endoscope 1853

In 1852 at the Necker Hospital in Paris, Antonin-Jean Désormeaux prepared to insert a rigid tube into the urethra of one of his patients. The tube was linked to a curious object that incorporated a lamp at its base burning a mixture of turpentine and alcohol. The light produced by the flames travelled through a lens set at a 45° angle into the rigid tube. Désormeaux was thrilled to discover that, on peering through the viewer attached to the tube, he could examine the interior of the patient's urethral canal. He sent a description of his invention to the Academy of Medicine the following year, and the birth of the modern endoscope was officially recognised. The word 'endoscopy' was subsequently accepted by the medical community as the term for examining internal organs by means of a tube.

From the lichtleiter to the fibroscope

Like most technological innovations, Désormeaux's endoscope had precursors. One such was the lichtleiter, devised by a German physician named Philip Bozzini in 1806 to examine the interior of the vagina. Literally meaning 'light-guider', it featured an arrangement of mirrors and lenses lit by candlelight. In France Pierre Ségalas devised a 'urethral speculum' that incorporated two silver tubes. It was Ségalas who pointed out to Désormeaux the need to light the endoscope from behind rather than in front – a crucial step in development. After a series of trials, Dr Adolph Kussmaul of Germany succeeded in looking into the stomach of a living human body for the first time in 1868. His endoscope was tested on a sword-swallower able to gulp down a straight, 47cm metal tube with a diameter of 13mm.

Endoscope technology steadily improved in the years that followed. From 1886 the invention of the incandescent bulb led to the development of endoscopes lit by electricity. In 1957 another important step was taken with the invention of the fibroscope, employing fibre-optics technology to transmit an image.

Désormeaux's endoscope
Endoscopy provided a less invasive means of investigating and treating internal disorders, reducing the need for surgery that cut open the flesh. Nowadays it is employed in many different fields of medicine.

TACKLING STDS

Sexually transmitted diseases (STDs) caused untold suffering in the 19th century. One of the most common was gonorrhea, which led to the formation of granulation tissue inside the urethra, sometimes blocking it to the point where surgery was needed. Endoscopes enabled doctors to localise and treat the problem as well as to practice urethrotomies to remove any obstruction.

Metamorphosis of a 19th-century city

The capital first of Prussia and then of the German Second Reich, Berlin saw unprecedented changes in the course of the 19th century. Under the impulse of industrialisation its population soared and the urban environment was transformed. Museums, scientific institutes and a university were all founded as the city came to symbolise the growing might of Prussia.

By the mid 19th century there was little left to recall the early days of Berlin. Originally there were two neighbouring villages, Berlin and Cölln, located on opposite banks of the River Spree. The earliest known reference to the first of these dates from 1237, and that year has since become officially ensconced as marking the foundation of the city.

Capital of Prussia

Built on the sandy plain of Brandenburg, the town was repeatedly razed in the course of the Thirty Years' War, which raged across central Europe from 1618 to 1648. Its fortunes were subsequently restored with the help of Huguenots, who were chased out of France by the revocation of the Edict of Nantes in 1685, which ended an era of religious tolerance for Protestants in Catholic France. At the time Berlin was little more than a rest

Fruit market
Fruit sellers on the quays of Berlin's Museum Island in the 1870s.

halt for travellers, with few permanent residences other than a handful of official buildings. That situation changed under Frederick the Great, king of Prussia from 1740 to 1786. Famous as a patron of the arts, Frederick made Berlin not just the capital of his kingdom but also a refuge for some of the finest minds of the day, notably the Enlightenment philosopher Voltaire. Eminent visitors stayed at Potsdam on the city's outer edge, where Frederick's Sanssouci palace arose.

In 1815 the Prussian army played a decisive part in the defeat of Napoleon at Waterloo, marking the kingdom's arrival as a significant player on the European stage. Over the ensuing decades industrialisation transformed a predominantly agricultural state into the Continent's leading economic power. Berlin itself developed into a buzzing metropolis, as the population surged from roughly 200,000 in 1816 to 425,000 in 1850, then more than 1.3 million by 1896. Horse-drawn trams criss-crossing the main thoroughfares symbolised the city's progress, as did the appearance of gas lighting on Unter den Linden. This famous avenue, whose name translates as 'Under the Lime Trees', led then as now to the Brandenburg Gate, a monument inspired by the Acropolis in Athens and topped by the Quadriga, a statue of Victory riding her chariot. Napoleon temporarily removed the statue as a spoil of war, but following his defeat it was returned to its rightful home.

Berlin's burgeoning industries
The Borsig factory (top) on Chausseestrasse in the Wedding district (now part of the Mitte district of central Berlin) employed more than 5,000 workers, most of them building locomotives (above). Other great industrial names followed in its wake: Siemens engineering in 1847, Schering pharmaceuticals in 1851, and AEG electrical goods, established in 1883.

The other side of the coin

Heavy industry flourished in Berlin, providing employment for a growing labout force drawn in from the surrounding lands. The locomotive manufacturing plant set up in 1837 by August Borsig, the 'railway king', was typical. The massive influx created serious social problems in its wake. Each evening the workers found their way back to the city's northern suburbs, where they clustered in a slum district known as Vogtland after the region of Saxony from which the first incomers had arrived. A 23-year-old Swiss student called Heinrich Grunholzer spent a month exploring the darker corners of the city in the 1840s and left an account of the misery and squalor he saw there. There could hardly have been a greater contrast with the sculpted stairs and marble-paved porches decorated with frescoes that adorned the western residential districts where the city's elite traditionally lived.

In March 1848 the dire poverty drove workers, craftsmen and students out onto the streets. The insurrection, which was put down that November by the army, did little to slow the explosive growth of the city or the nation. The years between 1850 and 1870 saw the creation of a plethora of banks and more than a thousand factories in the capital, along with three man-made waterways carrying goods traffic: the 11km Landwehr canal, the 12km Berlin-Spandau navigation canal and the 38km Teltow canal. Berlin was becoming an economic crossroads of central Europe.

THE FIRST RAILWAY

Prussia's first railway line, the Berlin – Potsdamer Eisenbahn, entered service in 1838. The opening of the Potsdam station marked the start of a period of rapid growth in the German rail network.

City of scholarship

In 1810 the University of Berlin was set up in a palace that previously belonged to Frederick the Great's younger brother Henry. It quickly attracted the finest teachers and students in Germany. The philosopher Fichte became the first rector, and his colleague Hegel taught there from 1818. An obstetric clinic attached to the university opened in 1817, and an eye clinic followed in 1828.

The city became famous for its salons, where intellectuals gathered to exchange ideas. There was also an active Jewish community. In 1737 Frederick William I had ordered that Jews without property should settle in the Scheunenviertel district. This area now entered an era of prosperity that culminated in 1857 in the building of a synagogue seating 3,000 people, designed in ornate Moorish style.

Scholarly circle
Alexander von Humboldt greets recipients of the Order of Maximilian II, created in 1852 by the king of Bavaria to honour artists and scientists.

A SATIRE BOOM

Pre-publication censorship of newspapers, magazines and artwork was temporarily suspended in mid-19th-century Berlin, sparking a sudden satire boom. For a time some 35 of the capital's 135 periodicals came under that heading, among them such titles as *Satyr, Satan, Der Teufel in Berlin* ('The Devil in Berlin'), *Staats-Zeitung der Hölle* ('Official Chronicles of Hell') and *Kladderadatsch* (approximately 'Crash Bang Wallop'). Some of the journals attracted substantial readerships: the *Berliner Krakehler* ('Berlin Brawler') and *Berliner Gro Maul* ('Berlin Bigmouth') both had circulations in excess of 20,000.

BROTHERS WITH BIG AMBITIONS

In 1810 Wilhelm von Humboldt was given the task of setting up the University of Berlin. He was the elder brother of the great naturalist and explorer Alexander von Humboldt, who in 1802 undertook the ascent of Chimborazo, a 6,310m (20,700ft) volcano in Ecuador, the highest peak climbed at the time.

An intense cultural life

On 18 June, 1821, the audience at the Schauspielhaus theatre cheered the first performance of Carl Maria von Weber's *Der Freischütz* ('The Marksman'), Germany's first Romantic opera. Eight years later music lovers thrilled to a revival of Johann Sebastian Bach's *St Matthew Passion*, which had gone unperformed since his death 79 years earlier. The event was a significant milestone in Western musical history.

The city also had plenty to offer lovers of painting and sculpture. The two arms of the River Spree encircled an island that became home to the Altes Museum, Prussia's principal public gallery, which was commissioned in 1828 by Frederick William III from the architect Karl Friedrich Schinkel to house the royal collections. In later years the building would play host to the celebrated bust of Nefertiti, one of the masterpieces of ancient Egyptian art.

Another prominent attraction was the city's zoo, open to the public two days a week from 1844 on. Some 850 animals were on display there, including monkeys, kangaroos, llamas, eagles and giraffes, whose attenuated form would inspire the poet and journalist Theodor Fontaine to claim in his only novel, *Effi Briest*, that they resembled 'elderly daughters of the aristocracy'.

Although Prussia's nobility was viscerally conservative, it proved skilful at adapting to the changing economic situation. From the middle of the century on, the aristocracy showed no scruples about linking fortunes with the rising business class. Despite a crash in 1874 and subsequent temporary crises, the German economy as a whole boomed in the last decades of the century. New lifestyles became the norm in Berlin as in other Western cities, marked by greater social and geographic mobility, a widening family circle and the separation of home and workplace. There were also new cultural reference points, notably a growing interest in science and technology.

Museum Island
Located between two arms of the River Spree, the island (centre) houses five separate museums devoted primarily to ancient art and archaeology

Bust of Nefertiti
The bust was found at Tel-el-Amarna in Egypt in 1912 in excavations led by Ludwig Borchardt.

The Brandenburg Gate
Built between 1788 and 1791 at the western end of Unter den Linden (below), the monument is the only survivor of 18 gates that once gave access to the city.

CHRONOLOGY

The timeline on the following pages outlines key discoveries and inventions from the heyday of the Industrial Revolution. Selected historical landmarks are included to provide chronological context for the scientific, technological and other innovations listed in the columns below them.

1800

- Napoleon conquers Italy (1800)
- Act of Union comes into force, creating the United Kingdom of Great Britain and Ireland (1801)
- The USA acquires lands west of the Mississippi River through the Louisiana Purchase (1803)

- Joseph Marie Jacquard's loom boosts textile production and reduces manpower needs

- William Herschel discovers the infrared band of the spectrum

- Johann Wihelm Ritter discovers ultraviolet light

- Alessandro Volta develops a battery that supplies a continuous electric current

- Invention of the keyed trumpet, chromatic in all its registers

▲ Spectroscope with seven prisms, made in the second half of the 19th century

1805

- Muhammad Ali becomes ruler of Egypt (1805)
- Dissolution of the Holy Roman Empire (1806)
- Slavery is declared illegal in the British Empire (1807)
- The Peninsular War begins in Spain (1808)

- Friedrich Sertürner isolates morphine, the analgesic ingredient of opium

- The Italian chemist Luigi Brugnatelli discovers electroplating, a process that uses electric current to coat metals

- Ralph Wedgwood, a cousin of the potter Josiah Wedgwood, invents carbon paper

- Sir William Congreve invents the Congreve rocket, equipped with an explosive warhead for military use

▶ Pyramidal metronome designed by Johann Maelzel

▶ John Dalton collecting natural gases for use in his experiments

1810

- Napoleon's retreat from Moscow marks the beginning of the end of his tenure of power (1812)
- The USA declares war on Britain (1812)
- Mexico declares itself independent from Spain (1813)
- Napoleon abdicates and is banished to Elba (1814)

- Joseph von Fraunhofer lays the foundations of the science of spectroscopy

- Jöns Jacob Berzelius introduces the use of chemical symbols

- Cumberland-born chemist and physicist John Dalton discovers that atoms of different elements have different atomic weights and that the weight of compound groups of atoms (molecules) corresponds to the sum of the atoms composing them; these discoveries laid the foundations of modern atomic theory

1815

- Napoleon suffers his final defeat at Waterloo and is exiled to the Atlantic island of St Helena (1815)
- The Congress of Vienna redefines the frontiers of Europe (1815)
- Argentina declares its independence from Spain (1816)

- David Brewster invents the kaleidoscope

- Humphry Davy patents his version of the miners' lamp

- René Laennec invents the stethoscope

- Johann Maelzel patents the metronome

- Louis Jacques Thénard discovers hydrogen peroxide

- John Loudon MacAdam develops the road surfacing technique that will come to bear his name

- Augustus Siebe develops a new model diving helmet

- Hans Christian Œrsted discovers that an electric current passing through a wire can deflect a compass needle, thereby establishing the link between electricity and magnetism

- Several inventors patent new types of handgun

▲ Examples of the miner's lamp designed by Humphry Davy

▲ Steamroller macadamising a path in Hyde Park, London

◄ Stethoscope that once belonged to René Laennec

1820

EVENTS

- Simon Bolivar establishes the Republic of Gran Colombia (1821)
- Liberia is founded as a home for former US slaves (1822)
- Brazil achieves independence from Portugal (1822)
- US President declares the Monroe Doctrine (1823)

INVENTIONS

- Michael Faraday invents the first homopolar electric motor

- Charles Barbier de la Serre devises 'night writing', designed to send military messages silently by night, which will later provide the inspiration for Louis Braille's reading system for the blind

- Jan Evangelista Purkyně develops the first system for classifying fingerprints

- Marc Seguin invents the multi-tubular boiler, which will be adapted for use in steam locomotives and boats

- The French scientist Sadi Carnot spells out the Carnot cycle in his *Réflexions sur la Puissance Motrice du Feu* ('Reflections on the Motive Power of Fire'), the work that founds the science of thermodynamics

- Trade union activity is legalised in Britain

- The first modern suspension bridge is built in France to a design by Marc Seguin

- The Belle Jardinière, the world's first department store, opens its doors in Paris

1825

- John Nash remodels Buckingham Palace (1825-35)
- Death of Ludwig van Beethoven (1827)

- The world's first passenger railway line opens between Stockton and Darlington, with George Stephenson's *Locomotion No.1* pulling the carriages

- William Sturgeon invents the first electromagnet

- Gas lighting appears in the streets of Berlin

- Patrick Bell invents a mechanical harvester drawn by horses

- Two horse-drawn omnibuses enter service in the French city of Nantes, inaugurating a new era in public transport

- The French scientist André Marie Ampère – a mathematician as well as a physicist and chemist – publishes his *Memoir on the Mathematical Theory of Electrodynamic Phenomena, deduced from Experiment Alone* (1826), a cornerstone of the scientific discipline of electromagnetism

▲ Marc Seguin's locomotive, employing a multi-tube boiler

▲ Department store elegance in Harrods' food hall

▲ French scientists François Arago and André Ampère studying electromagnetic phenomena

1828

- The Duke of Wellington becomes prime minister of Britain (1828)
- Greece wins independence from Turkey (1829)

- Benoît Fourneyron develops the turbine

- Nicéphore Niépce takes the first black-and-white photographs

- The Altes Museum, the first of its kind in Prussia, opens to the public in Berlin

- Encouraged by his success in Nantes, Stanislas Baudry starts a horse-drawn omnibus service in Paris

- Louis Braille invents the reading and writing system for the blind that will come to bear his name

- James Blundell carries out the first successful human-to-human blood transfusion

1830

- France takes control of Algeria (1830)
- Belgium wins independence from the Netherlands (1831)
- The Great Reform Bill passes into law in Britain (1832)

- Barthélemy Thimonnier invents a handle-operated sewing machine, the world's first functional model

- Walter Hunt invents the modern safety pin

- Edwin Beard Budding takes out a patent on a prototype lawn mower

- Walter Hancock puts the world's first steam-operated motor bus into service in London

- Michael Faraday makes a number of important scientific discoveries: electromagnetic induction (1831), the laws of electrolysis (1832-4) and the concept of the electromagnetic field (1835-9); he will also do important work in optics and lay the foundation for the later development of nanoscience

- Hyppolite Pixii uses Faraday's discoveries to develop the principle of the modern dynamo

- Charles Wheatstone invents the stereoscope, creating a 3D effect when viewing images

- America's first horse-drawn tramway line opens in New York City

- Anselme Payen discovers cellulose

◀ The safety pin, used to secure nappies since the 1830s

▲ Michael Faraday's homopolar motor, generating electric current by mechanical movement

▼ Horse-drawn omnibus in service in Paris in the 1850s

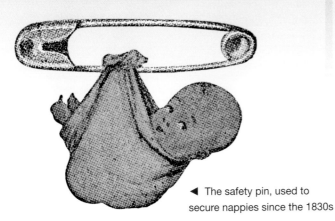

1835

- Boer farmers launch the Great Trek in South Africa (1836)
- A Mexican army storms the Alamo (1836)
- Victoria becomes queen of Great Britain (1837)
- The First Opium War breaks out between Britain and China (1839)

- Gaspard-Gustave Coriolis describes the Coriolis force, which determines local effects of the Earth's rotation

- John Ericsson develops the screw propeller for use in ships

- James Marsh invents the test that bears his name, used to detect the presence of arsenic – an important step forward for forensic medicine

- Prussia's first railway line, the Berlin–Potsdamer Eisenbahn, comes into service

- William Cooke and Charles Wheatstone demonstrate telegraphy over a line more than a mile long

- Louis Jacques Daguerre invents the daguerreotype, a photographic process that produces a positive image

- Edmond Becquerel demonstrates the photovoltaic effect

- Samuel Morse patents the telegraphic code that comes to bear his name (1839)

- Louis Braille invents decapoint, a system designed to allow blind people to communicate efficiently with the sighted

- Charles Goodyear discovers the vulcanisation process for treating rubber

1840

- New Zealand becomes a British colony (1840)
- Lower and Upper Canada are merged by the Act of Union (1840)

- William Talbot invents the calotype, also known as the talbotype, a photographic process producing negatives from which prints can be repeatedly made

- François-Pierre Foucault mechanises Louis Braille's decapoint system and invents the raphigraph, an ancestor of the dot-matrix printer

▶ Screw propeller designed by Frédéric Sauvage

▲ An autopsy at the turn of the 20th century

▲ Equipment used by Justus von Liebig while researching fertilisers

1842

- The First Opium War ends with China ceding Hong Kong to Britain (1842)
- Britain annexes Natal in South Africa and Sind in India (1843)

- Crawford Long uses ether as an anaesthetic in the USA
- Cigarettes are manufactured in France at a factory in Paris
- Samuel Morse establishes his first telegraph line in the USA
- Friedrich Gottlob Keller patents a wood-pulping machine
- Francis Rynd invents the hypodermic needle

▶ Cooke and Wheatstone's five-wire telegraph

1845

- Start of the Irish Famine (1845)
- Karl Marx and Friedrich Engels publish the *Communist Manifesto* (1846)
- Repeal of the Corn Laws in Britain (1846)
- Europe goes through a 'Year of Revolutions' (1848)
- Start of the Californian Gold Rush (1848)

- Anton von Schrötter finds a way of processing red phosphorus
- Richard Hoe patents a rotary printing press
- Astronomers at the Berlin observatory confirm the first observation of the planet Neptune
- Ascanio Sobrero discovers nitroglycerine
- William Morton attempts to patent the use of ether as an anaesthetic
- William Thomson (the future Lord Kelvin) calculates a temperature value for absolute zero
- Hippolyte Fizeau conducts an experiment to determine the speed of light

▼ William Morton and his team perform the first successful public operation conducted under anaesthesia

▼ Rotary press in a New York printing works

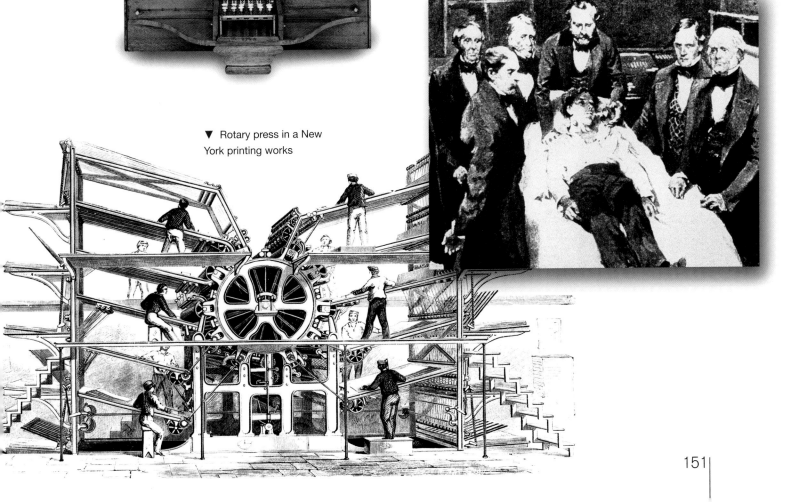

1850

EVENTS

- Taiping rebellion in China (1850-6)
- The Second Empire is established in France under Napoleon III (1852)
- Crimean War begins (1853)

INVENTIONS

- The first international telegraph cable enters service between Paris and London

- Léon Foucault demonstrates the rotation of the Earth in an experiment involving hanging a pendulum from the dome of the Pantheon in Paris (1851); the French physicist will also do important work in the fields of astronomy, optics and electromagnetism

- The Great Exhibition opens in London's Hyde Park, staged in the specially constructed Crystal Palace (1851)

- The Swedish inventor Johan Ervard Lundström invents the safety match

- Charles Gabriel Pravaz and Alexander Wood independently invent the hypodermic syringe

- Antonin-Jean Désormeaux invents the endoscope.

- Death of the French physicist, astronomer and politician François Arago (1853), a leading proponent of the wave theory of light and a pioneer in the field of electromagnetism, who collaborated with Ampère to build an early electromagnet; his meteorological observations played a part in the development of a national weather service in France

1855

EVENTS

- Alexander II becomes tsar of Russia (1855)
- Second Opium War breaks out between Britain and China (1856-60)
- Indian Mutiny challenges British rule in India (1857)

INVENTIONS

- Henry Bessemer invents a process for producing steel on an industrial scale

- William Henry Perkin develops the first aniline dye, mauveine

- The remains of Neanderthal man are found in Germany

- Gail Borden creates condensed milk

- Joseph Gayetty is the first man to market toilet paper, promoted as a health product

- Edwin Drake successfully drills for oil in Pennsylvania, starting a boom

- Charles Darwin publishes *On the Origin of Species*, his ground-breaking account of the theory of evolution by natural selection (1859)

- Henri Dupuy de Lôme designs the first ironclad battleship

- Étienne Lenoir builds the first internal combustion engine, powered by coal gas

▲ Galvanometer designed by William Thomson

Equipment for laying an underwater telegraph cable installed on the deck of the SS *Great Eastern* ▶

1860

- Wilhelm I becomes ruler of Prussia (1861)
- Alexander II emancipates Russia's serfs (1861)
- The American Civil War breaks out (1861)
- Victor Emmanuel II becomes the first ruler of a united Italy (1861)

- Linus Yale creates the modern pin tumbler lock with a notched key

- Germain Sommeiller pioneers the use of the pneumatic drill for excavation work

- Richard J Gatling patents the rapid-fire gun that will bear his name

- George Fellows Harrington invents the dentists' drill

- The Football Association, founded in London, draws up the rules of soccer

- Louis Pasteur develops the method of preserving food that will bear his name: pasteurisation

- The world's first underground railway opens in London

- James Clerk Maxwell discovers radio and electromagnetic waves

1865

- The American Civil War ends with victory for the Union; US President Abraham Lincoln is assassinated (1865)
- Second Reform Act passed on male suffrage in Britain (1865)
- Creation of the Dual Monarchy of Austro-Hungary (1867)
- The modernising Meiji era gets under way in Japan (1868)

- Joseph Lister promotes the use of antiseptics in surgery

- Georges Leclanché invents the Leclanché cell battery

- Barbed wire makes its first appearance in the USA

- Hippolyte Mège-Mouriés invents margarine

- The Suez Canal is opened to shipping

- Ives McGaffey patents the first vacuum cleaner

- Gregor Mendel publishes the results of his pea breeding experiments (1866)

◀ Swedish safety matches

▲ The *Gloire*, a propeller-driven French warship in service in the second half of the 19th century

◀ Gyroscope designed by Léon Foucault to illustrate the rotation of the Earth

Picture credits

ABBREVIATIONS : t = top, c = centre, b = bottom, l = left, r = right

Front cover: main image, 'Iron Rolling Mill', painting by Adolph Menzel, 1875, Old National Gallery, Berlin; inset: reproduction of John Hadley's octant, Cosmos/Science Museum/SSPL. **Spine**: early metronome, Bridgeman Giraudon/ Musée de la Musique, Paris. **Back cover**: diving helmet, Cosmos/SSPL/Science Museum.
Page 2, left to right, top row: AKG-Images/ engraving on wood, 1880, after R Wimmer; Cosmos/SSPL/Science Museum; Picture Desk/ Coll Dagli Orti/Gunshots; 2nd row: Cosmos/ A Pasieka; Corbis/LLC/Swin Ink 2; Leemage/Aisa; 3rd row: Cosmos/SSPL/Science Museum; Corbis/CSA Images/Printstock; Musée de la Marine, Paris; bottom row: Bibliothèque nationale de France, Paris/Trois Mousquetaires poster J Chéret; Cosmos/SSPL/Science Museum; Bridgeman Giraudon/Musée d'Histoire de la médecine, Paris.
Pages 4/5: © Getty Images/AFP/Patrick Kovarick; 6tl: AKG-Images/H Champollion; 6tc: AKG-Images/ engraving on wood, 1880, after R Wimmer; 6b: RMN/Metropolitan Museum of Art/Image of the MMA, New York; 6/7c: Cosmos/SSPL/Science Museum; 7t: Cosmos/SSPL/Science Museum; 7r: Leemage/Costa; 8l: Bridgeman Giraudon; 8c: Leemage/Photo Josse; 8/9: AKG-Images/ Science Photo Library; 9c: Corbis/Ch O'Rear; 9tr: Cosmos/SSPL/Science Museum; 9b: Cosmos/ SSPL/National Railway Museum, York; 10tl: Picture Desk/Dagli Orti Collection/E Tweedy; 10tr: © Musée des Arts et Métiers-CNAM, Paris/JC Wetzel; 10bl: Cosmos/SSPL/Science Museum; 10/11b: Bridgeman Giraudon/Science Museum, London, colour engraving by by C Hunt after W Summers; 11tl: Cosmos/SSPL/NMeM; 11cr: Cosmos/SSPL/NMeM; 12tl: Leemage/Costa; 12r: SparkMuseum/J D Jenkins; 12b: Picture Desk/Dagli Orti Collection/Musée de la Marine, Genoa, colour engraving by J W J Howkins; 13c: AKG-Images/E Bohr; 13tr: Leemage/MP; 14t: RMN/dist BPK, engraving on wood after W Trautschold; 14bl: Leemage/Heritage Images/ Oxford Science Archive, fom 'The Illustrated London News' of 16 April,1884; 14br: Collection NLC; 15tl: Cosmos/SSPL/Science Museum; 15tr: NASA/DR; 15b: Cosmos/SSPL/NRM/Pictorial Collection, Hexham Station, colour engraving J Archer after J W Carmichael; 16tl: Bridgeman Giraudon/Musée d'Histoire de la médecine, Paris; 16cl: Musée des Arts et Métiers-CANAM, Paris/ J C Wetzel; 16b: Cosmos/SSPL/Science Museum; 16/17t: AKG-Images/Stiftung Stadtmuseum, Berlin; 17tr: Ministère de la Culture, Inventaire général/Collection École polytechnique/D Lebée; 17b: AKG-Images; 18/19: Cosmos/SSPL/NRM-Pictorial Collection, Liverpool-to-Manchester line, engraving after I Shaw; 20: AKG-Images/ engraving on wood, 1880, after R Wimmer; 20/21: AKG-Images/H Champollion; 21cl: Cosmos/SPL/Science Museum, Spectroscope made by J Browning for Norman Lockyer; 21br: Cosmos/SSPL, sunspots by L Trouvelot; 24tl & 25tr: Cosmos/SSPL/Science Museum; 22br: Bridgeman Giraudon/Musée de la Musique, Paris; 25br: Jupiter Images 2010; 24tl: Cosmos/ A Pasieka; 24b: Corbis/Mediolmages; 25: Corbis/ Bettman; 26b: Picture Desk/Dagli Orti Collection/ Gunshots; 26t: Corbis/T Wright; 26cr: RMN/ Metropolitan Museum of Art/Image of the MMA, New York; 27: Corbis/Bettman; 28t: Cosmos/SPL/ portrait of John Dalton, engraving by C Cook; 28b: Leemage/Heritage Image, Ann Ronan Picture Library, Quaker meeting, artist unknown, 1839; 29: Cosmos/SSPL/Science Museum; 30t: Bridgeman Giraudon/Manchester Town Hall; 30b: Cosmos/SPL/CCI Archives; 31tl: Cosmos/ SPL; 31tr: Corbis/DK Limited; 31br: Cosmos/ SPL/R Kightley; 32t: Cosmos/SSPL/Science Museum Pictorial, lithograph by W Kolder, 1845; 32b: Cosmos/SSPL/Science Museum; 33tr: Cosmos/Aurora/J Azel; 33b: Musée de la Marine, Paris; 34t: Corbis/L de Selva; 34b: Académie des sciences/Institut de France, Paris; 35t: Librairie Armand Colin/Christophe; 35b: Musée Ampère, Poleymieux, France; 36tr: Académie des sciences/Institut de France, Paris; 36l: Corbis/DK Limited; 37b: Cosmos/SPL/CERN; 37tl: Cosmos/SPL/S Terry; 37tr: Leemage/Costa; 38tl: Cosmos/SPL/J King-Holmes; 38b: Corbis/Hulton-Deutsch Collection; 39t: Corbis/Ch O'Rear; 39l (insert): Collection NLC; 39bd: Library of Congress Prints and Photographs Division, Washington, photo Bashford & Thomson (ph Coll 290.36); 40bl: Bibliothèque nationale de France, Paris; 40c: Corbis/LLC/Swin Ink 2; 40/41t: RMN/ H Lewandowski/Musée d'Orsay, Paris, la Belle Jardinière, lithograph F Sorrieu, 1870-80; 41: Bibliothèque nationale de France, Paris; 42: Corbis/Bettman; 43tr: Leemage/Delius, 1927; 43cl: Leemage/Selva; 43b: Corbis/P Aprahamian; 44l: Bridgeman Giraudon; 44r: Picture Desk/Dagli Orti/private collection; 45: Leemage/Photo Josse; 46b: Corbis/Negri; 47l: Cosmos/SPL/R Harris; 47r: Cosmos/SPL/Victor Habbick Visions; 48bl: Cosmos/SPL; 48c: Cosmos/SSPL/Science Museum; 49: RMN/G Blot/Châteaux de Versailles et Trianon, Lazare Carnot; 50/51t: AKG-Images/ Science Photo Library; 50bl: Bridgeman Giraudon/ Science Museum, London, watercolour by T Rowlandson; 51: Cosmos/SSPL/National Railway Museum, York; 52tl: Bridgeman Giraudon/National Railway Museum, York; 52b: Picture Desk/Coll Dagli Orti; 52/53t: Cosmos/ SSPL/NRM-Pictorial Collection; 53b: Picture Desk/Dagli Orti Collection/Bibliothèque des arts décoratifs, Paris/G Dagli Orti; 54t: Leemage/Selva; 54c: Bridgeman Giraudon/Musée de l'Île-de-France, Sceaux; 55b: Bridgeman Giraudon/Peter Newark American Pictures; 55t: Cosmos/SSPL/ NMeM/Walter Nurnberg; 56bl: Bridgeman Giraudon; 56cl: Corbis/Milepost 92 1/2/C Garrat; 56/57b: Corbis/Milepost 92 1/2/W A Sharman; 56tr: Cosmos/SSPL/National Railway Museum/York; 57t: Bridgeman Giraudon/Peter Newark American Pictures; 57tr: Corbis/DPA/ H Weisser; 57tl: Corbis/Lake County Museum; 57br: Corbis/Robert Harding World Imagery/ Ch Kober; 58l: Bridgeman Giraudon/Peter Newark American Pictures, h/t N C Wyeth, private collection; 58tr: Cosmos/SSPL/Science Museum; 59t: Corbis/Gehl Company; 59b: Corbis/ L Kennedy; 60tl: Musée départemental Dobrée, Conseil général de Loire-Atlantique, Nantes/ H Neveu-Derotrie; 60tr: Bridgeman Giraudon/ Musée Carnavalet, Paris; 61t: Collection NLC; 61b: Bridgeman Giraudon/Bibliothèque nationale de France, Paris; 62b: Bridgeman Giraudon/ Science Museum, London, colour engraving by C Hunt after W Summers; 62/63t: Bridgeman Giraudon/The Stapleton Collection; 63b: AKG-Images/Ullstein bild; 63t: Library of Congress, Washington; 64/65t: Picture Desk/Dagli Orti Collection/E Tweedy; 64c: Leemage/Photo Josse, Fourchambault forge, detail from a painting by F Bonhomme; 65c: © Musée des Arts et Métiers-CNAM, Paris/JC Wetzel; 65b: Région Centre, Inventaire général/M Hermanowicz 1996/ADAGP, Paris 2010; 66tl: Deutsches Museum; 66cr: Collection NLC; 66b: Leemage/Lee, engraving by Bourdelin, in 'Le Monde illustré' n° 104, 9 April 1859; 67: Corbis/J C H Grabill; 68t: AKG-Images; 68b: W P Wuzur/Deutsches Museum; 69t: AKG-Images; 69b: Corbis/Underwood & Underwood; 70: Bibliothèque nationale de France, Paris; 71t & bl: Cosmos/SSPL/NMeM; 71br: Cosmos/SSPL/ Science Museum, photographer unknown; 72t: Cosmos/SSPL/NMeM; 72cg: Cosmos/SSPL/ Science Museum; 73bl: Bridgeman Giraudon/ Victoria & Albert Museum, London, photograph by R Fenton; 73r: Leemage/J Bernard; 74tr & br: Cosmos/SSPL/NMeM; 74cl: Leemage/Heritage Images; 75tr: AKG-Images; 75c: Bridgeman Giraudon/Royal Geographical Society, London; 76tr: Cosmos/SSPL/Science Museum; 76b: Leemage/Photo Josse; 77br: Corbis Sygma/Vo Trung Dung; 77t & 78bl: Corbis/Bettmann; 80bd: Leemage/Aisa; 79b: Corbis/CSA Images/ Printstock; 79tl, 80tr & bl: Cosmos/SSPL/Science Museum; 81t (insert): Corbis/Beateworks/ S Mayoral; 81b: Leemage/Selva; 82t: Bridgeman Giraudon/Châteaux de Versailles et Trianon, A Sheffer; 82bl: Leemage/Lee, engraving from 'Histoire populaire des sciences' by A Bitard, 1880; 83br: Paris Observatory; 83tl: RMN/Musée des Arts et Traditions populaires/Direction des musées de France, 2005; 84: Cosmos/M Henley; 85tl: Leemage/Costa; 85tr: Cosmos/SPL; 86l: Cosmos/SSPL/Science Museum; 86br: Leemage/ North Wind Picture Archives; 87tr: Leemage/ Heritage Images; 87br: Picture Desk/Dagli Orti Collection/Musée de la Marine, Paris; 88t: Cosmos/SSPL/Science Museum; 88bl: Musée de la Marine, Paris; 88br: Corbis/M Keller; 89t: Picture Desk/Dagli Orti Collection/Musée de la Marine, Genoa, colour engraving by J W J Howkins; 89cr: Cosmos/SSPL/NRM/Pictorial Collection, colour engraving after E Weedon; 90t: Cosmos/SSPL/Science Museum; 90b: Musée de la Marine, Paris, Lauvergne c1860; 91r: Corbis/D Guravich; 92t: Cosmos/SSPL; 92b: Cosmos/SSPL/Science Museum; 93: SparkMuseum/J D Jenkins; 94t: Cosmos/SSPL/ Royal Institute; 94b: Corbis/DK Limited; 95tl: Cosmos/SSPL; 95r: Cosmos/P Menzel; 96: Corbis/Zefa/G Rossenbach; 97: AKG-Images/ Postmuseum, Berlin; 98bl: AKG-Images/E Bohr; 98tr: Cosmos/SSPL/Science Museum; 99tr: Leemage/Costa; 99bl: Cosmos/SSPL/Science Museum; 99br: Bridgeman Giraudon/Museum für Kommunikation, Frankfurt; 100t: Cosmos/SSPL/ Science Museum Library, lithograph after R Dudley, 1866; 100c & b: Cosmos/SSPL/Science Museum; 101t: Picture Desk/Dagli Orti Collection/ Culver Pictures; 101bl: Cosmos/SSPL/Science Museum; 101br: Corbis/Bettmann, colour engraving by Currier and Ives, 1876; 102t: Cosmos/SSPL; 102b: Leemage/MP; 103t: Picture Desk/Dagli Orti Collection/A Dagli Orti; 103b: Corbis/Hulton-Deutsch; 104/105t: Cosmos/SPL/ D Van Ravenswaay; 104c & b: Cosmos/SSPL/ Science Museum; 105: NASA/DR; 106: Bridgeman Giraudon/Stapleton Collection; 107: Corbis; 108tl: Collection NLC; 108r: National Museum of American History, Behring Center, Smithsonian Institution/DR; 109t: Prod DB/TCD/Charles Chaplin/United Artists/DR; 109b: Cosmos/SPL/ J Scriba; 110tr: Cosmos/SSPL/Science Museum; 110bl: RMN/dist BPK, engraving on wood after W Trautschold; 111t: AKG-Images; 111br: Corbis/D Turnley; 112c: Corbis/LLC/Swin Ink 2; 112/113t: Corbis/Zefa/K Leidorf; 112bl: Cosmos/SPL/R Brook; 113b: Corbis/Science Faction/Ed Darack; 114b : Corbis/J Springer Collection; 114tl: Cosmos/SPL/V de Schwamberg; 115tr: Bibliothèque nationale de France, Paris/ Trois Mousquetaires poster J Chéret; 115b: Bridgeman Giraudon; 116b: Cosmos/SPL/S Terry; 116t: Cosmos/SSPL/Science Museum; 117t: AKG-Images/W Forman/Topkapi Palace Library, Istanbul, from a manuscript of Yousouf al Maswilli, 1228; 117b: Bridgeman Giraudon/Bibliothèque nationale de France, Paris; 118c: Boerhaave Museum, Leiden; 118tl: Corbis/Bettmann; 119cl: Cosmos/P Goetgheluck; 119b: Cosmos/SPL; 120/121t: AKG-Images/Lain Art Gallery, watercolour of Murton Colliery by Thomas Miles Richardson; 120c: Bridgeman Giraudon/ Bibliothèque des arts décoratifs, Paris, engraving from 'l'Illustration' magazine of 27 October, 1849; 121b: Cosmos/SSPL/NRM/Pictorial Collection, Hexham Station, colour engraving J Archer after J W Carmichael; 122r: Bridgeman Giraudon, Bidonville, engraving C A Ferrier; 122b: Corbis SABA/S Sherbell; 123b: AKG-Images/photograph by Lewis W Hine, 1908; 123t: Picture Desk/Dagli Orti Collection/Galleria Brera, Milan, 'La Fiumana' by G Pellizzza da Volpedo; 124: AKG-Images/ photographer unknown, 1858; 125bl: Cosmos/ SPL; 125tr: Cosmos/SPL/Laguna Design; 125r Jupiter Images © 2010; 126tl: AKG-Images/ photograph by P Bouillant, 1900; 126b: Corbis/ Sygma/Ph. Caron; 126c: Leemage/Heritage Images/Oxford Science Archive, fom 'The Illustrated London News' of 16 April,1884; 127: Corbis/Sygma/D Vander Zwalm; 128t: Cosmos/ SPL/NASA; 128b: NASA/DR; 129b: Bridgeman Giraudon/Bibliothèque nationale de France, Paris/Archives Charmet; 129t : Picture Desk/Dagli Orti Collection/Bibliothèque des arts décoratifs, Paris/G Dagli Orti; 130tr: Bridgeman Giraudon/ CNAM/Archives Charmet; 130cl: Picture Desk/Dagli Orti Collection/Culver Pictures; 130/131b: Leemage/Bianchetti; 131cl: Cosmos/SPL/NASA; 131tr: Musée des Arts et Métiers-CANAM, Paris/J C Wetzel; 132bl: Cosmos/SSPL/Science Museum; 132t: Paris Observatory; 133tr: Cosmos/SSPL/Science Museum; 133bl: Leemage/Selva, engraving from 'Les Merveilles de la science' by L Figuier; 134b: Cosmos/SPL/CERN; 134tl: Cosmos/SSPL/ Science Museum; 135cl: SIPA Press/Pouzet; 135tl: Leemage/Selva; 135br: Ministère de la Culture, Inventaire général/Collection École polytechnique/D Lebée; 136tr: Corbis/Blue Lantern Studio; 136/137t : Corbis/M Agliolo; 136bl: Cosmos/SSPL/Science Museum; 137br: Corbis/The Francis Frith Collection; 137tr: Cosmos/SSPL/Science Museum; 138tl: Bridgeman Giraudon/Musée d'Histoire de la médecine, Paris; 138r: Cosmos/SPL/J Farrow; 139bl: Cosmos/A Tsiaras; 139tr: Musée d'Histoire de la médecine, Paris; 140/141t: AKG-Images/Stiftung Stadtmuseum, Berlin; 140bl: Leemage/North Wind Picture Archives; 141b: AKG-Images/engraving after a fresco by P Meyerheim; 142tl: AKG-Images/Maximilianeum Foundation, Munich, E Seibertz, 1858; 142/143: AKG-Images/R Wulf; 143br: AKG-Images; 143c: Leemage/Aisa/Berlin Museum, bust of Nefertiti; 144/145: Bridgeman Giraudon/Old National Gallery, Berlin, 'Iron Rolling Mill' by A Menzel, 1875; 146/147b: Bridgeman Giraudon/ Manchester Town Hall; 146l: Cosmos/SPL/ Science Museum; 146r: Bridgeman Giraudon/ Musée de la Musique, Paris; 147tl & bl: Cosmos/ SSPL/Science Museum; 147br: Corbis/Bettman; 148cl: Bridgeman Giraudon/ National Railway Museum, York; 148bg: Corbis/P Aprahamian; 148br: Cosmos/SPL/ S Terry; 149b: Bridgeman Giraudon/Musée Carnavalet, Paris; 149cl: Corbis/CSA Images/ Printstock; 149r: Corbis/DK Limited; 150tr: Corbis; 150br Cosmos/SSPL/ Science Museum; 150bl: Musée national de la Marine, Paris; 151bl: Bridgeman Giraudon; 151r: Cosmos/SPL/ S Terry; 151tl & 152bl & br: Cosmos/SSPL/ Science Museum; 153tl: Corbis/Blue Lantern Studio; 153b: Cosmos/SSPL/Science Museum; 153tr: Musée de la Marine, Paris.

Illustrations on pages 46 (the Carnot cycle), 66 (Fourneyron's turbine) and 93 (how screw propulsion works) by Jean-Benoît Héron.

THE ADVENTURE OF DISCOVERIES AND INVENTIONS
Revolution in Industry – 1810 to 1855
Published in 2010 in the United Kingdom by Vivat Direct Limited
(t/a Reader's Digest), 157 Edgware Road, London W2 2HR

Adapted from *Au Temps de la Révolution Industrielle*, part of a series entitled
L'ÉPOPÉE DES DÉCOUVERTES ET DES INVENTIONS, created in France by
BOOKMAKER and first published by Sélection du Reader's Digest, Paris, in 2010.

Translated from French by Tony Allan

Series editor Christine Noble
Art editor Julie Bennett
Designer Martin Bennett
Consultant Ruth Binney
Proofreader Ron Pankhurst
Indexer Marie Lorimer

Colour origination FMG
Printing and binding Arvato Iberia, Portugal

FOR VIVAT DIRECT
Editorial director Julian Browne
Art director Anne-Marie Bulat
Managing editor Nina Hathway
Picture resource manager Sarah Stewart-Richardson
Pre-press technical manager Dean Russell
Product production manager Claudette Bramble
Production controller Sandra Fuller

We are committed to both the quality of our products and the service we provide to our
customers. We value your comments, so please feel free to contact us on 08705 113366
or via our website at **www.readersdigest.co.uk**

If you have any comments or suggestions about the content of our books, you can
email us at **gbeditorial@readersdigest.co.uk**

CONCEPT CODE: FR0104/IC/S
BOOK CODE: 642-006 UP0000-1
ISBN: 978-0-276-44518-7
ORACLE CODE: 356400006H.00.24